Object-Oriented Software Engineering

Steve Halladay
Michael Wiebel

R & D Publications, Inc.
Lawrence, Kansas 66046

R & D Publications, Inc.
1601 West 23rd Street, Suite 200
Lawrence, Kansas 66046-0127
USA

The programs in this book are presented for instructional value. The programs have been carefully tested, but are not guaranteed for any particular purpose. The publisher does not offer any warranties and does not guarantee the accuracy, adequacy, or completeness of any information and is not responsible for any errors or omissions or the results obtained from use of such information.

Distributed in the U.S. and Canada by
Publishers Group West
P.O. Box 8843, Emeryville, CA 94662

0-87930-446-4

Cover Design: T. Watson Bogaard

```
ject(Requirements),
scribe the objects externals
tSpec = CreateSpec(Requiremen
 the object until it passes
all veri  the  tests
Do {
    // Describe how th
    ObjectDesign = DesignO
    // Find or build subordina
    Subordinates = CreateSu
    // Implement this objec
    Code = CodeObject(O
    // Create boundary v
    TestSet = CreateBlac
    // Create condition
    WhiteBoxTes
```

Preface

This book is not an introduction to C++ and object-oriented programming. Lots of books are available to teach you the C++ programming language. This book goes beyond C++ programming to show you how to engineer an application using object-oriented principles.

The current challenge in software development is to understand how to harness the power of Object-Oriented Programming (OOP). Popular OOP approaches amount to brainstorming objects using ad hoc techniques. Seasoned OOP developers have little trouble with this approach on moderate-sized development efforts. Those developers with less experience or those involved in larger development efforts have a more difficult time using OOP.

This book describes a methodology that combines the strength of OOP with a pragmatic process. The authors empirically derived this methodology by studying how successful developers create OOP software. The concepts presented herein reflect pragmatic working practices as opposed to blue-sky theory. The method minimizes bureaucracy while maintaining a high standard of software reliability.

This methodology addresses the complete software development life cycle — from initial requirements to final maintenance. This cradle to grave perspective has the effect of minimizing total development cost. Because development phases of the methodology will be more expensive than their less disciplined counterparts, these less disciplined approaches may appear to have an immediate lower cost. When all costs are considered, such short cuts will generally have a negative impact on the total cost of the software project.

Who Should Read This Book

To get the most from this book, you should have some prior exposure to OOP and be comfortable with C++ syntax and semantics. We explain the "how" of OOP, but assume you are familiar with the "what" of OOP. We present examples in C++, but seldom explain language features.

This book is for experienced programmers who want to develop industrial strength object-oriented software *products*. You will learn how OOP affects the *entire* product development process.

Those who have moderate experience with software product development and OOP will greatly benefit from the structure of the development process outlined in this book. While OOP-based software development is a great breakthrough, some programmers use OOP as a license to hack. This book will help you harness the power of OOP by introducing you to an empirically-derived, process-based methodology. This methodology can greatly leverage your skills.

How This Book Is Organized

Each chapter develops a different facet of the methodology by explaining the concepts and demonstrating them with examples. Throughout the book, we continuously refine a more comprehensive example, thus showing how the methodology works in large scale projects. A set of exercises at the end of each chapter reinforces concepts as they are introduced.

Chapter 0, the introduction, identifies some basic attributes of OOP and discusses why these attributes are useful. This chapter also defines the concept of a methodology, and explains why methodologies are critical in sophisticated software development.

Chapter 1 is an overview of the methodology. It discusses the major steps in this development process and shows how they relate. Chapter 1 introduces abstraction as the basis for OOP. This chapter also discusses the expert perspectives used by each step of the development methodology.

Chapter 2 focuses on the requirements gathering process. This chapter explains why it is so important to identify the requirements early in the development project. It also shows how to gather requirements and how to distinguish between functions, attributes, constraints and preferences.

Chapter 3 discuses why and how to do an object specification. This chapter defines what a specification is and explains how the specification relates to the requirements. This chapter also discusses some tools and techniques for developing object specifications.

Chapter 4 centers on the nuts and bolts of object-oriented design as defined by this process. This chapter shows how and when to identify objects and their methods. It also describes the various relationships between objects. This chapter also shows how to represent object designs without fluff or hieroglyphics.

Chapter 5 deals with the issues of translating an object-oriented design into code. This chapter identifies some common OOP constructs and gives rules of thumb for their use. This chapter also explains some useful defensive OOP coding techniques.

Chapter 6 concentrates on object verification or testing. It describes a test strategy that incorporates test plans, test drivers and benchmarks. This chapter uses additional examples to explain how to perform object verification from an external perspective.

Chapter 7 explains object testing from an internal perspective known as white-box testing. This chapter discusses white-box test strategies and shows their relationship to the testing strategies previously discussed in Chapter 6.

Chapter 8, the final chapter, discusses many important maintenance aspects of an OOP software product. These issues include how to use and update software product artifacts, how to schedule OOP product development, and how to enhance and tune existing OOP products.

Chapters 1 through 8 describe a development process. Each chapter has an algorithmic summary to describe the section of the methodology discussed by the chapter. Appendix A is the combination of the algorithmic summaries from each chapter. Once developers have read the book and understand the development methodology process, Appendix A is a useful ready reference to remind developers of the development sequence. Appendix B contains the complete listing of the source code for the comprehensive programming example.

```
ject(Requirements);
scribe the objects externals
tSpec = CreateSpec(Requirements
 the object until it passes
all veri    tests
Do {
    // Describe how th
    ObjectDesign = DesignO
    // Find or build subordina
    Subordinates = CreateSu
    // Implement this objec
    Code = CodeObject(O
    // Create boundary v
    TestSet = CreateBlac
    // Create condition
    WhiteBoxTes
```

Table of Contents

Table of Contents — *Cont'd*

```
ject(Requirements
scribe the objects externals
tSpec = CreateSpec(Requirements
the object until it passes
all veri  tests
Do {
    // Describe how th
    ObjectDesign = Design
    // Find or build subordina
    Subordinates = CreateSu
    // Implement this objec
    Code = CodeObject(O
    // Create boundary v
    TestSet = CreateBlac
    // Create condition
    WhiteBoxTes
```

Chapter 0

Introduction to Objects and Methods

Software development paradigms, methodologies and tools have improved dramatically since the appearance of the first computers. Instead of using stone axes like the original front panel switches and arcane punch cards, software developers now use power tools like context-sensitive editors and high-level languages. Yet, even with these significant advances in software development technology, today's software is more difficult to build than ever. The difficulty of current software development lies with software development technology's inability to keep pace with user expectations.

To narrow the gap between user expectations and what software development technology can provide, software engineers are continuously improving their development methodologies and paradigms. A recent software development breakthrough is known as the Object-Oriented Paradigm (OOP). By coupling OOP with a sound development methodology, software developers improve software quality while decreasing development time. This chapter introduces two fundamental concepts: OOP and "methodologies."

What is the Object-Oriented Paradigm?

For those steeped in traditional software development paradigms, the Object-Oriented Paradigm (OOP) is a new way of looking at a familiar world. Each person has a different understanding of the world. To work together individuals must hold some views in common. These shared views of the world are a paradigm. Everyone uses paradigms to explore and explain the interactions and relationships that they see in the world. Sometimes, as people look at the world in a different way, they discover ideas that simplify their paradigm but continue to explain important phenomena about the world. When people discard an old standard paradigm and adopt a new one, they make a paradigm shift.

A famous paradigm shift occurred early in the 16th century. Prior to this time, people believed that the Earth was the center of the Universe. Astronomers devised complicated models to explain the irregular movements of the Sun and planets as they careened around the Earth. In 1543, Copernicus presented an alternative view of the Universe. Copernicus proposed that the Sun was the center of the planetary system. By assuming this revolutionary perspective, Copernicus greatly simplified our understanding of the Solar System. Using the Copernican model, scientists can explain the orbits of the planets so plainly that even grammar school children can understand them.

OOP has had much the same effect on the software development community. Contrast OOP with more conventional paradigms. Some

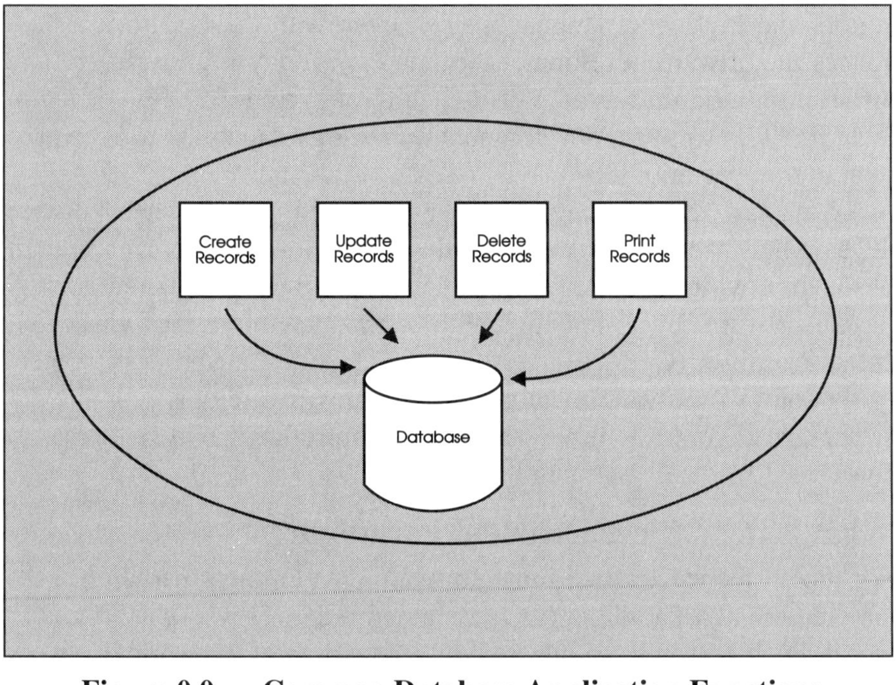

Figure 0.0 — Common Database Application Functions

traditionally structured methodologies advocate decomposing programs into source, transformation, and sink modules. The source module assumes the input functions. The transformation module changes the data in some useful way. The sink module outputs the result of the transformation. An OOP approach maintains the same functionality, but organizes the software differently.

An Example of OOP Advantages

To compare OOP with a more traditional paradigm, consider a common database application that supports creating, updating, deleting, and printing records. Figure 0.0 shows these functions in the database application.

A traditional design for this application would probably create a module for each operation (i.e., create, update, delete, and print). Figure 0.1 shows such a traditional design of the database application.

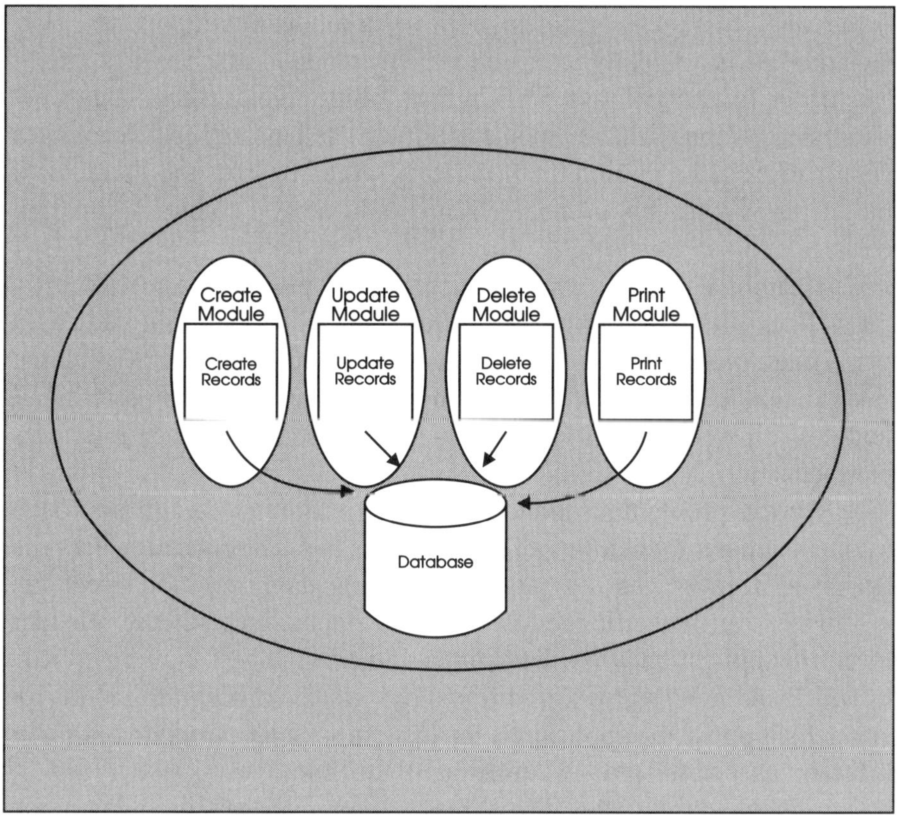

Figure 0.1 — Traditional Database Application Design

Each module has the responsibility of handling all the details of its operation, including user interaction and database access. For example, the Update Module would perform four steps:

- ❑ Query the user for the record to update.
- ❑ Retrieve the record from the database.
- ❑ Interact with the user to make the necessary changes to the record.
- ❑ Write the record to the database.

The traditional reasoning binds all functions of a given operation together. This seems to make sense because it allows developers to treat each operation like a separate program. Since each operation works like a separate program, developers think they can design, implement, and debug each module independently.

In reality, this traditional design misses a subtle, but important, point. Each module is not really independent. The modules all share a common data format for the database. The Create Module creates records that have a format common with the Update Module. The Update Module updates records that can be printed by the Print Module. Besides the shared data format, each module's user interface should have a common look and feel.

Conventional design solves these problems by creating a specification that defines the data format and the user interface look and feel. This seems like a painless solution, but consider the ramifications. Writing the specification takes time. In addition, the only way to be certain all modules follow the specified look and feel is to review each module's interface.

A second problem introduced by the traditional design approach becomes apparent when one of the modules has a bug that corrupts the database. Because the symptoms of such a bug may not direct the developer to any specific module, the developer must carefully consider the entire application when searching for the bug.

Third, and most serious, traditional designs are difficult to modify or enhance. Suppose the application developers want to introduce a slightly different user interface, or to expand the database. These types of modifications require the developers to change each module in the application. Any changes will tend to introduce errors to the application.

Because the developers have to change all modules to modify the application, they have no idea where to look for the errors.

Now consider the same application designed using an object-oriented perspective. Figure 0.2 shows an OOP design for this application.

Using the OOP perspective, developers can view the database application as two large objects. These objects are the user interface object, and the database object. The purpose of the user interface object is to handle all interaction between the application and the user. Because it is the only object that handles all the user interaction, the user interface object can guarantee the user interface is consistent from operation to operation.

The database object takes care of data storage and retrieval for all operations. This object hides the actual format of the stored data records from the rest of the application by providing a procedural interface for the required operations. The database object manages the physical access

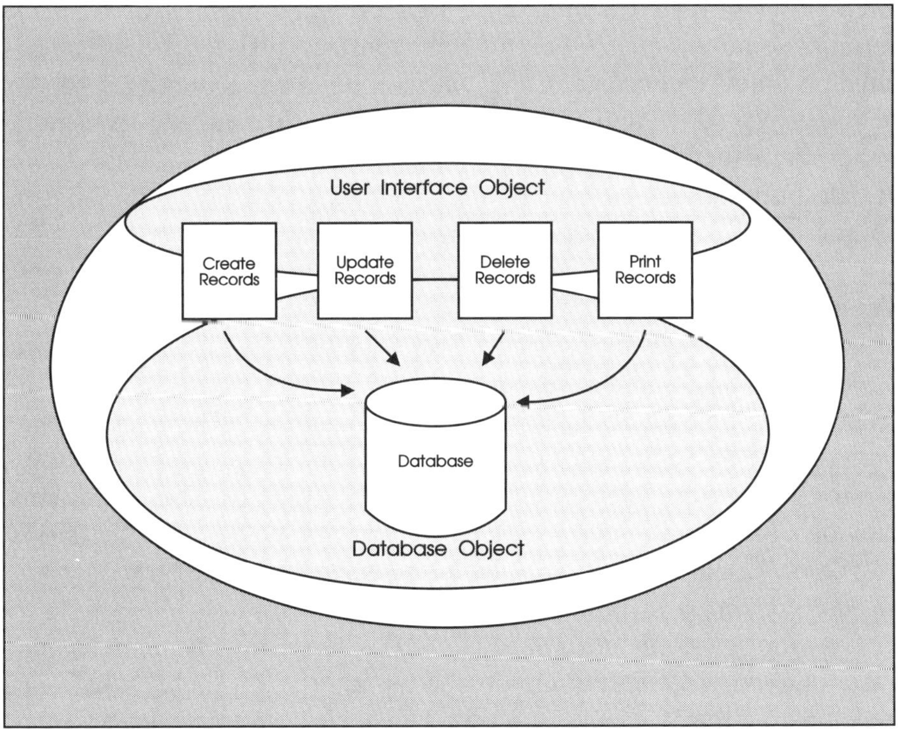

Figure 0.2 — OOP Database Application Design

to the database. If the database should ever become corrupted, the source of the bug must exist in the database object.

Making a modification to the application shows one of OOP's greatest strengths. To use dialog boxes instead of forms in the user interface, the developers only need to change the user interface object. If the developers also want to add additional data fields to the database, they make the change only to the database object. In either case, the developers have limited the impact of changing the application.

What Are Objects?

The previous section described some of the benefits of objects. This section describes what an object is. Abstract data types (ADTs) are the basis of objects.

Historically, software developers focused on the program's control flow. An archeological study of software from the control flow era reveals artifacts known as flow charts. Flow charts specify the sequence of operations the processor uses when executing a program. The structured programming revolution focused on program control flow by defining some reasonable control flow constructs. Each of these structured programming constructs has one entry and one exit point.

As software development evolved, developers learned there was more to a program than just control flow. They began to realize the importance of data in programs. As the significance of data became paramount in programs, software developers began to focus exclusively on data analysis. This created a flurry of data flow diagrams and data dictionaries. These artifacts, like the flow charts, are useful but incomplete.

ADTs combine software control flow with the relevant data to produce a module with a specific responsibility. Each ADT includes a set of related functions which encapsulate a responsibility. The related functions operate on a common data structure, and are the programmer's only means of accessing or manipulating the data structure. These functions provide a procedural interface that represents the boundary of the ADT. The object-oriented world calls the functions in this procedural interface *member functions* or *methods*.

Operating systems used the first ADTs. Operating systems use the encapsulation provided by the procedural interface to help enforce the operating system's security. A good historical example of an early operating system ADT is the third level programmer interface to the

UNIX file system. C programmers now recognize this ADT as part of the standard C run-time library. The ADT provides the following functions:

fopen	Creates or reopens a file.
fread	Reads data from a file.
fwrite	Writes data to a file.
fprintf	Writes formatted data to a file.
ftell	Determines the current location within a file.
fseek	Changes the current location within a file.
fclose	Closes a file.

When a program calls *fopen*, *fopen* allocates and initializes a data structure (called a *FILE*) that contains information about the file to be opened. The information in the data structure includes the file index, buffer space and pointers, and the file's access permissions. The definition of the *FILE* structure usually looks something like the following:

```
typedef struct  {
    int                 _cnt;      /* buffer character count  */
    unsigned char       *_ptr;     /* current buffer position */
    unsigned char       *_base;    /* buffer base pointer */
    char                _flag;     /* file status flags */
    char                _file;     /* file index */
}   FILE;
```

This data structure is the ADT's *control block*. When *fopen* completes, it returns a pointer to the control block (called the *handle*). The handle identifies the instance of the open file. Since *fopen* creates a separate handle for each open file, programs may have multiple concurrent open files. Programs pass the handle as the first parameter to each member function (except *fopen*) to identify a specific file.

After a program calls *fopen*, it can then use any of the other member functions. Figure 0.3, shows the legal sequence of file operations. *fclose* is the last member function called when using this ADT. *fclose* flushes file buffers and deallocates the control block. After *fclose* deallocates the control block, the handle is invalid and should not be used.

Since *fopen* constructs the ADT control block, in object-oriented terms, *fopen* is the *constructor* function. *fclose* is the inverse of *fopen*.

`fclose`, and similar functions, are *destructor* functions. All ADTs have constructor and destructor functions. The job of the constructor is to allocate and initialize the control block. The job of the destructor is to do any clean up and deallocate the control block.

ADTs provide public interfaces that support their specified functions. While the specification for the UNIX file system ADT tells what the functions do and how to use them, it explains very little about exactly how the functions work. Appropriately, C programmers seldom concern themselves with the contents of the `FILE` control block. When using an ADT, programmers should let the member functions or methods do all manipulation of the control block. The ADT purposefully hides this information from ADT users.

Hiding implementation detail increases the independence of the ADT. Portable C programs do not realize how the `FILE` control block varies from compiler to compiler. All access to the control block is through the defined procedural interface. This allows ADTs to be easily built, tested, maintained, and reused.

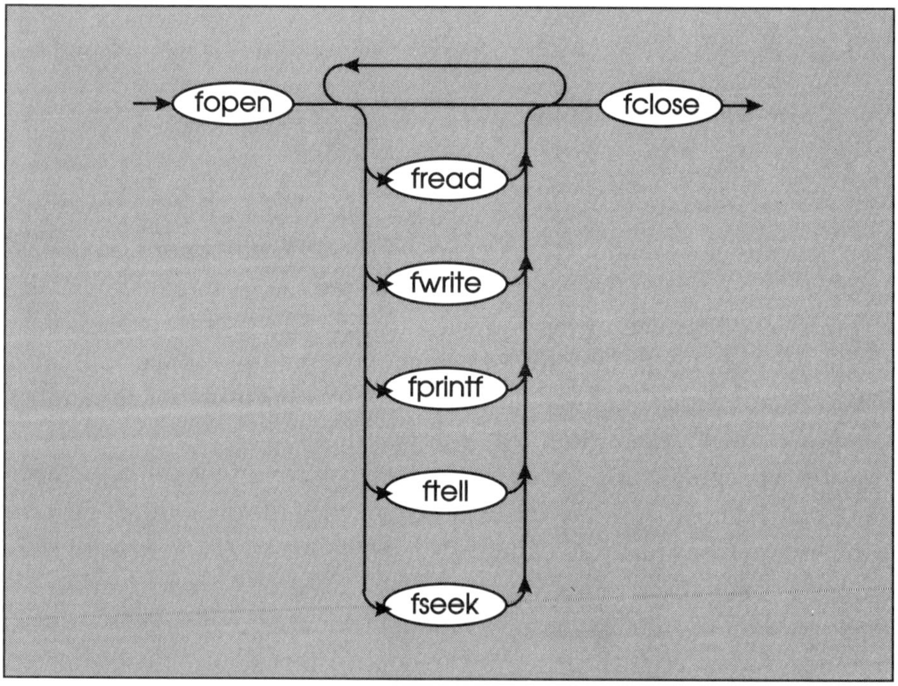

Figure 0.3 — UNIX File System ADT Calling Sequence

ADTs distinguish the hidden details of the ADT from the visible aspects. Hidden ADT details are considered *private*. The visible portion of an ADT is *public*. The ADT *public* information is the interface to the ADT and constitutes a contract between the ADT and its users.

There are many other examples of ADTs. Obvious examples include common data structures like binary trees, linked lists, hash tables and stacks. Listings 0.0 and 0.1 show a simple example stack ADT. Listing 0.0, the header file, shows the public section of the stack ADT. Listing 0.1 shows the C file that contains the private implementation details.

To use the stack ADT the programmer includes *stack.h* (Listing 0.0) in the source files that read stack access. Listing 0.0 shows the interface to the five member functions of the stack ADT. *StkConstruct* is the stack ADT constructor. *StkDestroy* is the ADT destructor. *StkPush* pushes an item on an instance of a stack. *StkPop* retrieves the top item from a stack. *StkIsEmpty* determines if any items exist on the stack.

The *typedef* in Listing 0.0 defines *STK*, the stack handle type, as a void pointer even though these handles are really pointers to *Stacks* (see Listing 0.1). Defining the handle on a *void* pointer in the public interface hides the implementation details of the *Stack* control block from stack users.

The stack ADT in Listing 0.1 implements the stack with an array. This implementation is simple but restricts stack storage to *STACK_SIZE* (*10*) items. Since the ADT hides the implementation details, one could reimplement the stack ADT as a linked list, if necessary, without changing any of the code which uses the stack ADT.

Listing 0.0 — Stack ADT Public Section (*stack.h*)

```
/*
*   stack.h - Stack abstraction header file
*/

typedef void*    STK;

STK       StkConstruct();
void      StkDestroy(STK);
void      StkPush(STK, void*);
void      *StkPop(STK);
int       StkIsEmpty(STK);
```

Listing 0.1 — Stack ADT Implementation Details (*stack.c*)

```
/*
*   stack.c - An example of a stack abstraction
*/

#include <stdlib.h>
#include <assert.h>
#include <stack.h>

#define   STACK_SIZE   10

typedef   struct {
   char   *stk_magic;      /* stack magic number */
   int    stk_top;         /* top of stack index */
                           /* actual stack storage */
   void   *stk_stack[STACK_SIZE];
}  Stack;

/*
Each member function can confirm that it has been given a
pointer to a valid stack control block by checking the
stk_margin signature stored in the stack control block
*/

static char      *magic = "Stack";

#define MAGIC_ON(p)     ((p)->stk_magic = magic)
#define MAGIC_OFF(p)    ((p)->stk_magic = NULL)
#define MAGIC_CHECK(p)  assert(((p) != NULL) && \
                           ((p)->stk_magic == magic))

/* Create a stack */
STK    *StkConstruct() {
Stack  *stk;

   stk = (Stack*) malloc(sizeof(Stack));
   if (stk != NULL) {
      stk->stk_top = 0;
      MAGIC_ON(stk);
      MAGIC_CHECK(stk);
   }
   return((STK) stk);
}
```

Listing 0.1 — *Cont'd*

```
/* Destroy a stack */
void  StkDestroy(STK stk) {
Stack  *s;

   s = (Stack*) stk;
   MAGIC_CHECK(s);
   MAGIC_OFF(s);
   free(s);
}

/* Push an item on the stack */
void  StkPush(STK stk, void *item) {
Stack  *s;

   s = (Stack*) stk;
   MAGIC_CHECK(s);
   assert(s->stk_top < STACK_SIZE);
   s->stk_stack[s->stk_top++] = item;
}

/* Pop an item from the stack */
void  *StkPop(STK stk) {
Stack  *s;

   s = (Stack*) stk;
   MAGIC_CHECK(s);
   assert(s->stk_top > 0);
   return(s->stk_stack[--(s->stk_top)]);
}

/* Determine if the stack is empty */
int   StkIsEmpty(STK stk) {
Stack  *s;

   s = (Stack*) stk;
   MAGIC_CHECK(s);
   return(s->stk_top == 0);
}
```

So far, this section has identified several important components of ADTs, including member functions or methods, control blocks, handles, constructors, destructors, public and private sections. Objects are ADTs that automatically incorporate these aspects. Object-oriented languages, such as C++, have language constructs that support each of these constructs. Listing 0.2 and Listing 0.3 reimplement the stack ADT as a stack object using C++.

The first noticeable difference between the stack ADT with the stack object, is the *class* construct. A class is a definition of an abstract data type. Objects are instances of classes. The class definition contains both private and public information. The first section of the class shows the private data items and member functions. These items and functions can only be used directly by the stack object itself.

The second section of the class, starting with the *public:* directive, shows member functions that can be accessed by users of the stack class. This section is the contract that describes the functionality the class will

Listing 0.2 — Stack Object C++ Public Interface (*stack.h*)

```
//
// stack.h - Stack class
//

#include <stream.h>
#include <assert.h>

#define   STACK_SIZE   10     // stack capacity

class  STK{
   char   *magic;          // magic number
                           // stack storage area
   void   *stack[STACK_SIZE];
   int    top;             // stack index
   void   MagicCheck();    // check for a valid stack
public:
   STK();                  // create a stack
   ~STK();                 // destroy a stack
   void   Push(void *);    // push an item onto the stack
   void   *Pop();          // pop an item off the stack
   int    IsEmpty();       // is stack empty?
};
```

Listing 0.3 — Stack Object Implementation Details (*stack.cpp*)

```
static char   *Stack = "stack";   // arb. magic number value

//make sure this is a valid stack
inline void  STK::MagicCheck() {
   assert(this != NULL);
   assert(magic == Stack);
}

// create a stack
STK::STK() {
   top = 0;               // initialize the stack index
                          // to empty
   magic = Stack;         // set the stack magic number
   MagicCheck();          // make sure the magic is set right
}

// destroy a stack
STK::~STK() {
   MagicCheck();          // make sure this is a valid stack
   magic++;               // make the magic number invalid
}

// push an item on the stack
void   STK::Push(void *item) {
   MagicCheck();                 // check for a valid stack
   assert(top<STACK_SIZE);       // check for overflow
   stack[top++] = item;          // store item on the stack
}

// pop an item off the stack
void   *STK::Pop() {
   MagicCheck();                 // check for a valid stack
   assert(top > 0);              // check for underflow
   return(stack[--top]);         // remove and return the item
}

// determine if the stack is empty
int    STK::IsEmpty() {
   MagicCheck();                 // check for a valid stack
   return(top == 0);             // check for a zero index
}
```

provide to the outside world. Listing 0.3 contains additional private implementation details that are not visible to users of stack classes.

The class declaration provides a complete and explicit list of methods or member functions. The explicit list clarifies how users can manipulate classes. Separating the external interface from the implementation clarifies how to use a class by eliminating irrelevant clutter.

Notice that the class declaration recognizes both data and control flow. Data items previously contained in ADT control blocks are now contained in classes. In addition, classes expand upon the control block concept by adding declarations of the procedures that manipulate the data items.

A class contains both public and private sections, allowing limited access to the internal data structure. In an object-oriented language the programmer can hide the class internals without resorting to tricks like defining the handle as a *void* pointer. Because the language directly supports the hiding of private members, the compiler can enforce strict type checking without sacrificing the object's integrity.

In ADT-based programs the application programmer must remember to explicitly destroy an ADT when it is no longer needed. When programs inadvertently create, but do not destroy, ADTs, the ADTs slowly fill memory until the program can no longer run. Object-oriented languages alleviate this problem by implicitly invoking constructors and destructors.

The C++ compiler identifies the correct member function to invoke it as a constructor or destructor by looking for a member function with the same name as the class (e.g., *STK*). The name of the destructor is the same as the class with a prepended tilde (e.g., *~STK*). By relying upon this naming convention, the compiler can automatically generate code to invoke the appropriate constructor and destructor when an object comes into and goes out of scope.

Unlike ADTs, classes created with an object-oriented language are manipulated through implicit handles. The stack ADT uses an explicit stack pointer in all of its member functions to reference data items in the control block. In contrast, the stack class references the class data items as if they were global data. This difference generates a subtle benefit by removing one level of indirection.

More Than Just a Fancy ADT

The previous section discussed how objects can more conveniently represent ADTs, but objects are more than just fancy ADTs. OOP also provides *inheritance* and *polymorphism*, capabilities which enhance the power of OOP by making objects extensible, yet simple.

Inheritance is a relationship among classes that allows one class to take on attributes of other classes. Typically OOP uses inheritance to construct a new class from an existing class if the new class can be described as "a type of" the existing class. For example, Ferrari is "a type of" car, or dog is "a type of" animal. This "type of" relationship is characterized by a taxonomy or classification hierarchy. Figure 0.4 shows an example of a classification hierarchy that could be implemented using inheritance.

In Figure 0.4 *animals* could have the attribute that they can move around and that they have parents. One might represent these attributes in an animal class as follows:

```
class animal {
    ...
public:
    animal();               // create an animal object
    ~animal();              // destroy an animal object
    void      Move();       // move an animal
    animal    *Mother();    // determine the animal's mother
    animal    *Father();    // determine the animal's father
};
```

Mammals are a type of animal that has hair and feeds offspring. This relationship implies that mammals have all the attributes of any other animal, plus those specific to mammals. We can represent this relationship as a class by showing that *mammal* inherits the attributes of *animal* as follows:

```
class mammal:public animal {
    ...
public:
    int    HasHair();    // indicate that mammals have hair
    void   Feed();       // feed mammals' offspring
};
```

Dogs are a type of mammal that barks. Besides their specific attributes, dogs inherit all the attributes of mammals (i.e., they move, they have parents, they have hair, and they feed their offspring). We can represent this relationship as follows:

```
class dog:public mammal {
   ...
public:
   void   Bark();       // dogs bark
};
```

Polymorphism and Dynamic Binding

Consider a program that computes the area of different geometric shapes. A C program might use the shape of the object to decide which area function to apply. Such a program might have a statement such as:

```
switch(shape->shape_type){
    case CIRCLE: CircleArea(shape);
        break;
    case TRIANGLE: TriangleArea(shape);
        break;
    case RECTANGLE: RectangleArea(shape);
        break;
    default: fprintf(stderr,"Error Message\n");
        break;
}
```

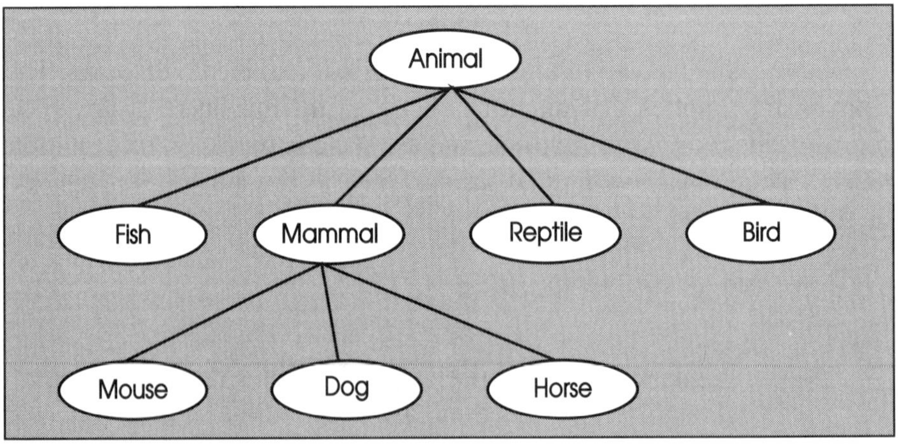

Figure 0.4 — Example Classification Hierarchy

Using each *shape* to decide the area function requires a discriminating record in the `struct`. This record is a disadvantage, because adding new *shapes* requires modifications to existing code at the risk of introducing bugs to the program. Because C requires the type of *shape* to be known at compile time, every *switch* statement using the discriminating record must be rewritten to include the special case of the new *shape* type. Proliferating these changes in a large program quickly becomes a maintenance nightmare.

Another OOP feature, polymorphism, allows different objects to respond differently to the same message. For example, if *shape* is a base class, from which each distinct geometric shape inherits common characteristiscs, C++ would allow every class to use *Copy* as the name of a member function. (See Listing 0.4.)

Listing 0.4 — Polymorphic Use of *Copy()*

```
class shape {
   stype shape_type;      // stype is an enumerated type.
public:
   virtual void    Copy();
   virtual void    Draw();
   virtual double  Area();
};

class circle : public shape {
   ...
public:
   void      Copy();
   void      Draw();
   double    Area();
};

class rectangle: public shape {
   ...
public:
   void      Copy();      // polymorphism allows different
                          // objects to have identical
                          // member function names.

   void      Draw();
   double    Area();
};
```

Because it uses polymorphism, the solution presented in Listing 0.4 allows programs to pass the same message to different objects like:

```
switch () {
...
case CIRCLE:
   MyCircle.Draw();
   d = MyCircle.Area();
   break;
case RECTANGLE:
   MyRectangle.Draw();
   d = MyRectangle.Area();
   break;
...
}
```

Notice in the preceding example each shape receives the same message (e.g., *MyCircle.Draw()*, *MyRectangle.Area()* ...). This solution uses polymorphism but is still unacceptable. This solution, like the geometry program, still imposes the programming overhead associated with the discriminating record. This discrimination code can be eliminated by using dynamic binding.

With dynamic binding an object's type does not have to be revealed until run time. The previous examples used a *switch* statement to send the program to the appropriate block of code based on the type of object. By executing this *switch* at run time the program will alter its stream of execution depending upon the value of the discriminating record. The maintenance is difficult because adding objects requires modification to every *switch* statement making use of the discriminating record. Consider a solution that takes advantage of dynamic binding:

```
shape *shapes[] = {   new circle,
                      new rectangle,
                      new triangle
                    };
// creates and initializes an array of shapes.
...
  shapes[i].Draw();
```

This code segment will pass the message *draw* to the shape pointed to by *shapes[i]*. The keyword *virtual* (in front of the public member function *Draw* in the base class *shape*) signals the compiler that this function may be called by pointer. With dynamic binding the program determines the type of object at run time, eliminating the need for the discriminating record and the associated switch statement. Thus, discriminating records and associated switch statements become an indication to the object-oriented software developer that there may be something seriously wrong with the design.

Why Use OOP?

The most commonly touted benefit of OOP is software reuse. In the earlier database example, conventional software development paradigms decompose the application into modules that create, update, delete and print items from the database. Imagine trying to reuse any one of these modules in another application. Since the modules are so tightly coupled (i.e., they rely heavily on each other), it is nearly impossible to envision reusing any of this software without a significant amount of rework.

In contrast, an OOP design strategy decomposes the application into a database class and a user interface class. Other applications can easily make use of either of these objects. Since reuse is such a major emphasis in OOP, reusability is the acid test for a good class definition. The concepts of inheritance and polymorphism enhance the reusability of classes since they allow users of classes to customize a class without affecting its internals.

Some might argue that reusability was the driving force behind the invention of OOP. While there is some truth to this, reusability is really a byproduct of a superior design philosophy. Other side effects of OOP include the ability to understand, design, test and maintain OOP software.

The same aspects that make software easy to reuse also make it easy to handle in other ways. Two important aspects of classes are independence and completeness. The independence of classes makes them easier to test and debug. Because the class descriptions are complete, they are easier to understand and design.

To test and debug software modules effectively, one must isolate the module from any surrounding software. This allows the test driver to control thc cnvironment in which the module operates. Since classes are isolated modules, they are ideal for testing. By studying the public class interface definition, testers can easily determine how to interact with the class to control its environment.

The nature of OOP classes also makes it easier to change working software without introducing bugs. Since any changes to a class are confined to the class itself, other classes will not be affected by the maintenance.

What is a Methodology and Why Use One?

This section explains how methodologies influence software development. We'll use the "Jumping Pawn Puzzle" to illustrate the effect of methodologies. The puzzle begins with six pawns on a board with seven positions. Pawns one, two and three occupy the leftmost positions. Pawns four, five and six occupy the rightmost positions. Figure 0.5 shows the initial condition of the board.

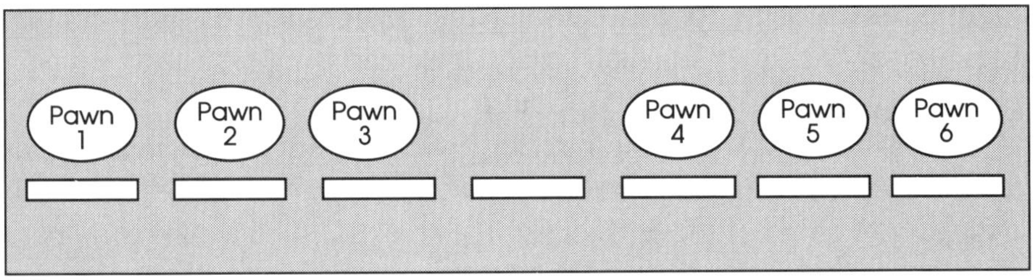

Figure 0.5 — Starting Positions of the Jumping Pawn Puzzle

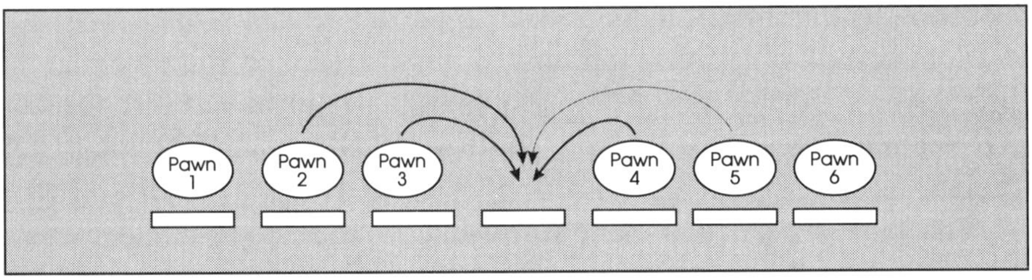

Figure 0.6 — Possible Opening Moves of the Jumping Pawn Puzzle

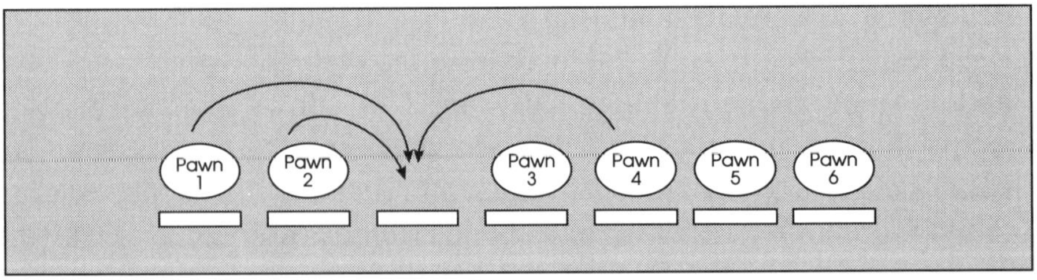

Figure 0.7 — Possible Second Moves of the Jumping Pawn Puzzle

The pawns can move to an adjacent open position or they may jump one other pawn to move to its adjacent open position. Pawns one, two and three can only move right. Pawns four, five and six can only move left. For example, from the initial position, any of the four inner pawns can move to the open position between Pawns three and four. Figure 0.6 shows the possible initial moves.

Moving Pawn three to the open position limits the next move to one of three possibilities shown in Figure 0.7: moving Pawn two to the open position to the right, jumping Pawn two with Pawn one, or jumping Pawn three with Pawn four. Note that Pawn three cannot move because it may not move left.

The puzzle is solved when Pawns four, five, and six occupy the leftmost positions and Pawns one, two and three occupy the rightmost positions. Figure 0.8 shows the solution to the puzzle. Before reading any further, take a few minutes to try to solve this puzzle.

If you have not yet solved the puzzle, consider the following hints:

- ❑ From any board state, there are at most four possible moves (i.e., move left to the open position, move right to the open position, jump left to the open position, and jump right to the open position).
- ❑ Some moves prove to be unsuccessful and should be eliminated.
- ❑ By keeping track of past moves, you waste less time repeating mistakes. The list of moves is a permanent record, tracing the steps taken to solve the puzzle.

This puzzle is deceptively difficult. Most individuals seem confident they can solve this problem with little forethought. They generally begin by attempting to move pawns in an intuitive manner. Once the initial attempt fails, they continue trying similarly. After a second or third failure, the person trying to solve the problem begins to realize that the problem is more difficult than it appears.

Once stumped, many individuals will change gears mentally. They will stop thinking about solving the puzzle itself, and start thinking about the *process* of solving the puzzle. The earlier hints are most useful to a person who has reached this point. If you were successful, you probably consciously, or unconsciously, developed a strategy for attacking the puzzle. It may have been similar to the following:

```
Start at the initial state and analyze the state.
```

We recursively define *analyze the state* as:

```
For each possible move...
   If the move is legal in this state,
      Create a new state by making the move.
      If the new state is the solution state then,
         we solved the puzzle.
      Otherwise analyze the new state.
      If we have not yet found a solution then,
         this move is not part of the solution.
```

This approach allows one to traverse the tree of possible moves quickly to find a path from the initial state to the solution state. The rate at which someone solves the puzzle is a function of the number of dead ends they attempt and the amount of time they spend at each state. Without knowing the answer in advance, it is difficult to know when a path is going to result in a dead end. It is impossible to eliminate trying dead ends, but using the previously described process will eliminate the useless effort of re-exploring the same erroneous paths. Additionally, since it is clear what to think about at each state, a person can quickly make the necessary decisions and move on. Ultimately the approach reduces the amount of wasted mental effort expended while solving the puzzle.

The set of principles and practices which guides one through a puzzle is a methodology. Once practitioners understand a methodology, they can

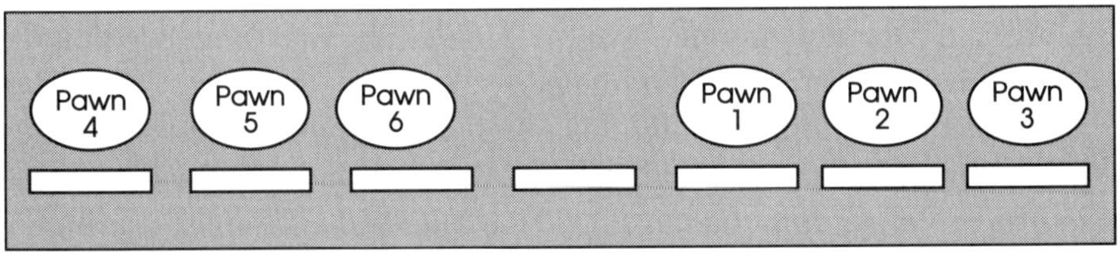

Figure 0.8 — Ending Positions of the Jumping Pawn Puzzle

reduce it to a process description like the one used to solve the Jumping Pawn Puzzle.

For years software developers have been trying to define a concrete software development methodology to solve the software development puzzle. Initially software developers built software by intuition, but like the Jumping Pawn Puzzle this was seldom successful. Developers recognized they needed to identify a methodology to eliminate development waste and reduce development cycle time.

Software developers identified many practices and principles to guide them along the way. The acceptance of OOP has propelled the software community into a new phase of software development. But if developers are to harness all the potential that OOP provides, they must define a concrete development process. As with the Jumping Pawn Puzzle, a concrete software development process will eliminate redundant dead ends. It also reduces the amount of mental energy spent at each state in the development process.

There are some in the software development discipline that resist the use of a methodology. They give several fallacious reasons for avoiding a methodology.

Fallacy 1: Methodologies stifle creativity.

Some programmers believe that conforming to a set methodology will stifle their creativity. Inexperienced developers often confuse creativity with chaos. Forcing them to use a methodology may alienate them. Yet those who choose to adopt a good methodology will magnify their creativity. They will create more software in less time. The genuine delight of creative software development comes from identifying innovative ways of solving problems. The purpose of a good methodology is not to eliminate the creative elements of software development. A good development methodology should stimulate the creative process by eliminating the drudgery of reinventing the wheel.

As with the Jumping Pawn Puzzle, software development has lots of opportunities to go down blind alleys. Running down a path can be mysterious and adventurous. If developers do not use a methodology to help them identify redundant paths, they may fool themselves into believing they are trying something new or creative. In reality, the frustration of revisiting the same dead ends will eventually far outweigh the enjoyment they derive from the self-deception of simulated creativity.

Fallacy 2: Methodologies are bureaucratic.

Some feel that software development methodologies require too much tedious, yet unproductive work. This feeling usually indicates that either the development management or the software implementors don't fully understand the methodology. When management does not fully understand the purpose of a development methodology, they may impose extravagant policies and procedures. It is easy for project managers to mistakenly believe that if a little structure is good, more structure must be even better. These policies and procedures are usually a result of developers trying to obey the letter of the law without understanding the principles behind it. Such a situation is truly bureaucratic and should be relaxed. A dose of common sense can go a long way toward preventing unwarranted overhead.

Software implementors who don't fully understand the development methodology can easily rationalize skipping steps that have little immediate payoff. This is especially true for developers who lack experience in the full software development life cycle. Experience is a sure cure for those with short sight. Developers may grumble about doing software customer support or software maintenance, but experience with these tasks is necessary to the growth of a well-rounded software developer.

The best protection against these problems is to fully understand the principles behind the methodology and to use common sense in applying the processes. Structure, policies, and procedures should be used precisely when needed; no more, no less. The effort and practice required to find this balancing point will be rewarded with a trim development effort that produces quality products within reasonable time constraints.

Fallacy 3: Development methodologies take too long.

Ultimately a methodology should reduce the cost of the full software development life cycle. Every process and procedure required by the methodology must support this goal. Even so, employing a reasoning that defies logic, developers often throw their methodology to the wind when faced with a tight schedule. Any methodology worth using should represent the formula for the shortest distance between two points. If a methodology represents the best course of navigation for a project, throwing the methodology out is really an act of panic. Panic mode does not produce quality products.

In defense of those who believe these fallacies, we must admit that working without a methodology might be better than some of the methodologies that developers have tried. Some developers have come to believe these fallacies because they worked on a project that abused a methodology. To avoid a methodology-related fiasco you must understand the methodology and use common sense.

Often development teams will start a new effort with a completely new methodology — a methodology that none of the team members know or understand. To successfully apply a development methodology, one must take the time to understand the principles behind each step of the methodology. You can test whether a development team understands a specific methodology by having the team practice on a small project first. Sometimes trying out a new methodology on a simple mock program will reveal strengths and weaknesses with the methodology or its implementation. As developers get enough experience, the methodology will become second nature.

Once developers understand a methodology, they must maintain an attitude of common sense. One can easily get carried away with policies and procedures that implement a methodology. If developers allow this to happen, they will awake one morning to find their development process crumbling under its own weight. Remember, the purpose of a methodology is to reduce the total development effort. You can never do enough up-front work to guarantee that the program will never require maintenance. But, you also can't afford to reduce development time if the result is software that requires an expensive life support system. The optimum balance lies somewhere between perfect and slipshod — that's only common sense.

Despite the potential for misuse, as the Jumping Pawn Problem showed, a good methodology is an important tool. Consider some additional benefits a development methodology can yield.

Benefit 1: Methodologies can improve the development project's chance of success.

Imagine a problem much more complex than the Jumping Pawn Puzzle. If developers do not use a methodology and the problem is sufficiently complex, they may get lost in a labyrinth of possibilities and never emerge. If developers use a methodology that helps them track where they have been and where they are going, they have the assurance of making progress.

Benefit 2: Methodologies can reduce the overall development effort.

Since a methodology can eliminate redundant unsuccessful effort, a methodology reduces the development effort. The focus of a good development methodology is to do the right work at the right time. In software development, the right work at the right time means knowing what issues to resolve at specific points in the development process. Resolving the issues too early may lead to blind alleys, while resolving issues too late causes expensive rework. A methodology helps assure that design issues are resolved in proper sequence.

Benefit 3: Methodologies can improve product quality.

Besides making sure developers do not redo work, methodologies can help make sure all the work gets done. Errors of omission can result in limited functionality or even defects. A methodology guarantees developers will consider all the issues.

Benefit 4: Methodologies can make software development more predictable.

A serious problem in the software development industry is estimating software development time and effort. Estimating development time and effort is like projecting a time of arrival for a long trip. If travelers know the type of transportation they will be using and what route they will be taking, they can accurately estimate the amount of time required to complete the trip. Without this information, their estimates can easily be off by orders of magnitude.

If developers cannot describe their development process, time and effort estimates are an intuitive guess. If developers follow a methodology, they know what they will be doing at each phase of development. By knowing what needs to be accomplished at each phase, developers can more accurately estimate the amount of time and effort involved.

Since methodologies describe repeatable processes, developers can use historical data to help estimate development effort. Without a methodology, each development effort is different. This makes comparing development efforts between projects like comparing apples and oranges.

Very little can be learned from previous development efforts because the next one will be different. By applying a complete methodology, developers will identify similarities in the development process and effort.

Summary

This chapter has discussed the Object-Oriented Paradigm (OOP) and methodologies. The chapter defined OOP as a way of looking at software problems in terms of abstract data types with inheritance and polymorphism. Abstract data types are sets of related functions that operate on a common set of data items. Inheritance is a relationship of attributes from one class to another. Polymorphism is the ability of classes to implement the same functions differently. This chapter also showed how developers use these features of OOP to improve the software they build.

Methodologies are repeatable and predictable problem solving process descriptions. This chapter discussed fallacious reasons for avoiding methodologies. The chapter also showed how methodologies simplify software development by giving it a better chance of success, by reducing the development effort, by improving the resultant software, and by making the development process predictable.

Exercises

0. List the similarities between ADTs and classes. List their differences.
1. Write a binary tree package as both an ADT and a class. The package should insert and search for values. Don't forget the constructors and destructors.
2. List the reasons for using OOP.
3. Define the term methodology. List the reasons for using a methodology in problem solving.
4. Solve the Jumping Pawn Puzzle for eight pawns and nine positions.

ject(Requirements,
scribe the objects externals
tSpec = CreateSpec(Requirements
the object until it passes
all verif... tests
Do {
// Describe how th...
ObjectDesign = Design...
// Find or build subordina...
Subordinates = CreateSu...
// Implement this objec...
Code = CodeObject(O...
// Create boundary v...
TestSet = CreateBlac...
// Create condition...
WhiteBoxTest...

Chapter 1

Overview of the Methodology

The previous chapter highlighted the importance of OOP and the use of methodologies in software development. This chapter introduces a specific OOP-based software development methodology. Most software development methodologies focus on the design phase of software development. This chapter discusses a methodology that distinguishes itself by taking a macroscopic view of software development — a view that describes the complete software life cycle from initial requirements to final maintenance. This methodology also recognizes that each phase of this life cycle is essential to developing quality software.

Two independent concepts lie at the core of the methodology described in this chapter. These concepts are *abstraction* and the use of differing *expert perspectives*. The first part of this chapter demonstrates the concepts of abstraction and expert perspectives, tells why these concepts are helpful, and describes how to use them. The last part of this chapter gives a high level, step-by-step description of the development methodology. The latter part of the chapter also shows how abstraction and expert perspectives support this methodology. This chapter identifies each step of the methodology and explains why each step is necessary. Later chapters will describe in more detail how each step works.

Abstraction

Examine Figure 1.0 and make a mental note of what you see. Most viewers immediately conclude the image in Figure 1.0 represents a butterfly. Now look at the Figure 1.0 again. This time look for something besides a butterfly. As you investigate the image you will see that Figure 1.0 is a butterfly composed of triangles. If you look at the image a third time, you may even see Figure 1.0 as a set of organized line segments. Though all three explanations correctly describe Figure 1.0, the image of the butterfly jumps out at first glance. The butterfly image is unmistakable because the mind applies a concept called abstraction to the line segments and triangles.

Humans use *abstraction*, a natural mental tool, to deal with complexity. By masking insignificant detail, abstraction accents the elements of central importance to any given level of detail. For example, a complex ecosystem of trees, plants and animals is abstracted to "forest." The combination of a power supply, electronic components, a cathode ray tube and a keyboard is a "computer." Since the mind can only deal with a finite amount of complexity, it is necessary to use abstraction to understand complex systems. Abstraction prevents complexity overload by masking irrelevant detail.

The differing amounts of detail are levels of abstraction. For example, the butterfly image is one level of abstraction. The triangles are a second level. The line segments are a third. More detailed concepts, such as the line segments, are lower levels of abstraction. Conversely, more general concepts, like the butterfly image, are higher levels of abstraction. The mind consciously moves from one level of abstraction to another by deciding what details to consider.

Levels of abstraction naturally have consistent amounts of detail. It is difficult to imagine Figure 1.0 as a picture of a part of a butterfly mixed with some triangles and some line segments. The mind sees the image either as a complete butterfly, or as a set of triangles, or as a set of lines. Mixing levels of abstraction creates confusion. The concept of maintaining uniform levels of detail is called *abstraction consistency*.

Abstraction compels the mind to isolate individual elements or aspects of a system. Focusing on individual elements frees the mind from maintaining details about indirectly related parts of the system. Since the mind can devote full attention to the element at hand, it can easily understand the specifics of that element. For example, when you investigate each element of the butterfly in Figure 1.0 individually, you can make sure that each element is a triangle consisting of three connected line segments.

While abstraction is a naturally occurring mental process, one can strengthen the results by exercising conscious discipline over the process. When faced with a complex system, be certain to look for multiple levels of abstraction. Analyze each level separately, being careful to maintain abstraction consistency. Finally, be certain you understand what to avoid when using abstraction. The four most common mistakes are:

- ❑ Illogically partitioning elements for a level of abstraction.
- ❑ Collapsing or skipping levels of abstraction.
- ❑ Not identifying all the elements for a level of abstraction.
- ❑ Identifying non-existent elements for a level of abstraction.

One might view the objects that compose the butterfly in Figure 1.0 as V-shaped objects. This would be an illogical partitioning, because V-shaped objects do not represent the subordinate objects of the butterfly

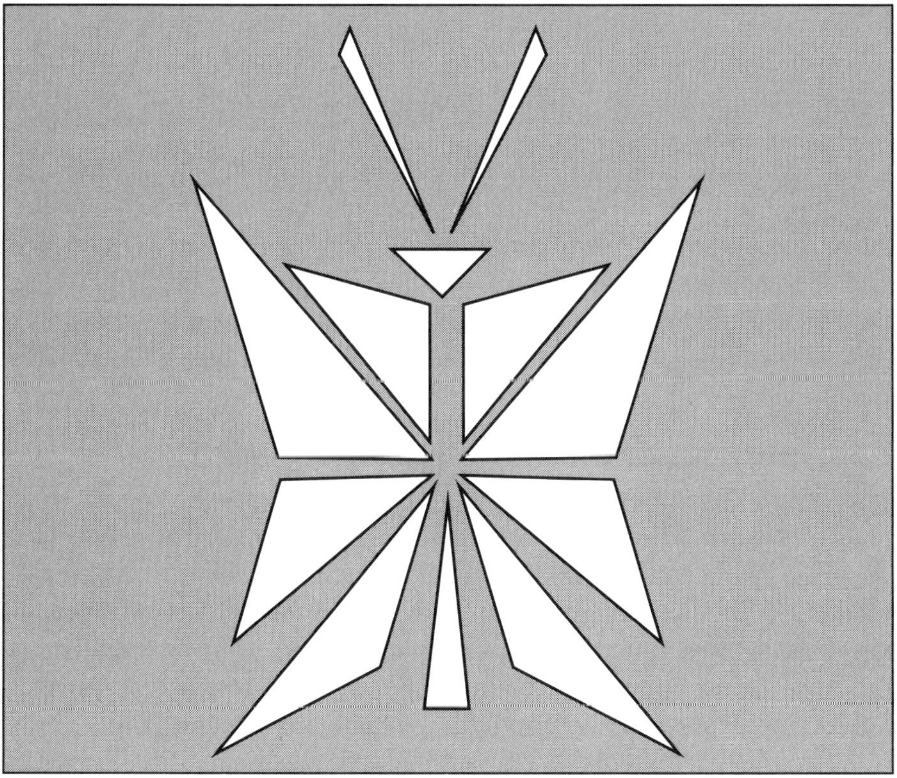

Figure 1.0 — An Abstract Image

well. To completely describe the butterfly with V-shaped objects, requires that the V-shaped objects overlap one another. The resulting description is not as clear, concise, or intuitive as a description based on triangles.

Skipping or collapsing levels of abstraction adds complexity. Imagine overlooking the triangle level of abstraction and viewing the subordinate objects of the butterfly in Figure 1.0 only as lines. There are 11 triangles in the butterfly image and 33 lines. A description of the butterfly image, in terms of its lines, is much more complex than a description of the same image in terms of its triangles. It is simpler to understand and describe the butterfly in terms of its triangles, and the triangles in terms of their lines.

Decomposition using abstraction must account for all the subordinate elements. Since the wings of the butterfly in Figure 1.0 are mirror images of each other, one might describe the butterfly as two wings (each wing consists of four triangles). At first glance this seems to simplify the description of the butterfly since the two-wing description consists of only two objects instead of 11. The two-wing description fails, though, because it overlooks the head of the butterfly. Therefore, the two-wing description is not complete.

Individuals sometimes make the mistake of assuming they know what the subordinates of an object are. Those who have studied butterflies know that butterflies have two wings, a head and a body. But when applied to Figure 1.0, this description fails because this butterfly image does not have a body. To be useful, an abstraction must describe only those subordinate elements that exist. Adding subordinate elements that do not exist results in confusion and wasted effort.

Using Abstraction for Software Development

In software development, abstraction organizes software to introduce detail as the detail becomes important. Abstraction in software development also can keep the level of detail consistent and prevent complexity overload. Applying abstraction during software development yields software that is easy to understand. Software that is easy to understand is also easy to design, test, and maintain. Thus, using abstraction shortens the development cycle and improves the software's quality.

Abstraction is especially important to object-oriented development because it helps the designer avoid common object-oriented design pitfalls. In one common approach to object-oriented design, the development team begins by enumerating all the objects contained within a system. Armed with the list of objects, the developers attempt to enumerate all the methods that each object needs. Because this approach tends to ignore the many different relationships between objects, it tends to yield an illogical partitioning and overly complex objects. In complex systems, even the best developers will overlook some objects and create other useless objects. The developers' chance of missing or creating the wrong objects grows geometrically as the size and complexity of the software increase. The number of objects also increases the complexity of determining the relationships between objects.

When developers do not apply abstraction to object-oriented systems, each additional object geometrically increases the complexity of the system. Consider the two diagrams in Figure 1.1, which represent systems of objects. The circles in the diagrams represent the objects and the lines represent the possible relationships between the objects. The system with three objects (the first diagram) has only three possible relationships. The system with eight objects (the second diagram) has 28 possible relationships. While the second system has only five more objects than the first system, the number of relationships increases by 25.

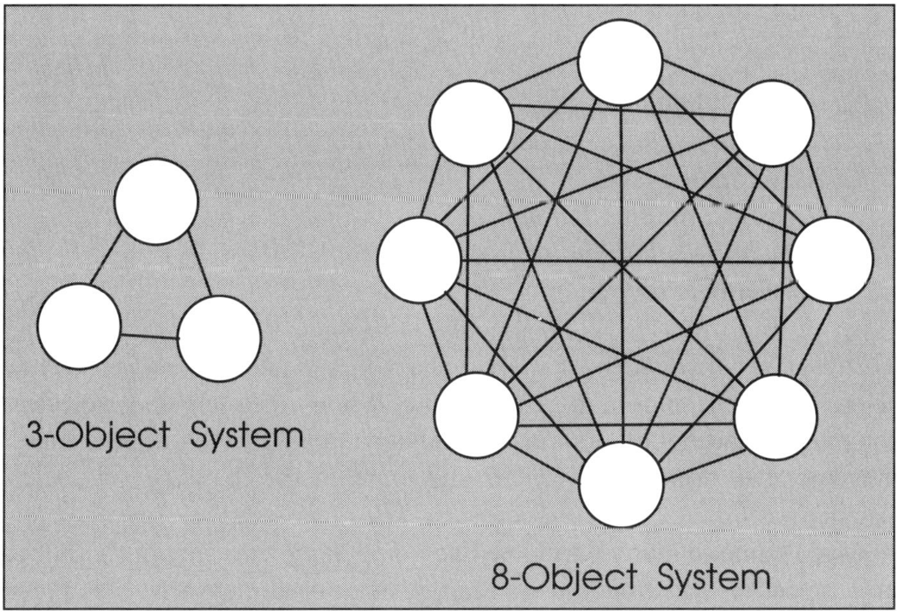

Figure 1.1 — Object Relationship Diagrams

Developers can avoid common object-oriented design pitfalls by carefully considering the levels of abstraction within a system. To find levels of abstraction within a system and understand how the levels relate, the developer first describes the system in terms of its component parts or elements. The elements of the system are the subordinate objects that form a new level of abstraction. Given the elements of the new level, the developer then describes each element in terms of its component parts or elements. By recursively identifying the layers of abstraction, developers completely identify all the objects that make up the system. This recursive process also helps developers understand the relationships between objects.

The diagram in Figure 1.2 shows how abstraction simplifies system architecture. The developers of this eight-object system recursively applied abstraction to identify and organize the eight objects within the system. This abstraction-based design limits the number of possible relationships to a maximum of 12. Thus, applying abstraction to the eight-object system architecture example reduces the complexity of the architecture reflected in the number of relationships by more than half.

Expert Perspectives

If you were to sketch a map of the area around where you live and work, which of the following would be included in your map? Why?

- ❑ Roads and highways
- ❑ City, county, state, or other borders
- ❑ Land topology
- ❑ Historical or other landmarks
- ❑ Population information
- ❑ Mass transit routes

In our experience, most individuals will include one or two of the above items, but seldom more than three. When asked why they selected some items and not others, respondents generally answer that the items they included somehow seemed important to the map they chose to sketch.

Maps come in many varieties. Each map has a specific point of view or perspective. Most people are familiar with road maps that help them figure out how to get from one place to another. Backpackers are familiar with topographical maps that explain the terrain. If you have ever explored an unfamiliar shopping mall, you may have even used a map to find all the computer bookstores. Each map includes only the details that are relevant to its intended use.

It is important to consider each potential application perspective individually. At first, an "all-purpose" map, one that contains all the items in the list above, might seem like a good idea. However, to represent so many different items, such a map would need to use every different color and line style. The map would become so crowded that it would become difficult to read. Instead of being helpful for many different purposes, the map would become nearly useless for all. Even though they all describe the same area, multiple maps, each with a different perspective and purpose, are more useful than a single, overly-complex, general-purpose map.

Similarly, complex systems are more easily understood when studied from several different perspectives. Different perspectives focus on different attributes, though they describe the same thing. Combining all the perspectives yields a complete understanding of the system.

The most useful perspectives are *expert perspectives*. An expert is a person who knows a lot about a specific domain. Because of their specific knowledge, experts lend useful insight. When experts voice descriptions

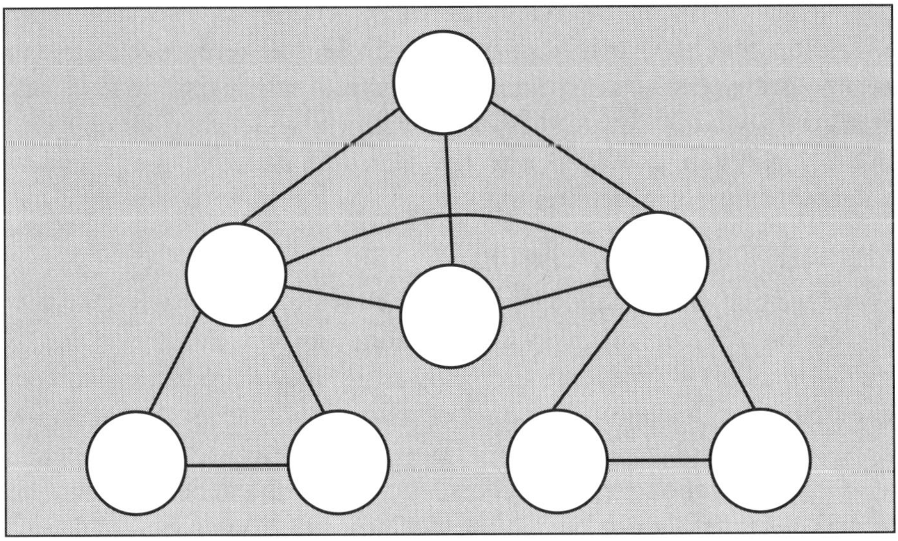

Figure 1.2 — Eight-Object System With Abstraction

of their domains of expertise, they are giving expert perspectives. Combining several expert perspectives from the same specific domain yields an in-depth understanding.

For example, there are many expert perspectives that describe different facets of the human body. Specialists with an expert perspective of the human body include internists, bone specialists, brain surgeons, eye doctors, and dentists. While no single perspective completely describes how the human body functions, the sum of all perspectives yields a complete understanding.

This book describes a methodology which employs expert perspectives to understand and develop software. The relevant experts are:

- the customer
- the user
- the architect
- the implementor
- the referee
- the detective

The customer defines the requirements. The user specifies what the solution looks like. The architect designs the software. The implementor codes the software. The referee judges the software. The detective inspects the software's internals. These expert perspectives do not imply a development staff of six people. A single software developer can assume each perspective when appropriate. These perspectives work together to yield software that the developers understand completely. Because software quality is directly related to the developer's understanding of the software, multiple perspectives produce better software.

Methodological Description

The development methodology described here, the Object Creation Process, is a recursive process for creating objects. Each level in the recursion uses the object requirements as input and produces an object as output. The design of the target object dictates the requirements for the subordinate objects. Given a set of subordinate object requirements, the Object Creation Process recurses to create the subordinates. The recursion continues until the decomposition identifies subordinate objects that already exist.

Figure 1.3 illustrates the recursive nature of the Object Creation Process. The circles represent objects and the lines show the relationships between levels of abstraction. Object A is the highest level object (the complete program). By applying the Object Creation Process to object A, the developer identifies the need for subordinate objects B and C. The developer then recursively applies the Object Creation Process to objects B and C to yield requirements for objects D, E, F and G. The recursion stops when the developer identifies requirements for existing objects. When all subordinate objects exist, the developer uses the subordinate objects to implement the target object. For example, when objects D and E exist, the developer can implement object B.

The Object Creation Process is one of *abstraction decomposition*. The abstraction decomposition always begins with the highest level object: the entire program. Decomposing the program object initiates the recursive Object Creation Process.

Priming the Process: The Customer Perspective

The Object Creation Process uses requirements as its input. Requirements describe what types of functions the object must perform. The first of the expert perspectives, the customer's, produces the requirements.

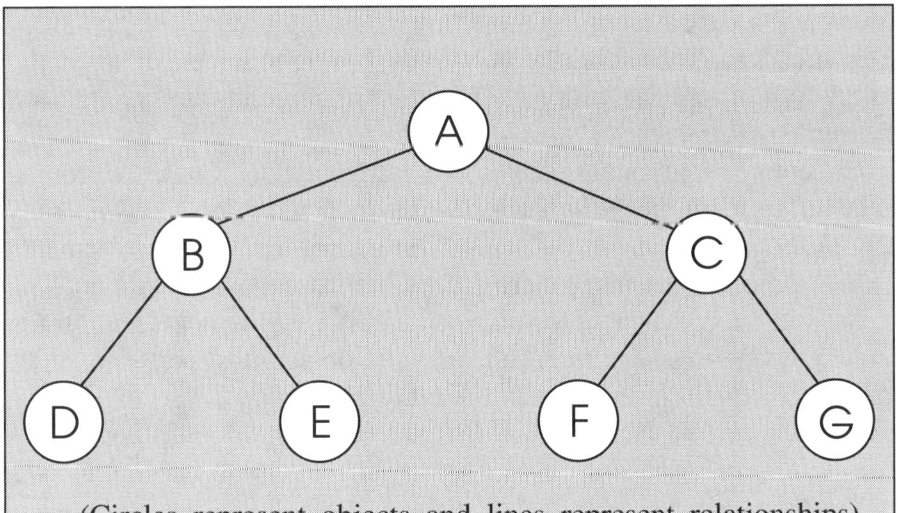

(Circles represent objects and lines represent relationships)

Figure 1.3 — Example System Abstraction Decomposition

A customer is one who needs a solution to a problem. The customer usually understands the problem very well and knows what functions an object must perform to supply an acceptable solution. As with the other perspectives, the customer perspective may or may not be represented by an actual customer. In the absence of an actual customer, a developer must assume the perspective of the customer.

Customers understand the problem and the requirements for the solution, but customers may not necessarily use the solution. For example, parents buy toys for their children, but the parents usually do not use the toys themselves. The parents are the customers for the toys while the children are the users of the toys. The parents understand the requirements for the toys. For example, the toys must be educational, entertaining, and safe. Parents may select from several solutions that meet these requirements.

It is the responsibility of those using the customer perspective to identify the requirements for an object. Programs consist of many objects, each of which has separate requirements. Therefore, each object needs a customer perspective to identify these requirements.

The most difficult requirements to identify are those for the entire program object. When the program object requirements are correct, it becomes easier for the developer to identify requirements of the subordinate objects within the program. The abstraction decomposition process naturally decomposes the requirements for subordinate objects from their superiors. Therefore, the initial program requirements "prime the pump." All subordinate objects derive their requirements indirectly from the initial requirements.

Collecting requirements serves two main purposes. First, the process of identifying requirements helps developers reach a detailed consensus about what an object must do to solve the problem. The requirements delineate those solutions that are acceptable from those that are not.

Second, requirements create an audit trail. Requirements audit trails remind developers of critical functions the object must perform. Audit trails also explain to latecomers the rationale behind the selected solutions.

The Object Creation Process

Once developers have established the requirements for a program, they can begin the recursive Object Creation Process. The process can be summarized in the following steps:

- ❑ Define what the target object is.
- ❑ Describe how the target object works (in terms of subordinate objects).
- ❑ Find or create all the subordinate objects.
- ❑ Implement the target object.
- ❑ Verify that the object fulfills its definition.
- ❑ Verify that the target object works as described.

To distinguish clearly between objects at the different levels of abstraction, the Object Creation Process refers to the object at the current level of abstraction as the target object. The target object defines the interaction of objects at the immediately lower level of abstraction. At any point in the recursive process, all other objects at higher and lower levels of abstraction are out of the scope of the Object Creation Process. Recursion brings the lower levels of abstraction into scope. The Object Creation Process naturally masks the unrelated objects to avoid overwhelming developers.

The Object Creation Process limits the number of concurrent objects developers need to consider by applying abstraction and recursion. Figure 1.3 shows how the Object Creation Process uses abstraction and recursion to bound the objects of interest. Remember that the circles in Figure 1.3 represent objects and the lines represent relationships between levels of abstraction. When designing object A, only objects B and C are in focus. Object B's design brings objects D and E into focus; object A goes out of focus. Similarly, object C's design brings objects F and G into focus and eliminates object A.

The Object Creation Process starts with the *specification phase*. In this phase the developers work to understand exactly what the object will look like when finished. The result of the specification phase is a description of all external views of the completed object. After the specification phase, comes the *design phase*. During the design phase the developer describes how the object works in terms of subordinate objects.

The design phase also identifies the subordinate objects for use in following phases.

Identifying the subordinate objects sets the stage for the *recursive phase* of the Object Creation Process. The recursive phase takes each subordinate object and recursively applies the Object Creation Process to create subordinate objects. The recursive phase is complete when all subordinate objects exist. The *coding phase* begins once the design is complete and the subordinate objects exist. The coding phase converts the design into executable code.

The final phases of the Object Creation Process focus on *object verification*. Given an object and its specification, the next phase is the *black-box test phase*. To create the black-box tests, the developers identify tests that can distinguish the desired object (as described in the specification phase) from other similar objects. Later these tests help verify that all phases of the Object Creation Process produce the desired results. Finally, the *white-box test phase* takes the executable code produced by the coding phase and uses it to identify white-box tests, tests which are based on the object's internal workings. The developer can combine the white-box tests with the black-box tests to create a solid regression test suite for the object.

The remainder of the chapter will describe each of these phases, explaining what each entails and why it is important. The chapter concludes by presenting an algorithm for the Object Creation Process.

The User's Perspective

Once the customer-based requirements are established, the developer turns to the user perspective. The user perspective describes what the object is. The user perspective differs from the customer perspective by describing how the object is used to solve the customer's problem (i.e., fulfill the requirements). The user identifies the solution by describing the object from multiple views.

Users may view the object from many different points of view, but the only legitimate user points of view, in this context, are external views of the object — views that describe the target object as a finished object. In other words, users should only describe what the object does; not how the object works. For example, a user might describe a black box in terms of its height, length and width. Users of the black box can describe the box's color, texture, weight, and maybe even smell. A user cannot describe what keeps the walls of the box rigid. Nor can a user explain why the box weighs as much as it does or why the box smells the way it does. These latter views of the black box are not legitimate user views. The latter views require some understanding about the construction of the box.

There are several reasons for defining the user perspective early in the Object Creation Process. The object developer must know what to build. By identifying what the object will be before any development takes place, the object developers can determine when the Object Creation Process is complete.

There are two extremes in object development. One extreme is knowing before initiating the development process exactly what the object will look like when it is complete. The other extreme is not knowing what the object should do or what it should look like. These extremes represent the bounds of a spectrum. Figure 1.4 shows the spectrum. No developer wants to attempt to create an object without knowing something about that object. Yet developers sometimes attempt to develop objects without a complete understanding of what the object should do. Without a description of what an object does, the object developer has little chance of successfully creating an object that satisfies the customer. The developer can only hope to iterate with the customer, building and changing objects until the customer happens to be satisfied. In this scenario, who is to decide when aspects of the object are bugs or features? By understanding what the object is from the beginning, developers avoid frustration and wasted effort.

Developers must agree upon what they are building. The same is true for all team endeavors. For example, if a construction team started building a house, without first deciding what the house will look like,

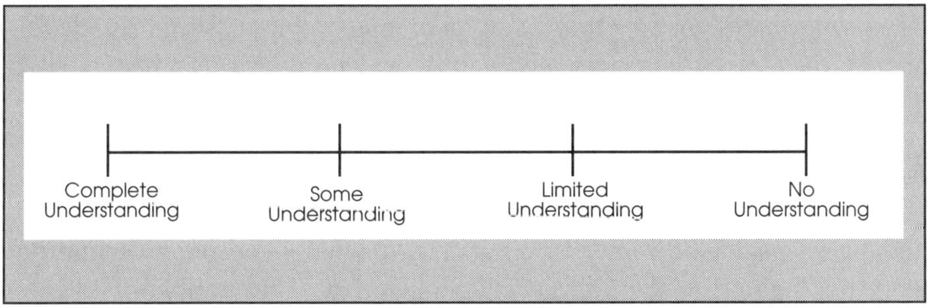

Figure 1.4 — The Object Specification Spectrum

they are likely to make some significant mistakes. For example, one builder might create a staircase only to find it blocked by a wall built by another builder. Or, if each builder assumes the other will run the gas or electricity they could end up with a house full of unusable appliances. In any case, the results would be disastrous.

The same concept applies to object development. By completely and concretely establishing what the object is before investing much effort, object developers reduce the amount of time and effort spent reworking their software.

Applying the user perspective early in the Object Creation Process helps developers avoid errors. The object may not be completely specified, or it may have external aspects that are not fully described. The object's specification may lack consistency. (Specification inconsistency occurs when different user points of view do not agree with each other. When different user views conflict it is impossible for the developer to succeed because the specification is ambiguous.) Viewing the object from the user's perspective may also generate some hints about how to develop the object. While specifying the dimensions of the doors and bathroom fixtures, for example, a home builder might realize that the bathtub will not fit through the doors, making it clear that the workers should install the tub before installing the door jambs. Similarly, applying the user perspective reduces object development time by identifying potential errors.

Completely specifying an object's external aspects also helps a developer assess the cost of developing the object. Imagine trying to project the cost of developing a house with no detailed specification about what the house looks like. The cost of building a Beverly Hills mansion is orders of magnitude higher than the cost of building a small grass hut. Given a detailed user description of a house, home builders can project the development costs within a few percentage points. Similarly, developers have a better chance of accurately projecting development costs if they understand what the object will eventually look like.

The Architect's Perspective

Once the object's external appearance and behavior are defined, the developer can decide how the object will work. The object's internal workings belong to the architect's perspective. The architect takes the user's external specification and creates an internal description of how the object works.

The architect relies heavily upon abstraction to describe the architecture of an object. The architectural description of the target object describes the operation of the object in terms of other subordinate objects. This description does not describe how the subordinate objects work. For example, an architectural perspective of printing data on a standard PC laser printer might have the following description:

```
While printable data exists...
    Get a buffer of data from the input port;
    For each page of data in the buffer...
        Get a sheet from the sheet feeder;
        Send the page of data and the sheet to the laser unit;
```

This description explains the entire operation of printing data within a laser printer. The description does *not* explain the details of subordinate objects, such as the buffer, the sheet feeder, or the laser unit. Each architectural description should be complete only for its level of abstraction. The architects of the subordinate objects fill in the details about the subordinate operations (such as how to get a sheet from the sheet feeder).

Architectural design descriptions have multiple uses. Since design descriptions are complete, developers can review the descriptions to verify that the design provides all the functionality specified in the user perspective. The implementation phase uses design descriptions to decide how to create the object.

Design perspectives also help developers understand the relationships among objects. Using a well ordered process to identify the objects within a program also helps the developer describe the relationships between objects. Developers can easily understand the purpose and function of each relationship by identifying and examining relationships in an independent and organized manner.

Architectural design perspectives help developers avoid unnecessary and unnecessarily complex objects. A wise rule of thumb for development is "don't be afraid to throw away excess baggage." Excess baggage means ideas, designs, or objects that do not contribute to the goal of the target object development. If a well designed, coded, and tested subordinate object does not contribute to the functions of its superior, the subordinate object is junk. As developers invest more development effort in an object, they become more committed to using the object. It is much easier to abandon a useless object if the developer has not made a large investment in the object's development. Coded and tested objects represent significantly more development effort than objects that are mere designs on paper.

The Implementor's Perspective

After designing how the object works, the next phase of the object's development is the implementation phase. During the implementation phase the implementor translates the design into actual executable code. Traditionally, developers refer to this phase as *programming*.

In the Object Creation Process, it is the responsibility of the implementor to produce a quality implementation of the object. Three independent variables are the basis for the quality of an object's implementation. These variables are:

- ❑ Function
- ❑ Clarity
- ❑ Performance

The most important aspect of an object is its function. If the object does not provide the functionality defined by the architectural or design perspective, the object is useless. It does not matter how quickly the programmer programmed the object, how pretty the object's code looks, or even how well documented the object is. If the object does not provide the necessary functionality, the other trappings associated with the object are not important.

The implementor's ability to deliver the necessary object functionality depends heavily upon the object's architectural perspective. It is critical to the success of the implementor that the architectural perspective is correct and understandable. When the architect and the implementor are different people, they need to work closely to be certain the implementor understands and provides the correct functionality for an object.

Once an implementor guarantees that the object provides the necessary functionality, it is the implementor's responsibility to make the implementation easy to understand. Implementation clarity depends on the object's documentation, comments, and the code itself. Developers find fewer defects and can fix the defects easier when the developers understand how the object works.

Another important aspect of object implementation is the object's run-time performance. While an implementor's coding finesse can never compensate for an inherently weak architectural design, the selection of actual data structures and algorithm specifics does affect the run-time performance. The implementor is responsible for understanding the performance impact of implementation details, and must use implementation techniques that maximize the object's run-time performance while preserving the object's implementation clarity.

The Referee's Perspective

The responsibility of determining if an object adheres to the user description is the job of the referee. The referee's perspective protects the user by testing the object to make sure the object is what the user specified. The referee also protects the object implementor by limiting any criticism to aspects dictated by the documented user specification.

The referee employs the user's perspective of the object to establish criteria for accepting an object. The referee's use of the user's perspective is analogous to a referee using a rule book at a sporting event to determine acceptable sporting behavior. The referee's perspective identifies tests that exercise the object's external interface. Traditionally, software engineering refers to this type of testing as black-box testing. Black-box tests make sure the object provides all the specified functionality. Black-box testing only considers the functionality of the object, it does not consider the object's design or internal workings. Tests that rely upon the internal software design are white-box tests. Referees cannot perform white-box testing because they employ only the user perspective and are unaware of the object's design. White-box tests are the detective's responsibility. (See the next section.)

The referee's perspective uncovers defects in the software. From the referee's perspective, software defects occur when software breaks the rules established in the user's object specification. The specification must be thorough and consistent because the user's object specification establishes the referee's bounds. It is impossible to establish bounds and identify bugs in software if the software specification is not consistent and complete.

The referee determines the completion criterion for object development. When developers think they have an instance of the object as specified by the user's perspective, the developer can use the referee's perspective to test the object. The developers cannot claim the object is complete until the referee agrees that the object meets the specification of the user's perspective.

The Detective's Perspective

Selective testing of an object's external behavior will not find all defects. Just as a stopped watch can give correct results twice a day, defective software can sometimes produce correct results. If you look inside a watch and see that its battery is missing, you'll know something is wrong, even if it appears to show the correct time. Similarly, some software problems are most easily found by looking *inside* the object.

Software can fool developers in much the same way as the watch without the battery might fool its owner. When developers create an object they expect it to work. After all, developers do not build software intentionally not to work. Black-box testing can even reinforce the belief that defective software works as desired. Developers need to open objects and look inside them to be sure they really work.

The detective perspective has the responsibility of looking inside the object. The detective creates tests based upon the object's internal structure. When detectives look inside objects, they must identify test cases that exercise all the object's code. Detective perspectives and referee perspectives work together to combine their tests. The difference between the detective's tests and the referee's tests is one of perspective. The referee determines how to test an object by looking at its outward functions while the detective considers the object's inner workings.

The perspectives of the referee and the detective combine to produce useful object regression tests. Object regression tests are essential for fully reusable software because most software, even OOP-based software, is not reusable without some modifications. (Inheritance lets developers extend objects without modifying the base object's data or methods. Sometimes it is more efficient to modify the original object than to extend it.) A rule of thumb for software development says that modified software is broken software. But if developers have a regression test suite to verify the operation of an object, they modify the object without fearing they will unknowingly violate the object's integrity. Both externally-based and internally-based tests are important in the regression test suite.

Internally-based tests help developers completely understand how objects act under various conditions. No matter how carefully one designs, codes, and inspects a program, the initial testing nearly always exposes some unanticipated behavior. Expecting to fully understand an object without benefit of the detective's perspective is equivalent to expecting a program to compile and run the first time. Cautious programmers only trust software after they have tested it.

The Object Creation Process Algorithm

The Object Creation Process relies on abstraction and expert perspectives. Each phase, in sequence, applies perspectives to produce artifacts. The full set of artifacts constitutes the complete product. So far in this chapter we've described both the process sequence and artifacts at a high level. However, the high level description of the process answers few questions about how to use the Object Creation Process for actual software development. The balance of this chapter describes the process in algorithmic form, adding some details for completeness. Subsequent chapters elaborate on how to use the Object Creation Process for each phase of the actual developement process.

The following algorithmic summary shows the starting point of the software development process. The starting point "primes the pump" for the Object Creation Process.

```
StartingPoint() {

    // Identify the program requirements
    ProgramRequirements = IdentifyRequirements();
    // Create the program
    CreateObject(ProgramRequirements)
}
```

Because the Object Creation Process needs requirements as its input, the first step in the creation of a program is to identify the program requirements. Given the program requirements, the developer begins the recursive Object Creation Process using the program as the highest level object. Decomposing the starting point operations provides insight into identifying and creating objects. (Chapter 2 describes how to identify program requirements in more detail.) Document 1.0 contains an algorithmic summary of the Object Creation Process.

The algorithmic summary of the Object Creation Process shows more detail than previously discussed, but the underlying ideas are the same. The first step is to use the user perspective and the object's requirements to describe the object as a black box. This is the specification phase. The result of the specification phase is an external specification of the object. Chapter 3 discusses the details of how to create an external specification.

After specifying what the object is, the Object Creation Process describes how the object works. The focus on abstraction directs developers to describe the object's operation in terms of subordinate objects. By relying heavily upon abstraction, developers can postpone detailed concerns until the time is appropriate. Chapter 4 shows how to use abstraction and how to describe objects' operations in terms of their subordinates.

With an understanding of how objects work with respect to their subordinates, the Object Creation Process finds or creates the necessary subordinate objects. Finding or creating subordinate objects is the recursive step of the Object Creation Process. Through this recursion, the developer acquires the necessary building blocks for implementing the target object. Once the necessary subordinate objects are known, the developer translates the external description of the object's operation into actual executable code. Chapter 5 describes some heuristics for performing the translation.

The next phase of the Object Creation Process uses the referee's perspective to create the black-box tests. Black-box tests determine if objects meet the external specification. Chapter 6 discusses black-box testing strategies and describes how to manage tests.

Finally, the Object Creation Process creates white-box tests to exercise all the object's code. Chapter 7 discusses white-box testing strategies. Developers create a complete test set by adding the white-box tests to the black-box tests. If the object does not pass the full object test set, the developer must reconsider and adjust the object's design. In the event that a change in design requires different subordinate objects, the developer finds or develops the new subordinates. Even if the design is sound and requires no new subordinates, the developer still may need to change the object's source code for the object to pass the tests. When the developer changes the object's implementation, the change may require some additional white-box tests to exercise all the object's code. The process iterates until the object successfully completes its tests.

By following the steps of the Object Creation Process the developer produces several important artifacts, including the object's external specification, the object's design, a complete regression test for the object, and the actual object's code. Each of these artifacts is critical to truly reusable software. Chapter 8 shows developers how to use these artifacts to ease product maintenance and improve software reusability.

Document 1.0 — The Object Creation Process

```
CreateObject(Requirements) {

    // Describe the objects externals
    ObjectSpec = CreateSpec(Requirements)
    // Work on the object until it passes
    // all verification tests
    Do {
        // Describe how the object works
        ObjectDesign = DesignObject(ObjectSpec)
        // Find or build subordinates
        Subordinates = CreateSubObjects(ObjectDesign)
        // Implement this object
        Code = CodeObject(ObjectDesign, Subordinates)
        // Create boundary value analysis tests
        TestSet = CreateBlackBoxTests(ObjectSpec)
        // Create condition coverage tests
        AddWhiteBoxTests(ObjectDesign, TestSet)
    } While the object does not pass the tests (TestSet, Code)
}

CreateSubObjects(Design) {

    // Identify the objects within the design
    ObjectRequirementsList = IdentifyObject(Design)
    For each of the ObjectRequirements in the list...
        If no object exists that meets the requirements
            // Create the object
            CreateObject(ObjectRequirements)
}
```

Software Quality in the Object Creation Process

The software methodology described in this book does more than streamline the software development life cycle. Every phase of the Object Creation Process emphasizes the development of a quality product. The primary goal of every software developer should be customer satisfaction. Developers have a better chance of producing error-free products that satisfy the needs of their customers if they apply a process that continuously focuses on developing quality software.

There are two questions developers must ask themselves to determine if their software product is of high quality:

- ❑ Did I build the right *product*?
- ❑ Did I build the product *right*?

The focus of the first question is requirements and specification. Product requirements and specifications result from the customer and user perspectives. It is possible to build the right product only if the product's requirements are complete and consistent and the product specification accurately fulfills the requirements. Conversely, it is impossible to build a quality product if the developer neglects the product's requirements and specifications.

Traditionally, developers attempt to inject quality into software by testing it. Unfortunately, software testing alone does nothing to add quality to the software. Software testing can only show how software lacks quality. The product will be no better than its design or implementation.

In the Object Creation Process, the responsibility for software quality lies with all expert perspectives. The software will only be as good as the weakest of the expert perspectives. Neither the referee nor the detective has total responsibility for the quality of the software. The detective's perspective makes sure the software works the way the architect and implementor intended. The referee's responsibility is to make sure the software meets the specification defined by the user's perspective. The user's perspective has the responsibility to define an object that fulfills the customer's requirements. The outcome is that each phase of the Object Creation Process has responsibility for the ultimate product quality. No one perspective can be singled out as the perspective responsible for quality.

Exercises

0. This chapter uses maps as an example of expert perspectives. Show how maps are also an example of abstraction.
1. List several expert perspectives one might employ to describe a car, the human body, or some other complex system.
2. List the six expert perspectives employed by the Object Creation Process and explain the purpose of each perspective.
3. Discuss abstraction and expert perspectives with respect to the Object Creation Process. Show how abstraction relates to the expert perspectives and how they differ in their use.

CreateObject(Requireme

Chapter 2

Priming the Object Creation Process

Every recursive level of the object-oriented program development process described in Chapter 1 (the Object Creation Process) needs information about its particular assignment. In programmatic terms, every invocation of the process needs a set of input parameters. Once the recursion is initiated, each level in the recursive process will generate input data for the next lower level.

The top level, however, is a special case. In a sense, one must "prime the pump" by creating the first set of input parameters, the *Program Requirements*, outside of the recursive process.

This chapter shows how to identify the initial program requirements. Many ideas in this chapter have their origins in *Exploring Requirements Quality Before Design* by Donald C. Gause and Gerald M. Weinberg (Dorset House Publishing, 1989). We highly recommend *Exploring Requirements* as a text for further study on the subject of general requirements gathering.

Requirements gathering has the following four important stages:

- ❑ Function Identification
- ❑ Attribute Identification
- ❑ Constraint Identification
- ❑ Preference Identification

The remainder of this chapter will describe and discuss each stage.

Function Identification

One can most effectively communicate an object's capabilities by explicitly stating what the object does. For example, which of these descriptions best exemplifies a word processor?

- ❑ A program that runs on a PC, drives a laser printer, employs columns, and uses four megabytes of disk space.
- ❑ A program that lets users edit, format, and print text.

The first description identifies features of word processors but does not describe what word processors do. The first description could also

The Cost of Ambiguity

Several years ago a comedy sketch illustrating the importance of eliminating ambiguity appeared on NBC's "Saturday Night Live." The story opens as a retiring nuclear power plant supervisor leaves his retirement party, giving his former crew this advice: "Remember, you can't put too much water in a nuclear reactor."

Moments later one technician floods the nuclear reactor with water. A coworker immediately questions this action. The first technician proclaims that their ex-supervisor just told them that a nuclear reactor needs lots of water. The second technician explains that the supervisor's last words meant just the opposite: they must avoid putting too much water in the nuclear reactor. The scene closes with the two men arguing over the meaning of the supervisor's last words as warning lights flash and sirens wail.

The next scene opens with the former supervisor of the nuclear facility ordering refreshment from a waitress while relaxing on the beach. Out on the horizon the pair see a brilliant flash of light followed by a mushroom-shaped cloud. The waitress wonders aloud what would cause the flash and the odd-shaped cloud. The retired supervisor explains that a mushroom-shaped cloud is the result of a nuclear explosion. As he prepares to leave the beach, he gives the waitress some advice. "Remember," he says, "you can't stare at a nuclear explosion too long."

The fictitious nuclear accident occurred because a critical operational

identify a spreadsheet application. In contrast, the second description focuses on the functions unique to word processors. Due to its focus on functionality, the second description eliminates many unrelated classes of applications. Identifying program functionality is the starting point for gathering requirements.

Attribute Identification

Attributes are qualities the customer desires in the program's functionality. Different programs may provide similar functionality, but have significantly different attributes. For example, two routes may lead to the same destination, but one may emphasize speed while the other emphasizes the view. The characteristics of "speed" and "view" are attributes.

guideline contained ambiguity. Both technicians felt they understood precisely what the last words of their former supervisor meant. The double meaning of "You can't put too much water in a nuclear reactor" remained hidden from the technicians until they attempted to implement the instructions. The technicians might have prevented the nuclear accident by removing the ambiguity from the supervisor's last statement before implementation.

If ambiguity exists in a requirements statement, a software developer may implement a solution based on the unintended meaning of the statement. Assume the statement, "You can't put too much water in a nuclear reactor," appears in the software requirements specification of a real-time control system for a nuclear power facility. The ambiguous phrase "too much" does not tell the control system developer the amount of water that must be present in the nuclear reactor at a given moment in time.

Software developers facing ambiguous statements in requirements specifications need to remove the ambiguity before proceeding with development. Ambiguity discovered late in the software development life cycle is expensive. Eliminating ambiguous statements from requirements gives the developer a better chance of developing exactly what the customer wants.

During the attribute identification stage developers list the attributes of the program. Attributes are characterized by adjectives or adverbs. For example, attributes of a laser printer might be:

- The printer should be *quiet*.
- The printer should create printed pages *quickly*.
- The printer should interface with PCs *easily*.
- The printer should support multiple *common* fonts.
- The printer should print *detailed* graphics.
- The printer should print *color* graphics.

The italicized attributes modify or describe the laser printer's functions. Each attribute must be associated with a function of the program. Attributes not associated with a specific function suggest an overlooked

Brainstorming

"Brainstorming" can be a useful technique for generating ideas about the program's functionality. During brainstorming, participants list as many ideas about the program's functions as they can. To identify program functionality, brainstorming participants complete the sentence, "The program should . . .."

For example, developers brainstorming about a PC laser printer might produce the following list of functions:

- The printer should *exist.*
- The printer should *create printed pages.*
- The printer should *interface with PCs.*
- The printer should *support multiple fonts.*
- The printer should *print graphics.*

The list of laser printer functions shows some example functions a laser printer might perform. The first function declares that the printer must exist. The existence function may seem so obvious that it is not worth mentioning, but the existence function is crucial. The existence function implies that the printer must be implementable. In addition, later stages of requirements gathering need and use the existence function.

During brainstorming, participants do not criticize or evaluate the ideas. Criticism inhibits partici-

function. To strengthen requirements, use dissociated attributes to identify overlooked functions and add them to the function list. Carefully scrutinize any function list additions to be certain the functions are necessary, desirable, and consistent.

Many legitimate attributes will modify only the "existence" function. For example, the laser printer uses the *quiet* modifier to describe the existence function. Phrases such as "the program should be..." or "the program is..." relate the existence function and its modifiers. If the developers omit the existence function from the requirements, many of these attributes may be overlooked or incorrectly discarded as "unrelated to any legitimate function."

Functions may have multiple modifiers. For example, the earlier laser printer attributes add both *detailed* and *color* to the graphics function's description. When using many modifiers with a single function, be

pation and creativity. Once participants have listed as many functions as they can, they review, discuss, and evaluate their ideas. The review of ideas reduces the list of functions by eliminating unnecessary or undesirable functions. When scrutinizing their ideas, developers must try to understand each function and its ramifications. Full participation during the review stage will also help developers reach a common understanding of the object's requirements.

Developers must be careful not to list solutions as functions. For example, a function requiring the printer to handle font cards is really a solution in disguise. The corresponding requirement is for the printer to *support multiple fonts.* The focus of requirements gathering should be to identify the functionality of the program. Because solutions describe the implementation of the program's functions they unnecessarily restrict the later development phases such as specification or design. Developers must maintain the customer's perspective during brainstorming to avoid "jumping to solutions."

certain the modifiers do not conflict. For example, the laser printer cannot be both quiet and noisy simultaneously. Conflicting attributes indicate unrecognized functions or incomplete attribute specifications.

Constraint Identification

Constraints strengthen the program's requirements by bounding the functions and attributes. Constraints are *measurable* bounds for the object's attributes. For example, the requirement of a race car to be fast must be bounded by an achievable speed constraint such as "120 miles per hour." Constraints answer questions like:

- ❑ How many...?
- ❑ How much...?
- ❑ How often...?
- ❑ How fast...?

Requirements should constrain every legitimate attribute. The requirement that a laser printer be *quiet*, is incomplete until the developers set bounds to specify an acceptable level of noise. For example, specifying that the laser printer must generate "less than two DBs of noise" sufficiently constrains the *quiet* attribute.

It is impossible to determine if an object fulfills the requirements if there are no bounds on the function's attributes. For example, does a printer that prints black ink on white paper meet the unconstrained requirement to print color? Some people may consider black to be a color while others may not. Here is the example list of printer requirements with the necessary constraints:

- ❑ The object should be quiet [less than 2 DB].
- ❑ The object should create printed pages quickly [greater than 10 pages per minute].
- ❑ The object should interface with PCs easily [using the standard parallel port and DB25 connector].
- ❑ The object should support multiple common fonts [Courier and Times Roman].
- ❑ The object should print detailed graphics [resolution greater than 300 dots per inch].
- ❑ The object should print color graphics [at least black, red, yellow and blue].

Preference Identification

Functions, attributes, and constraints delineate an *acceptable* instance of the target program. While two programs may both be acceptable, one program may be *preferable* to the other. For example, if you fly from Los Angeles to New York during an off-peak period, you may find the airplane nearly empty. On such a trip the airline might offer you the option of sitting in the first class section of the airplane. Your requirements for an acceptable flight are merely that you get to New York quickly and safely, but you will gladly sit in first class comfort if there is no additional charge for specifying a preference.

Preferences are functions, attributes, and constraints that are desirable but not mandatory. A preference must never add to the cost of the program either in terms of development time or money. Though preferences are not required, preferences are still valuable. Preferences can help customers decide between all acceptable alternatives. For example, flying first class or flying coach are both acceptable alternatives, but given the alternative at no extra cost most people will fly first class.

With adequate attributes and constraints, functions can be measured against their acceptance criteria. Since preferences are not measured against acceptance criteria, associating attributes and constraints with them is optional. Under some circumstances preferences should not have modifiers. The requirement that the laser printer *show status* is an example of a non-modified preference. The *show status* preference does not describe what type of status, but suggests any status is preferable to no status.

Preferences usually establish conditions where "more is better." Another possible preference may be for small laser printers rather than large laser printers. Still, the preference of printer size must not infringe upon the constraints of useful paper size or printing speed. Here are some more examples of preferences for the laser printer:

- ❑ The printer should handle odd sizes of paper [11x14, 3x5 and 11x18].
- ❑ The printer should be light.
- ❑ The printer should look technically sophisticated.
- ❑ The printer should attach to non-PC-compatible computers.

Any desirable characteristic is a preference if it is not mandatory. These examples of laser printer preferences show the variety in preferences. The preference for the laser printer to handle odd-size paper has attributes and constraints. The preference that the printer should be light is an unconstrained attribute of the existence function.

An Example of Requirements Gathering

Through the balance of this book, we will use a chess game program as an extended example. Most individuals are generally familiar with how to play chess, and a moderately complex chess program yields a sufficiently difficult programming example.

In fact, a chess program can become extremely difficult and complex. But in order for the chess program to be a good example, while it should still play well, the complexity must be limited as much as possible. To make the example chess program available to a large audience, we will design it to run on PCs under DOS and to have as few compiler dependencies as possible.

To be a good programming example, the chess game program needs to be easy to use. The chess program needs to play a single user and make moves in a reasonable amount of time (say, less than five minutes). The program needs to show the user the game's status so the user can follow the game and know what is going on. The user interface should be easy to master (say, learned in less than 15 minutes).

If these requirements had been produced in a brainstorming session, they might have started as a list like this:

- ❑ The program should play chess.
- ❑ The program should play a user.
- ❑ The program should be simple.
- ❑ The program should play chess with as much skill as possible.
- ❑ The program should run on PCs using DOS.
- ❑ The program should be compiler-independent.
- ❑ The program should make moves in under five minutes.
- ❑ The program should be learnable in less than 15 minutes.
- ❑ The program should display the game status.
- ❑ The program should explain what is going on to the user.

Once the brainstorming is completed, the participants should scrutinize the functions. In this stage, they try to combine or eliminate redundant functions, restate solutions in disguise, and make certain the list is complete. For example, the previous list might reduce to:

0. The program should exist.
1. The program should play chess.
2. The program should display the board.
3. The program should display the game status.

These four functions do not represent all the ideas identified during brainstorming; they are just the essential functions. Next the participants should use this function list to add modifiers to the functions. We can add the following attributes to the function list:

0. The program should exist:
   - ❑ The program should exist on a PC.
   - ❑ The program should be simple to build.
   - ❑ The program should be compiler independent.
   - ❑ The program should be easily learnable.

1. The program should play chess:
   - ❑ The program should play chess legally and honestly.
   - ❑ The program should play chess quickly.
   - ❑ The program should play chess intelligently.

2. The program should display the board:
   - ❑ The program should display the board clearly.

3. The program should display the game status:
   - ❑ The program should display the game status clearly.

In the final step of the requirements gathering the participants should constrain the attributes of the function list. The discussion during this stage will help distinguish preferences from attributes. The result might be:

0. The program should exist:
   - ❑ The program should exist on a PC [running DOS].
   - ❑ The program should be simple to build [preference].
   - ❑ The program should be compiler independent [preference].
   - ❑ The program should be easy to learn [less than 15 minutes].

1. The program should play chess:
   - ❑ The program should play chess legally and honestly [regular chess rules except for castling and *en passant*].
   - ❑ The program should play chess quickly [less than 5 minutes per move].
   - ❑ The program should play chess intelligently [preference].

2. The program should display the board:
   - ❑ The program should display the board clearly [displaying positions, pieces, and colors].

3. The program should display the game status:
   - ❑ The program should display the game status clearly [Display modes: thinking, select piece, place piece, computer wins, user wins, draw, illegal move].

Notice that some attributes' bounds are easy to identify because the constraints come directly from the brainstorming list. For example, the list answers the question of how quickly the program should play chess.

Other attributes are not bounded. Because unbounded functions and attributes are not testable, the customer must either identify the function/attribute constraints, identify the function/attribute as a preference, or eliminate the function/attribute. The brainstorming list did not explain exactly what the chess program should tell the user. The customer perspective added the list of display modes and board information. An attribute of the second function is to play chess intelligently. The initial function list qualifies this function/attribute with the bogus phrase "as much skill as possible." "As much skill as possible" is not measurable, yet the quality of play is important for a chess game. Therefore, the function/attribute for the program to play chess intelligently is classed as a preference. Developers often ask, "How do you know if the requirements are complete?" Unfortunately, you can never be certain the requirements are complete, but there are ways to increase confidence in the requirements. One technique is to envision a spectrum of objects, some of which obviously meet the requirements and some that obviously do not. Visualizing this spectrum can help you find a line that separates the acceptable from the unacceptable, using only the requirements for a particular object. If the point of separation seems comfortable and reasonable then there must be a high degree of confidence in the completeness of the requirements. If the division is uncomfortable, analyzing the reason for the sense of discomfort can lead to improvements in the requirements.

For the chess game example, one can easily construct such a spectrum of programs, as in Figure 2.0.

Objects at the left side of Figure 2.0 clearly meet the requirements. The right side of the spectrum represents those programs (e.g., word processors or spread sheets) that clearly do not meet the requirements. The middle of the spectrum contains those programs that meet many and maybe all the requirements. The customer gets feedback by using the

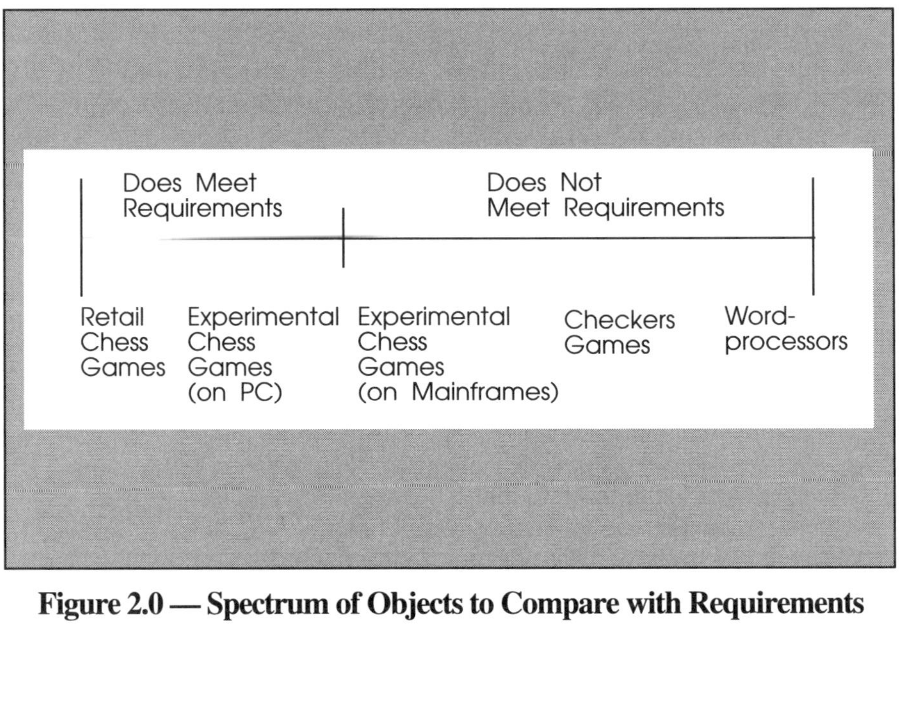

Figure 2.0 — Spectrum of Objects to Compare with Requirements

requirements to divide those objects that meet the requirements from those that do not.

Summary

As we pointed out in Chapter 1 the software development begins with the identification of program requirements. We can now detail the steps in this initial stage algorithmically.

The pseudocode description in Document 2.0 shows the details of gathering requirements. The *IdentifyRequirements* procedure shows the three major parts of requirements gathering: identifying functions and preferences, adding attributes, and adding constraints.

The function entitled *IdentifyFunctions* breaks the function identification process into function brainstorming and scrutinizing. The brainstorming loop puts as many functions into the requirements as possible. The scrutinizing loop eliminates redundant and unwanted functions. The scrutinizing loop also identifies those functions that are really preferences.

The *AddAttributes* function iterates and adds attributes to each function description. *AddConstraints* also iterates through each func-

Document 2.0 — The Top-Level Pseudocode

```
IdentifyRequirements() {

      // Create an empty requirements set
      new Requirements
      // Identify the functions and preferences
      IdentifyFunctions(Requirements);
      // Identify the attributes
      AddAttributes(Requirements);
      // Identify the constraints
      AddConstraints(Requirements);
}

IdentifyFunctions(Requirements) {

      // Brainstorm functions
      While customers can identify an additional function...{
            // Add the function to the Requirements
            Requirements += FunctionDescription
      }
```

tion and through each attribute, adding constraints as necessary. Remember that preferences need not be modified by attributes or bounded by constraints. This detail is not explicit in *AddAttributes* or *AddConstraints*, but is implied.

Document 2.0. — *Cont'd*

```
        // Scrutinize functions
        For each FunctionDescription in the Requirements... {
            // Eliminate unwanted functions
            If the FunctionDescription is redundant
            Or if the FunctionDescription is undesirable,
                // Delete the function from the Requirements
                Requirements -= FunctionDescription
            // Identify preferences
            If the FunctionDescription is really a preference
                Mark the FunctionDescription as a preference
        }
    }

    AddAttributes(Requirements) {
        // Assign attributes to each function
        For each FunctionDescription in the Requirements... {
            For each Attribute of the FunctionDescription... {
                // Modify the function with the Attribute
                FunctionDescription += Attribute
            }
        }
    }

    AddConstraints(Requirements) {
        // Set bounds to each attribute
        For each FunctionDescription in the Requirements... {
            For each Attribute of the FunctionDescription... {
                For each Constraint of the Attribute
                    Attribute += Constraint
            }
        }
    }
```

Exercises

0. Give two reasons for taking time to identify requirements.
1. Explain why gathering program requirements differs from gathering lower level object requirements.
2. Define functions, attributes, constraints, and preferences. Tell how to recognize each.
3. Gather requirements for a personnel database application. Be sure to show the functions, attributes, constraints, and preferences.

ObjectSpec = CreateSpec(Requiremer

Chapter 3

Object Specification

This chapter describes object specification and shows how to use requirements to create object specifications. In a formal sense, developing object specifications, `CreateSpec(Requirements)`, is the first step at any given level of the recursive Object Creation Process. Thus, with this chapter, we begin to detail the regular, recursive portion of the program development process.

Characteristics of Object Specifications

An object specification is a detailed description of the target object's external characteristics. The object specification describes the object from its user or external views. Any characteristic of the object that the user can identify, describe, feel, or sense belongs in the object specification. The specification of a robust object may need to describe many external characteristics. A good set of object specifications will completely and consistently describe each external characteristic.

Both the design and testing phases depend upon well conceived object specification. The architectural perspective uses the object specification as the blueprint for the object's design. The referee's perspective uses the object specification to drive the development of tests that determine valid instances of the object. The success of later phases of the Object Creation Process depends on the completeness and consistency of the external specification.

Incomplete object specifications are a major source of problems for developers. For example, a single view of a 3-D object, as in Figure 3.0, gives an incomplete external specification. The viewer can never know, based just on the view in Figure 3.0, that they are actually seeing the object in Figure 3.1. Attempting to sketch the object in Figure 3.1 given only the specification in Figure 3.0, would clearly demonstrate how an incomplete specification can misdirect and frustrate developers. A complete specification includes descriptions from enough different perspectives to fully describe the object. The complete specification of the object in Figure 3.1 must include the top, bottom, front, back, and side views.

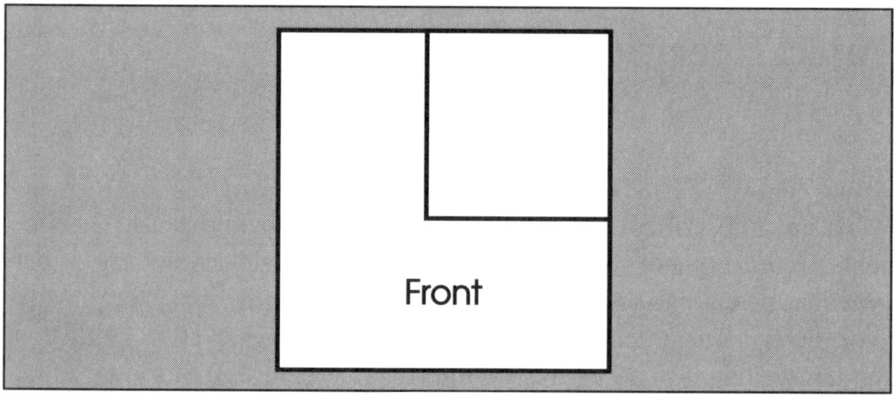

Figure 3.0 — An Incomplete Specification of a 3-D Object

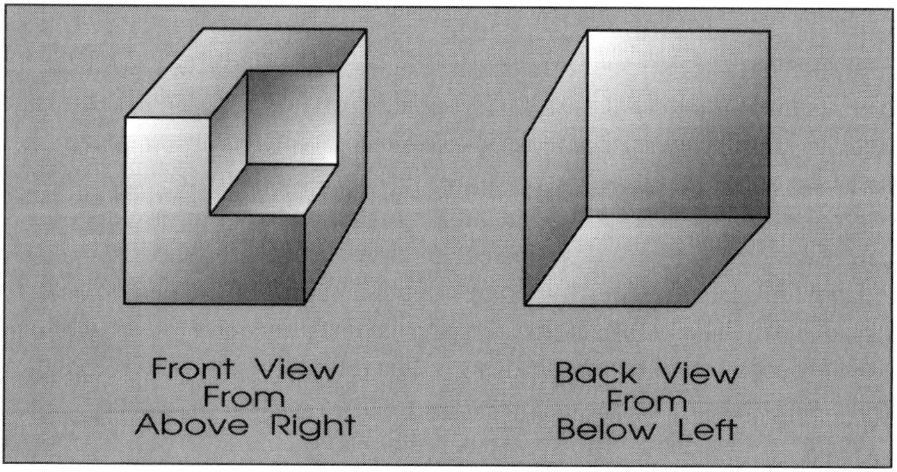

Figure 3.1 — A 3-D Object from the Incomplete Specification

Figure 3.2 shows a complete specification for another three-dimensional object. A careful inspection of Figure 3.2, however, will reveal many inconsistencies. The lines from one view do not correspond to the lines of the other views. The specification is *complete*, but it is not *consistent*. It is impossible to fulfill an inconsistent specification. Design decisions that satisfy one view of the specification will violate another. Developers must resolve all specification inconsistencies before beginning

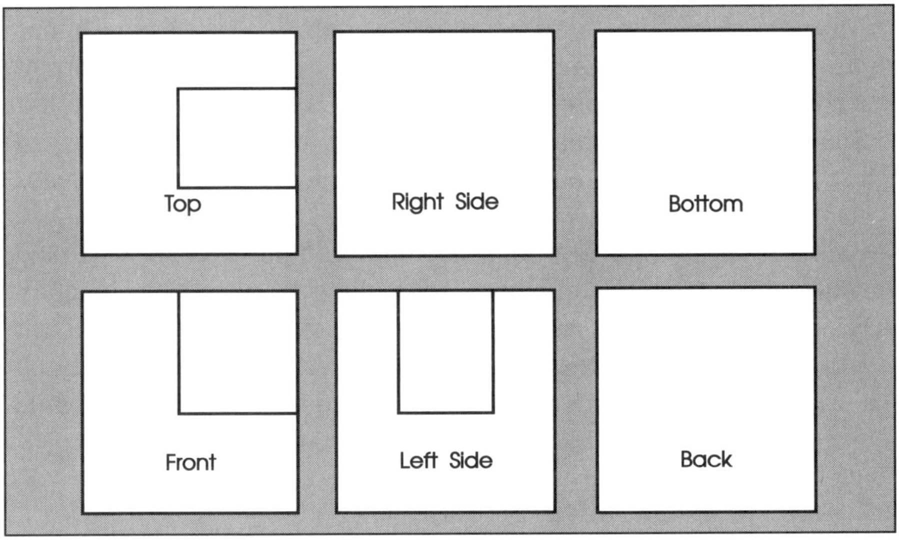

Figure 3.2 — Inconsistent Specification of a 3-D Object

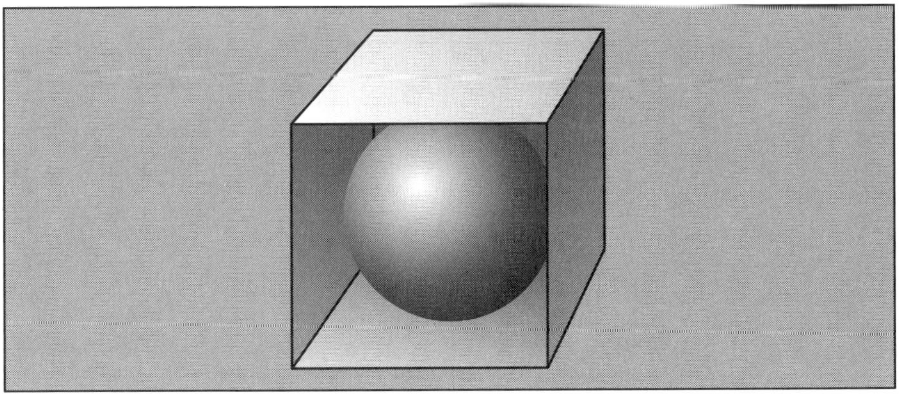

Figure 3.3 — Non-External Specification of a 3-D Object

the design process. Unresolved inconsistencies cause confusion later in the development process.

The 3-D image in Figure 3.3 illustrates another common external specification problem. The illustration gives a complete and consistent specification of the object, but includes information about its *internals*. Figure 3.4 shows the correct *external* specification for this object. These two figures also illustrate why only internal specifications aren't adequate. If Figure 3.3 showed *only* the sphere (only the internal specifications), how would the developer know to build the object in Figure 3.4?

An external specification must only describe an object's appearance from an external perspective. Developers must avoid including information about an object's internals in the external specification because internal information describes how an object works. Describing how an object works before fully understanding and describing the object leads to the development of the wrong object.

Useful external specifications must be complete, consistent, and contain only external information. Thus, the goal of the specification phase is to find all views, insure that the individual views are consistent with each other, and insure that each view is an external view. Verifying that the object's specification is complete, consistent, and external while in the specification phase eliminates rework during later phases of development.

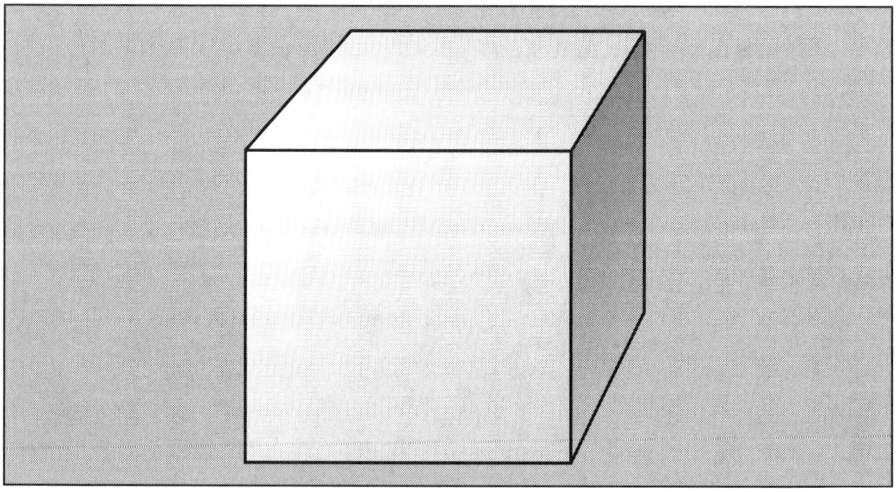

Figure 3.4 — A 3-D Object for the Non-External Specification

Software External Views

Admittedly, software objects present a less tangible external view than do physical objects. Users can directly sense only some of the outward views of software. Other views are sensed indirectly. Users see an application's screens, windows, and prompts, but they also become aware, sometimes indirectly, of the application's response time, and the amount of disk space required, and the application's mode of operation. Since users perceive each of these aspects of software, the object's specification must address each aspect.

One way to identify external views of software is to assume the perspective of the potential user. Internal views of the software, such as data structures and algorithms, are of little concern to the end user. Users generally have only executable forms of software and tend to focus on the software's external views. For example, the user of a word processor will focus on the user interface layout and the ease of integration with other software packages. The user of a set of math library subroutines will be interested in functionality, required inputs, and the data type of the output. A graphics library user will be interested in the hardware supported and the execution speed of the functions. It is essential that developers identify all potential views of the object to make certain they are building the right object. Any aspects of the software that the user can access are external views. Here is a list of common external aspects of software:

- ❑ Function
- ❑ User interface
- ❑ Programmer interface
- ❑ Response time
- ❑ Static and dynamic disk utilization
- ❑ Main memory requirements
- ❑ Additional hardware requirements (monitor, mouse, printer, etc.)
- ❑ Dependent software (operating system, compiler, linker, etc.)
- ❑ File formats (input and output)
- ❑ Report formats
- ❑ Operational states

The most significant external characteristic of an object is its functionality. Objects that execute quickly and use little memory are useless if they do not provide the desired functionality. Because functionality is so important, each object's specification must include a description of the object's desired functionality. Developers may more easily understand the functionality of some object if its description is intertwined with other aspects of the object's specification. Combining the description of the object's functionality with descriptions of other external characteristics of the object is satisfactory if the functional description is complete.

The specification for an object that interacts directly with the user must describe the interaction in detail. A detailed description of the user interaction includes the appearance of display presentations, allowed keyboard input, and mouse interaction.

The object specification serves much the same purpose as does the definition of a programming interface. For example, a developer may create a binary tree object for use by a coworker who is developing a database object. For the binary tree object to be useful, the specification must describe the object's programming interface, i.e., all the externally accessible data and member functions.

To describe each object's member functions, describe all the inputs, the purpose of the functions, and the outputs. Descriptions of the inputs and outputs must include a definition of their data types, passing mechanisms, and constraints. For example, one parameter to a modulo function is the divisor. The divisor's data type is integer and can have any legal integer value except zero.

Specification and OOP

Encapsulation simplifies the specification of the programmable interface by reducing the amount of externally accessible data.

The examples in this book simplify object interfaces even more by allowing only methods or member functions to access an object's internal data. This restriction significantly strengthens software by creating a common and consistent interface to all objects. Consistency is a primary ingredient in the development of quality software.

OOP languages, such as C++, support class definitions which enumerate an object's methods and concisely describe the method's inputs and outputs. If developers select meaningful, readable names for the methods (i.e., that describe the method's functionality) they can adequately specify objects by presenting the class definitions along with a limited narrative. The next section contains examples of how to use class definitions in specifications.

Most applications are not especially concerned with the execution speed of an object's actions. However, real-time applications usually have specific time constraints. Therefore, the specification for objects used in real-time applications must address the issue of response time. For example, when building specifications for the scheduler object within a real-time operating system the developer must specify the maximum and average times required to execute a context switch. Time specifications allow the user to determine the impact of using the object.

The object specification should also address resource dependencies and requirements, such as memory requirements, disk space requirements, other hardware requirements, or necessary support software. For example, the specification for a PC-based graphics library object must specify what graphics adapter cards it supports. The specification of a database object must address the issues of main memory requirements and disk space requirements. By detailing the resource dependencies of an object, developers make it clear to the user that the object is useful for a given application.

Some object's methods return secondary results along with their expected results. This side effect of the methods' operations may alter the way an object reacts to messages. The object's specification must identify and describe all side effects. For example, the member function that *pushes* data onto a stack may move the `stack` object from the empty state to the non-empty state. The reaction of the `stack` object to the *pop* member function differs from the empty state to the non-empty state. It is essential for the object specification to make note of all state changes that affect user interaction. Users often build mental models to help them explain how an object works. Explicitly describing the state transitions of an object helps uscrs cfficicntly construct mental models that describe the object's side effects.

Specification Techniques and Tools

The object specification communicates information about the object. Many different perspectives used in the Object Creation Process have an interest in the object's specification. The object's customers use the specification to determine whether the object meets the requirements. Those with a user's perspective need the specification to understand how to use the object. The object architect uses the specification to decide what to design. The object specification helps those with a referee's perspective decide what to test and decide if the object works correctly. A good object specification also facilitates software reuse by helping the customer understand what the existing object does and whether it meets the new requirements.

Because so many different perspectives make use of the object specification it must be easy to understand. However, the cost of developing the object increases as the cost of creating the object specification increases. Developers can minimize development costs by making use of the most efficient mechanisms for creating object specifications. Toward this end, developers need to be facile with a number of different specification tools and techniques. Examples of useful specification tools and techniques include:

- ❑ Technical reference entries
- ❑ State diagrams
- ❑ Timing diagrams
- ❑ Recursive Transition Networks (RTN)
- ❑ Backus Naur Form (BNF)
- ❑ Story boarding
- ❑ Screen generators

The *technical reference entry* is commonly used to describe library functions. Technical reference entries generally describe library functions with one entry per function (like the part of a compiler manual that describes standard library routines). Each entry includes sections for *synopsis*, *functional description*, *examples*, and *related entries*. The *synopsis* section gives a terse, formal description of the function's parameters and types. The *functional description* is an informal textual explanation of the function and its parameters. The *examples* section shows the function in use. The *related entries* section tells of other technical reference entries that may be useful. Here is an example of a traditional technical reference entry for C's `strcmp()` function:

Synopsis: *`int strcmp(char *s1, char *s2);`*

Function: `strcmp` compares its arguments and returns an integer less than, equal to, or greater than 0, according to whether `s1` is lexicographically less than, equal to, or greater than `s2`.

Related Entries: `strncmp`

Example:

```
#include <string.h>
#include <stdio.h>

int main(void) {
    char   *s1 = "aaa", s2 = "bbb";
    int result;

    result = strcmp(s1,s2);
    if (result == 0)
        printf("strings are equal\n");
    else if (result  < 0)
        printf("string s1 is less than s2\n");
    else printf("string s1 is greater than s2\n");
}
```

In OOP the technical reference entry concept expands to describe objects instead of only functions. The class definition replaces the synopsis because it describes the object's interface from a grammatical viewpoint. Each of an object's public members requires its own section to describe the member's function. The *examples* section may need to present several examples, one to illustrate the use of each member function. Since, by definition, an object contains all its related functions, the *related entries* section should include references to other related objects and not object members. For example, the technical reference entry for the example `stack` object in Chapter 0 might look like Document 3.0. Technical reference entries are most useful for specifying the programming interface to objects.

Document 3.0 — A Technical Reference Document

Class:

```
class STK{
...
public:
    STK();                  // create a stack
    ~STK();                 // destroy a stack
    void  Push(void *);// push an item onto stack
    void  *Pop();           // pop an item off stack
    int IsEmpty();          // check if stack is empty
};
```

Description: A stack is a general purpose last-in-first-out (LIFO) data item container. The stack holds a maximum of 10 pointers to items of an unspecified type (void).

Members:

STK: Constructs a valid instance of an empty stack.

***~STK*:** Destroys an instance of a stack. *~STK* frees up any resources held by the stack instance and invalidates the stack. Only valid stacks can be destroyed with *~STK*. Valid stacks are those that have been created by *STK* and have not yet been destroyed by *~STK*. *~STK* can be used to destroy both empty and non-empty stacks. Once a stack is destroyed, it can no longer be referenced by any of the *STK* member functions. Attempting to destroy an invalid stack will cause the program to exit with a termination value of *-1*.

***Push*:** Pushes a pointer of unspecified type (i.e., *void**) onto an instance of a valid stack. Each instance of a stack can hold a maximum of 10 pointers. Attempting to push more than 10 pointers onto the stack will cause the program to exit with a termination value of *-1*. Attempting to push a pointer onto an invalid stack will also cause the program to exit with a termination value of *-1*.

Document 3.0 — *Cont'd*

***Pop*:** Pops and returns the top pointer value of unspecified type from a non-empty, valid stack. A stack is considered empty when a call to *IsEmpty* returns a non-zero value. Attempting to pop an empty or invalid stack will cause the program to exit with a termination valueof *-1*.

***IsEmpty*:** Returns a non-zero value if the stack is empty. It returns zero if the stack is not empty. A stack is empty if there have been as many items popped from the stack as there were items pushed onto the stack. If a program calls *IsEmpty* with an invalid stack, the program will exit with a termination value of *-1*.

Related Objects: List, Queue

Examples:

```
#include <assert.h>
#include <streams.h>

int main() {
   STK stk;
   char   *s1 = "String 1", *s2 = "String 2";

   assert(stk.IsEmpty());
   stk.push((void*) s1);
   stk.push((void*) s2);
   while (!stk.IsEmpty()) {
      char *str = (char*) stk.pop();
      cout << "Popped " << str << endl;
   }
}
```

A second tool, the finite state machine, is widely used to specify reactive systems. Figure 3.5 shows the state machine for a trivial reactive system. When event `z` occurs in state *A*, the system makes a state transition to state *B*.

Treating objects as reactive systems can make them easier to describe. The `stack` object, for example, is awkward to describe because the *IsEmpty* method sometimes returns zero, and sometimes returns non-zero. The return value of the *IsEmpty* function depends on the *state* of the `stack` object. When a stack is created, it is in the empty state. Pushing the first item causes the stack to enter the non-empty state. Popping the last item causes the stack to return to the empty state. Other stack states include a full state and an error state. Figure 3.6 shows how a state transition diagram can clearly represent the behavior of the `stack` object.

In a state transition diagram the ellipses represent the various object's states. Each ellipse contains the label that corresponds to its state name.

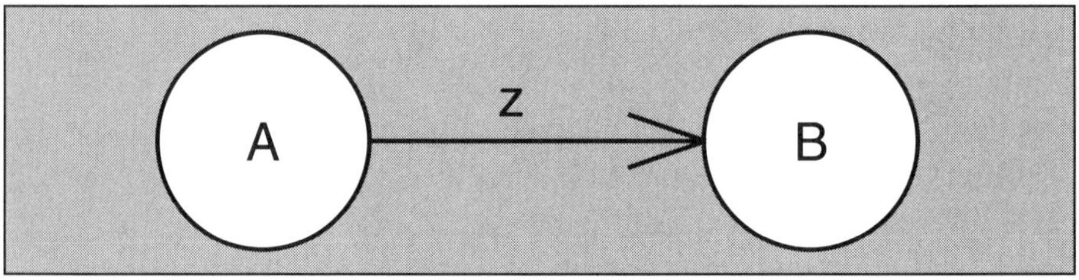

Figure 3.5 — A Simple Reactive System

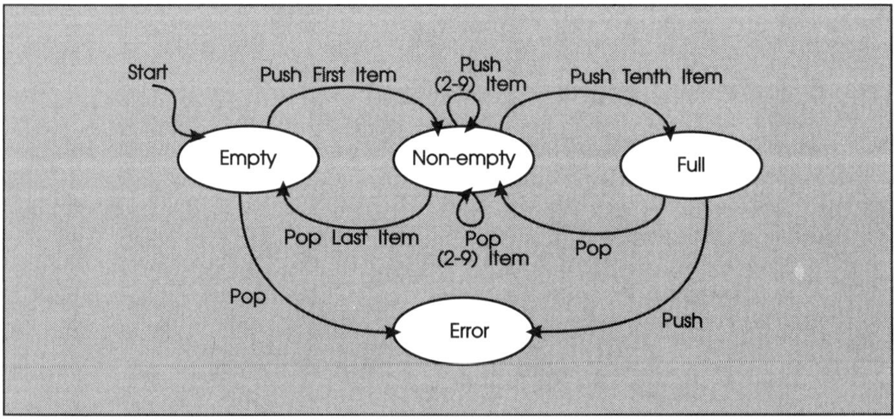

Figure 3.6 — A State Transition Diagram for a Stack

The arrows or arcs represent legal state transitions. Each arc is labeled with an event name. The event name designates the event that causes the associated state transition.

State transition diagrams describe only states and events that are visible on the exterior of the object. Internal state transitions are not visible to the user and should not be diagrammed in an external specification. For example, a `stack` object that uses a disk file for overflow purposes will have different states depending on the status of the file. Users of the stack do not need to know about the `stack` object's internal states. Internal states describe how the object works. External specifications limit their descriptions to the purpose of the object.

A third tool, timing diagrams, simplifies the specification of systems with time-dependent behavior. A home security system that turns on the outside lights in the evening is an example of a time-dependent state change. Figure 3.7 shows an example timing diagram for a home security system.

The horizontal lines in Figure 3.7 represent the passage of time with respect to the inside and outside lights. Raised horizontal lines represent the time when the lights are on. Vertical lines help align the beginning and ending of various state transitions.

Timing diagrams represent state transitions as a function of time. Another advantage of timing diagrams is their ability to illustrate the relationships of varying states. In Figure 3.7, initially both the inside and outside lights are off. The next state shows both the inside and outside lights are on. In the final state only the outside lights remain on.

When used as specification tools, timing diagrams should show only those states and transitions that are visible to the object's user. Timing

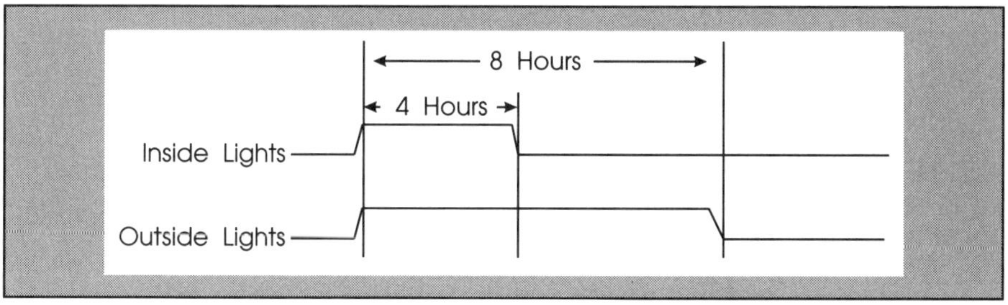

Figure 3.7 —Timing Diagram for a Home Security System

diagrams used as specification tools are not concerned with the internals of the object.

This section introduces a class of tools, *metagrammars*, which are helpful when specifying sophisticated objects that require input or produce output with elaborate syntax. A parser object that reads in a programming language source file and produces an intermediate output file is an example of such an object. The syntax of the input and the output of sophisticated objects such as parsers must be thoroughly defined in the object specification. Understanding, describing, and checking sophisticated syntax is an unavoidable task, requiring hard work and discipline. Undisciplined developers favor delaying complex specifications until later phases of the process. These developers run the risk of a costly rework effort resulting from their designing and implementing the wrong object. Accurate and complete specifications are always more cost-effective than scrapping a design and starting over.

A variety of tools is available for describing language syntax and grammar. Two commonly used tools for context-free grammars are Recursive Transition Networks (RTNs) and Backus-Naur Form (BNF).

RTNs consists of nodes linked by paths. The nodes represent language symbols and constructs that are combined to create valid sentences of the language. The paths represent unidirectional tracks that may be followed to construct the sentences. Figure 3.8 shows an example RTN that describes the syntax for an identifier in C/C++.

An RTN is an intuitive tool for describing language. RTNs are beneficial to developers because they are easy to understand. However, building simple RTNs to represent the language syntax may require some practice. RTNs generally require more effort to create than to read.

As Figure 3.8 shows, RTNs can also represent sequences of operations. RTNs are simple tools for describing the relationships between items in sophisticated sequences. The sequences may consist of language constructs, operations, events, or other types of items.

In contrast to RTNs, BNF is a strictly textual-based mechanism for describing context-free grammars. In place of the paths and nodes used in RTNs, BNF uses production rules. For example, the specification for a C/C++ identifier shown in Figure 3.8 can be written in BNF as:

```
Identifier   ::=Alpha AlphaNum
AlphaNum     ::=|
                AlphaNum AlphaNum |
                Alpha |
                Numeric
Alpha        ::='A'..'Z' |
                'a'..'z'
Numeric      ::='0'..'9'
```

Each BNF production rule has a left side and a right side. The left side identifies what the production rule is defining. The right side is the definition. For example, an *Identifier* is an *Alpha* followed by an *AlphaNum*. An *AlphaNum* is nothing or an *AlphNum* followed by an *AlphaNum* or simply an *Alpha* or a *Numeric*. An *Alpha* is an upper or lower case character constant, and a *Numeric* is a digit constant. The strength of BNF as a specification tool is that it is terse and requires only a text editor. However, BNF is not as intuitive as RTNs.

To close this section, we'll describe two tools that are especially useful for specifying an object's human interface. Human interfaces can be very complex since they can have many possible interaction scenarios. A technique called *story boarding* addresses this complexity by drawing

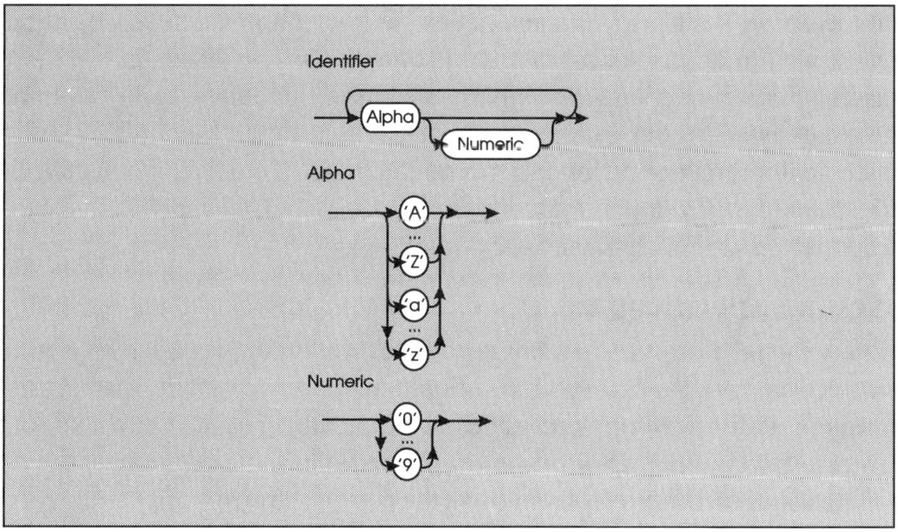

Figure 3.8 — A Recursive Transition Network for C Identifiers

representative snapshots. By combining snapshots a specification can tell the story of what the human interface looks like.

Like the RTNs, story boarding is intuitive. The major drawback of story boarding is that it lacks completeness and must be supplemented by other tools and techniques. For example, a video combat game that simulates a tank, might have three screens: one to show the view from within the tank, one to show the position of various tanks on a map, and one to show the tank status. A story board specification of the video tank game would show each of these screens, but would also need a state transition diagram to show how to move from one screen to another.

Alternatively, developers can *story board* an application by using screen generators or application generators to create "slide shows." Most screen interface library packages include a program that allows developers to interactively describe an application's human interface. Some of these programs will even simulate the running of the application. These approaches often produce more complete specifications than older, more manual approaches. With these tools a developer can easily describe both the appearance and the states of the interface.

To be most effective, developers should become comfortable with many different specification techniques. Developers who are well versed in a variety of specification techniques can be flexible and versatile. Developers should select specification tools and techniques appropriate to the object's intrinsic characteristics. While technical reference entries work well to describe programmable objects, timing diagrams are more useful for time-dependent objects. Versatile developers will combine techniques and tools when appropriate. A real-time object may require technical reference entries *and* timing diagrams. To develop solid specifications the developer must select the tools and techniques that best capture the salient characteristics of the object.

Testing Specifications

Every mistake or oversight during the development process adds defect correction time to the total development cost. Mistakes that persist through many development stages are typically the most expensive to correct. By eliminating errors before they contaminate subsequent development stages, developers minimize the cost of the errors. Unfortunately, most developers are loath to look for defects before implementation. Instead of testing the work product or artifact produced by each phase of development, most developers wait until the object is complete, and then test for valid behavior under adverse conditions.

Most developers are familiar with testing techniques that verify that the code works as expected. In the early phases of development, however, these techniques are ineffective since most artifacts are not executable. Developers must verify the artifact's validity by performing *inspections*.

Many developers are unfamiliar with effective inspection practices. If asked to inspect an object, they will simply read its contents. While this may turn up some major errors, simply reading an artifact is generally a superficial effort. Useful inspections require an honest, disciplined, and methodical effort. Inspectors prove more effective if they have *inspection objectives*. These objectives help inspectors focus their attention on the important aspects of the artifacts. Inspection objectives can be as simple as a "things to look for" list, such as:

- ❑ Is the specification complete?
- ❑ Is the specification consistent?
- ❑ Does the specification discuss the object's internals?
- ❑ Is the specification ambiguous?
- ❑ Does the specified object fulfill all of the object's requirements?
- ❑ What does the specification identify that has no basis in the requirements?

There are two types of incomplete specifications. First, a specification may fail to describe all perspectives of the object. A real-time object's specification is incomplete if it defines the object's *functionality* but omits a description of the object's *responsiveness*. Second, a specification may lack thoroughness in the described perspectives. For example, a technical reference description lacks thoroughness if it does not discuss all the parameters and return values.

A specification that contradicts itself is inconsistent. Such contradictions usually involve two different object perspectives. A story board description of an object might only represent five of the object's states, while the state transition diagram of the same object shows six states. Specification inconsistency is subtle and spotting it requires a concerted effort. Developers who invest the energy to identify specification inconsistency avoid costly rework efforts.

The specifications must not describe the object's internals, because such descriptions artificially limit the object's design. Describing the internals at this stage is like answering a question before hearing it. Premature design and implementation will result in waste, rework, or inadequate implementations.

Ambiguous specifications create many of the same problems as ambiguous requirements (see Chapter 2). Additionally, ambiguity in an object's specification robs the object of its reusability. Developers looking to reuse software will search for the software based upon the contents of its specification. A solid, reliable, and functionally correct object will not be reused if other developers cannot understand the object's external specification.

The specification must be compared with the object requirements to verify that the object specification fulfills all requirements. If the comparison suggests that some requirements are not covered in the object's specification, then the object's specification is incorrect. Object specifications must satisfy all object requirements or the resulting object will be unsatisfactory.

Additionally, the comparison between the object's requirements and specification highlights those aspects of the object that are neither requirements nor preferences. These are deviations from the requirements. Developers need to carefully question requirements deviations. What is the purpose of the deviation? What will the deviation cost? Some deviations add value to the object by improving its generality, reusability, performance, or aesthetics. However, added value usually adds complexity and cost.

The acid test of a good object specification is the visualization test. Based upon the contents of the specification, can someone visualize the appearance of the object and understand its functionality? A good specification describes an object so clearly that the reader knows exactly how to use it. For example, a good specification for a library function tells a programmer what features to expect from an object and how to apply them. A bad specification requires additional explanation from others and some prototype programs. Bad specifications are costly in terms of time and frustration. Conversely, good specifications are powerful tools in the hands of developers.The external characteristics of an entire program are often the most challenging to specify. Some important external views of a chess game include the program's function, user interface, and speed. A specification that incorporates these characteristics might look Like Document 3.1.

Document 3.1 — Chess Game Specification

Chess Game External Specification

The chess game is a PC-based program that allows a single player to play chess against the computer. The chess game allows and supports all conventional legal moves (excluding castling and *en passant*).

Display Specification

The chess game's terminal display consists of a single screen. The screen has two sections; the first 24 lines display the board, and the last line displays status information (see Figure Spec.0).

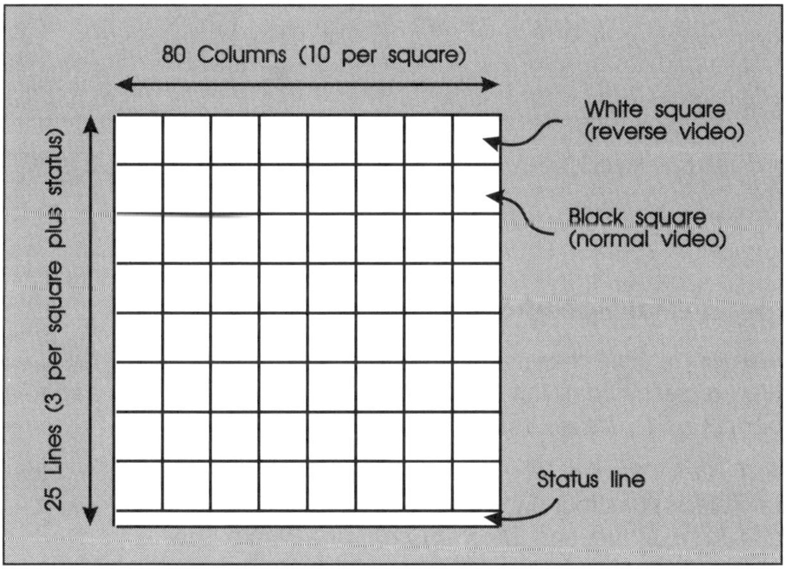

Figure Spec.0 — The User Interface Screen Display

Document 3.1 — *Cont'd*

When a piece occupies a board position, the square containing the piece displays its name (centered in the top two lines of the square). Figure Spec.1 shows how to construct valid piece names.

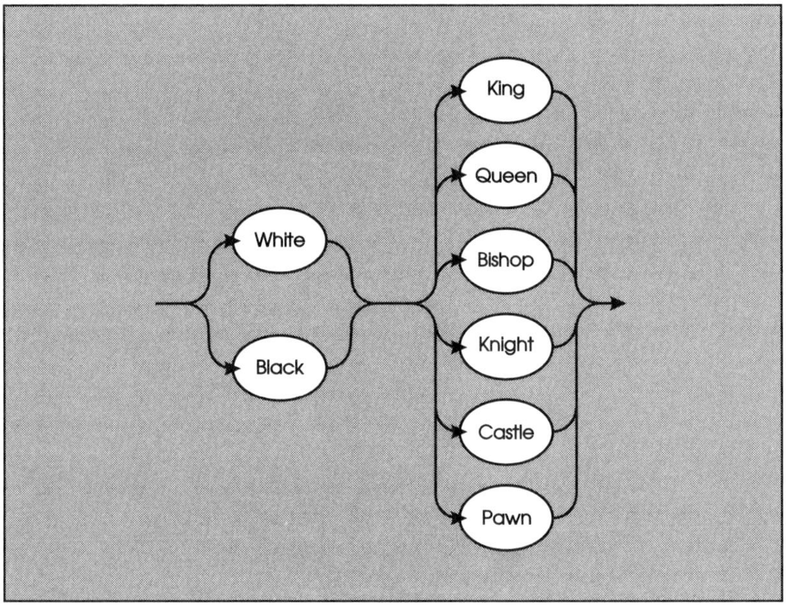

Figure Spec.1 — Valid Piece Name Construction Rules

Operational Specification

When running, the chess program switches among four major states. These states, represented by the state diagram in Figure Spec.2, include *Select Color*, *White Move*, *Black Move*, and *Game Result*.

The *Black Move* or *White Move* state (depending on which color the user selects) has four substates: *Select Piece*, *Place Piece*, *Validate Move*, and *Show Error*. See Figure Spec.3.

The program begins in the *Select Color* state. In this state the pieces occupy their initial legal positions. The white pieces occupy the leftmost

Document 3.1 — *Cont'd*

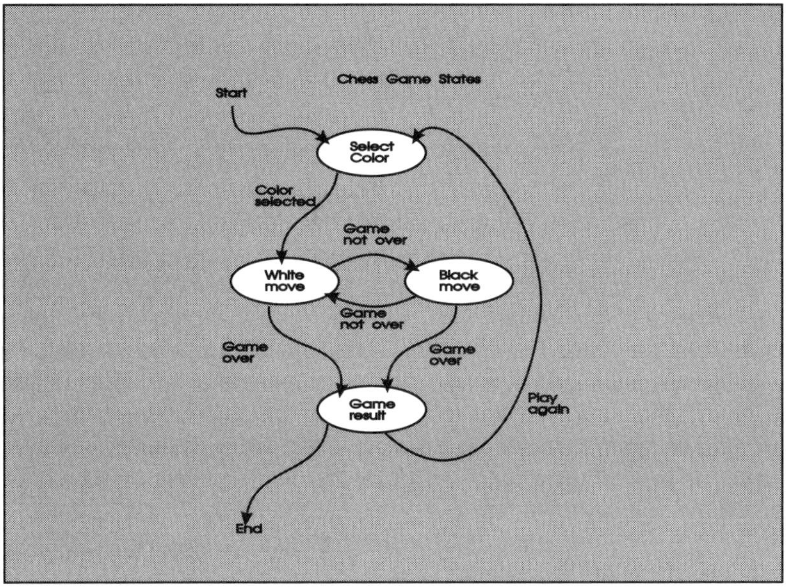

Figure Spec.2 — The Chess Game Program States

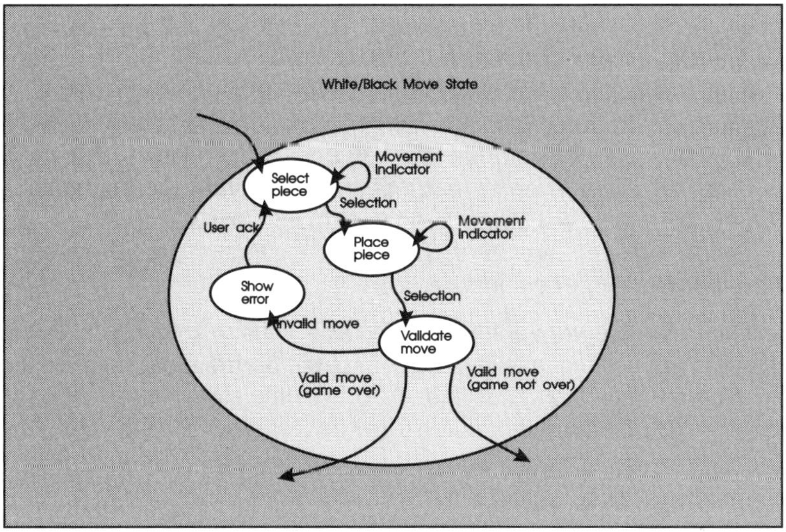

Figure Spec.3 — The White/Black Move Sub-States

Document 3.1 — *Cont'd*

two columns and the black pieces occupy the rightmost two columns. The status line displays the *Color Prompt*. The program remains in the *Select Color* state until the user presses the *B* or *W* key. Keys other than the *B* or *W* will cause a brief beep. Pressing the *B* or *W* key creates a *Color Selected* event, advancing the program state to the *White Move* state.

The program alternates between the *White Move* and *Black Move* states until the game is over. One of these states is controlled by the user while the other is controlled by the program. The state controlled by the user depends upon the color the user selected. In the program-controlled *Move* state, the status line displays *Thinking Status*. In this state the program moves a piece by erasing the piece's name at its current location and writing the name in a new location. The program requirements constrain the program to remain in this state less than five minutes. Having moved the piece, the program decides if the game is over. If the program detects a *Game Over* event, it advances to the *Game Result* state. If, the game is not yet finished, the program detects a *Game Not Over* event and moves to the user-controlled *Move* state.

Once in the user-controlled *Move* state, the program will use a blinking square to indicate the currently selected position. Initially the user's king will be selected (blinking). The user may direct the selection to a different position by pressing an arrow key. The program will recognize an arrow key *Movement Indicator* event. This event causes the currently selected position to stop blinking and causes an adjacent square (in the direction of the arrow) to begin blinking, making the adjacent square become the currently selected position. If there is no adjacent square, as is the case with squares on the edge of the board, the wraparound square (i.e., the square on the opposite edge of the board) will start blinking. After processing the *Movement Indicator* event, the program returns to the *Select Piece* substate.

Each time the program enters the *Select Piece* substate, it checks whether the user's king is in check. If so, the program displays the *In Check* prompt on the status line. Otherwise the status line displays the *Select Piece* prompt.

To select a piece to move, the user positions the blinking square at a user piece and presses *Enter*, causing a *Selection* event. Key strokes that do not result in a *Movement Indicator* or *Selection*

Document 3.1 — *Cont'd*

event cause a brief beep. The *Selection* event causes the program to bold the currently blinking square (the piece the user is moving) and enter the *Place Piece* substate.

In the *Place Piece* substate the user chooses the destination for the selected piece. The status line displays the *Place Piece Prompt*. The arrow keys have the same effect as in the *Select Piece* substate (i.e., they move the currently blinking square). The user positions the blinking square at the selected destination and presses *Enter*, causing a *Selection* event. When a *Selection* event occurs in the *Place Piece* substate, the blinking square stops blinking, the selected piece is unbolded, and the program enters the *Validate Move* substate.

In the *Validate Move* substate, the program determines whether the requested move is legal. If so, the program erases the piece's label from the source square and writes it to the destination square. Selecting a destination square that contains an opposing piece implies that the opposing piece is to be taken. In this case, the label for the opposing piece is erased from the destination square.

If the user requests an illegal move, the program will detect an *Invalid Move* event and enter the *Show Error* substate. In this substate the status line displays the *Illegal Move Status*. Once the user presses *Enter*, the *Show Error* substate causes the blinking to stop and the selected piece to be deselected (unbolded). At this point the *Ack* event occurs, causing the program to reenter the *Select Piece* substate.

After a valid move in the *Validate Move* substate, the program must decide if the game is over. If the game is not over, a *Game Not Over* event occurs and the program enters the program-controlled *Move* state. Otherwise, a *Game Over* event occurs and the program enters the *Game Result* state.

In the *Game Result* state, the status line displays the *You Win Prompt*, *I Win Prompt*, or the *Draw Prompt*. These three prompts also ask if the user wants to play again. If the user presses the *Y* key, a *Play Again* event occurs, placing the program back in the *Select Color* state. If the user presses the *N* key, an *End* event occurs, terminating the program's execution.

Document 3.1 — *Cont'd*

In the *White Move*, *Black Move*, and *Game Result* states, pressing *Q* will generate a *Quit* event. The *Quit* event stops the program immediately.

Status Line Specification

The status line will display the following messages:

Color Prompt:

"Black or White (B/W)?"

Thinking Status:

"Thinking..."

In Check Prompt:

"Check... Select the piece to move (use arrow keys to position
or the *Enter* key to select)"

Select Piece Prompt:

"Select the piece to move (use arrow keys to position
or the *Enter* key to select)"

Place Piece Prompt:

"Select the destination (use arrow keys to position
or the *Enter* key to place)"

Illegal Move Status:

"Illegal move (press any key to continue)"

You Win Prompt:

"You Win. Play again (Y/N)?"

I Win Prompt:

"I Win. Play again (Y/N)?"

Draw Prompt:

"Draw. Play again (Y/N)?"

Inspecting the Specification

A brief comparison of the chess game requirements with the specification shows that every constrained statement in the requirements is addressed in the specification. The specification notes that the program will run on a PC and is implicitly easy to learn. The specification suggests the program should play legal chess and make its moves quickly. The specification gives the complete details of the board display and status.

Preferences from the requirements, such as "the program should be simple to build," are not directly addressed in the specification. However, the specification defines a character-based interface that should eliminate any need for the complexities of graphics. Developers should use the preferences as guiding principles during specification, design, and implementation.

The specification also includes a "play another game" feature. Though the requirements don't mention this multiple game feature, it has been retained because it adds meaningful value without any appreciable change in cost.

The specification not only meets the requirements, it also fully captures the user viewpoint. With this specification a user can easily envision using the program. The specification explains what the user will perceive and how the user can affect the program.

Notice that the specification assumes a reasonable person as the audience. For example, the specification does not explain which keys are the arrow or `Enter` keys. This assumption keeps the specification from becoming excessively detailed and bureaucratic.

Summary

Given the requirements for an object, the Object Creation Process creates a specification of the object by describing all of the object's external perspectives. It is important that the specification be complete, be consistent, and describe only external dimensions of the object. This chapter enumerates different external views of software that may be needed in an object specification, and identifies tools and techniques developers can use to describe objects' external views. Specifications are tested by using inspections to compare the object's specification to the requirements.

We finish by giving the pseudocode that describes the specification phase of the Object Creation Process (following the exercises at the end of this chapter).

This pseudocode description shows the details of creating a specification as described in this chapter. The *CreateSpec* function loops until the function has created a specification of an object that meets the requirements. There are five major steps within the *CreateSpec* loop. The first step, *MeetRequirements*, identifies the specifications necessary to fulfill the requirements. The next three steps of the loop (*MakeConsistent*, *MakeComplete*, and *MakeExternal*) make sure that the specification is consistent and complete and that it only discusses user or external perspectives. The last step of the loop (*ScrutinizeAddedValue*) considers items in the specification that are not based on the requirements.

MeetRequirements looks at all the requirements of the object and creates specifications accordingly. As *MeetRequirements* creates the specifications, it adds the specifications to the set of the object's specifications.

MakeConsistent compares all the specification items in the specification set with each other. When *MakeConsistent* finds conflicting specifications, it resolves the conflicts.

MakeComplete combines the dimensions that the requirements identifies with any dimensions the user can identify. Using this set of dimensions, *MakeComplete* checks to see that the specification describes each of these dimensions. Finally, *MakeComplete* reviews each requirement item to see that it is complete.

MakeExternal inspects each of the specification's items to make sure the items only describe the object's external characteristics. *MakeExternal* removes any internal items from the specification.

ScrutinizeAddedValue identifies those specification items that do not relate to the requirements. *ScrutinizeAddedValue* then determines the cost and value of each of these items. If no one is willing to support the cost of the items, the items are removed from the specification.

Document 3.2 — Creating a Specification

```
CreateSpec(Requirements) {
    // Create an empty set of specifications
    new Spec
    // Fulfill all the requirements
    While the specifications do not meet the requirements... {
        // Identify object specifications that meet the requirements
        MeetRequirements(Spec, Requirements)
        // Make sure the specifications are consistent
        MakeConsistent(Spec)
        // Make sure the specifications are complete
        MakeComplete(Spec, Requirements)
        // Make sure the specifications only describe user views
        MakeExternal(Spec)
        // Scrutinize any added value in the specifications
        ScrutinizeAddedValue(Spec, Requirements)
    }
    return Spec
}

MeetRequirements(Spec, Requirements) {
    // Consider each requirement
    For each statement in the requirements... {
        If the spec does not address the statement
            // Alter the spec to address the statement
            Spec += StatementSolution
    }
}

MakeConsistent(Spec) {
    // Make sure all the specification items agree with each other
    For each item in the specification... {
        For each item in the specification... {
            If the items conflict {
                Make the items consistent
            }
        }
    }
}
```

Document 3.2 — *Cont'd*

```
MakeComplete(Spec, Requirements) {
	// Identify all dimensions of the object
	new DimensionList
	For each statement in the requirements... {
		For each dimension that the statement implies... {
			If the dimension is not yet in the dimension list
				DimensionList += Dimension
		}
	}
	// Try to think of any other interesting dimensions
	While the users can identify additional dimensions... {
			If the dimension is not yet in the dimension list
				DimensionList += Dimension
	}
	// Make sure the spec addresses all the dimensions
	For each dimension in the dimension list... {
		If the dimension is not described in the specification {
			Describe the dimension in the specification
		}
	}
	// Make sure all the specification items are complete
	For each item in the specification... {
		If the item is not described completely
			ItemDescription += missing item characteristics
	}
}

MakeExternal(Spec) {
	// Make sure the specifications only discuss user perspectives
	For each item in the specification... {
		If the item describes the object's internals
			// Remove the item
			Spec -= item
	}
}
```

Document 3.2 — *Cont'd*

```
ScrutinizeAddedValue(Spec, Requirements) {
    // Identify unfounded specification items
    new AddedValueList
    For each item in the specification... {
        // Look through all the requirements
        For each statement in the requirements... {
            If the statement relates to the item {
                The item has foundation in the statement
            }
        }
        // If no statements related to the item
        If the item has no foundation {
            // Add the item to the added value list
                AddedValueList += item
        }
    }
    // Consider each added value item
    For each item in the added value list... {
        Determine the cost of keeping the item
        Determine the value of the item
        If nobody will pay for the item {
            Spec -= item
        }
    }
}
```

Exercises

0. List the three significant aspects of a successful specification. Describe each of these aspects.
1. Explain why specifications that are incomplete or inconsistent can add to the object's development cost. Explain the costs associated with specifications that are based on an object's internals.
2. List six user views of an object that an object's specification might include. Describe what each view is and what types of objects might require each view.
3. List the tools or techniques developers can use to describe each view listed in the previous question.
4. Identify the four items of interest when inspecting a specification.

ObjectDesign = DesignObject(ObjectS

Chapter 4

Object-Oriented Design

Chapter 3 discussed how to describe objects from the user's perspective. Applying the user's perspective to the development process makes developers more aware of the responsibilities of an object. Once developers fully understand an object's required behavior, they are ready to describe how the object works from an internal or architectural perspective. Developers document the internal workings of an object in the object's design description. This chapter first discusses some general design principles and then shows the details of how to use the architect's perspective to create object design descriptions.

Object-Oriented Design and Cartoon Characters

The fundamental principle behind object-oriented design is abstraction. Abstraction allows people to ignore the details and remain focused on the big picture. Too much detail can overwhelm developers and cause them to lose focus. When that happens, development progress either stops or becomes completely disorganized, causing developers to "spin their wheels."

The sequence of steps involved in drawing a cartoon character illustrates how abstraction works. An artist starts by outlining the general shape of the character. At each stage of the cartoon character's development the artist adds a little more detail to the illustration. Figure 4.0 shows the various stages of development — or *levels of abstraction* — for a typical cartoon character.

For the character in Figure 4.0, the artist initially outlined the major shapes (i.e., the head, shoulders, and body) of the cartoon dog. At the next level of abstraction the artist added the shape of the legs, feet, and mouth. Each additional level of abstraction adds more detail to the cartoon until it is complete.

An artist could develop a cartoon character without applying abstraction. The artist could draw a fully developed face, and a fully developed tail, and then complete all the parts between the two extremes. A mistake made early in such a detail-first development process will result in tremendous amounts of wasted effort, time-consuming rework, and a general loss of morale.

By applying abstraction, the artist can create the desired character without much wasted effort. Notice how abstraction helps the artist to maintain the desired proportions of the character. Abstraction also ensures that the character's pose is correct. If the initial outlines had been out of proportion or the general outline had been incorrect, the artist would have started over. It's easy to start over if the amount of time invested in the project is minimal. Software architects should approach software development similarly by first creating a general outline of the software, using broad brush strokes and then building upon this outline, gradually adding more detail.

Like an artist, a good software architect cannot expect the first attempt to be a masterpiece. Developing the architectural skills to know how

Figure 4.0 — Using Abstraction to Draw a Cartoon

much detail to add at various levels of abstraction requires lots of practice. Architects should sharpen their skills by developing a variety of applications. Just as an artist improves with every sketch, painting, or sculpture, a software architect improves with every program designed and implemented. As architects build experience by applying abstraction to a variety of applications, they become more adept.

Applying abstraction to a design identifies dead-ends as quickly as possible. By drawing the first few ovals on the page, the artist can tell if the cartoon will be what the artist generally wants. If the artist decides early that the cartoon is not quite right, the artist changes the cartoon and limits wasted time and effort. The same principle applies to software design. It is impossible to completely avoid "dead-ends" or mistakes when developing software, but using abstraction helps identify the most serious mistakes with minimum effort.

Object Relationships

Early software development techniques focused almost exclusively on the software's control flow (i.e., on the software's sequence of operations). Flow charts epitomized this approach. As software development evolved, developers realized that control flow was not sufficient to fully describe a program's design. Developers realized programs were more than a sequence of operations. Programs were operations performed on *data*. This realization spawned a new set of techniques, which focused on data flow, as epitomized by tools such as the data flow diagram.

The object-oriented paradigm synthesizes these two views and adds new insight. Object-oriented designs describe both control flow and data flow *and* recognize the two are intimately related. Object-oriented design also recognizes the importance of *relationships between* objects. There are four general categories of interobject relationships. These are:

- ❑ The *Is-a-kind-of* relationship
- ❑ The *Uses* relationship
- ❑ The *Consists-of* relationship
- ❑ The *Contains* relationship

The classic *Is-a-kind-of* object-oriented relationship indicates set membership. For example, a queen "is a kind of" chess piece or a dog "is a kind of" animal. The object-oriented paradigm represents the

Is-a-kind-of relationship through inheritance. Inheritance implies that descendant objects receive the attributes of their base classes as described in Chapter 0.

The *Uses* relationship is a client-server relationship. In a *Uses* relationship, one object "uses" another object to accomplish some task. In a database application, a database object might store and retrieve data records for an application object. A client is the application that "uses" the server or the database object.

Objects can be both clients and servers. While the database object is the server for the application, the database object might be a client of a file system server. It is important for developers to focus on identifying the relationships between objects and not just the objects.

The *Consists-of* relationship occurs when an object is composed of other objects. A car "consists of" an engine, four wheels, a body, and an electrical system. *Consists-of* relationships are generally static. This means that a car always has four wheels and not sometimes two or 10.

Finally, the *Contains* relationship describes a potentially transient relationship such as cards in a poker hand or items in a box. Developers implement *Contains* relationships using container classes such as lists, queues, stacks, and trees. The transientness of the *Contains* relationship distinguishes it from the *Consists-of* relationship. For example, objects

A Common Mistake

Developers commonly confuse *Consists-of* relationships with *Is-a-kind-of* relationships. The confusion generally stems from classes that represent poorly understood abstractions. For example, is an arc "a kind of" circle or is a circle "a kind of" arc? Each of these relationships implies a different form of inheritance. Developers must fully understand the ramifications of inheritance before committing to its use. The convoluted inheritance hierarchies that result from improper use of inheritance obfuscate the software's function and limit software's reuse. Later sections of this chapter discuss different techniques for developing *Is-a-kind-of* and *Consists-of* relationships.

may be put into or taken out of a box, but in normal use, the engine never leaves the car.

The *Contains* relationship also represents set membership, but the transient nature of the *Contains* relationship distinguishes it from the *Is-a-kind-of* relationship. An item may come and go as a member of the set of things a box "contains," but a dog will always be a member of the set of animals. The transient nature of the relationships between the objects should help categorize the relationship.

To apply abstraction in the recursive design process, software designers must first concentrate on *Consists-of* relationships, i.e., on viewing programs as objects within objects. *Consists-of* relationships are the binding links between levels of abstraction. A book consists of a table of contents, chapters, appendices, and an index. The abstraction called the book is bound by the *Consists-of* relationship to the lower level abstraction's table of contents, chapters, appendices, and index.

For the recursive design process to be successful, developers must also recognize *Contains* relationships as links between levels of abstraction. Objects are potentially dynamic sets that decompose differently depending upon the changing constitution of the set. For example, the set of windows that makes up a screen of a Graphical User Interface (GUI) application may change as the application runs. The GUI screen might be considered an abstraction of the set of windows it contains. This *Contains* relationship binds the higher level screen abstraction to the lower level windows' abstractions.

Once software designers understand what the subordinate objects are, it becomes important to organize how the subordinate objects interact. As subordinate objects work to perform the functions of their superior object, they will require each other's assistance. These assisting relationships are the *Uses* relationships.

Finally, developers should identify *Is-a-kind-of* relationships. The *Is-a-kind-of* relationship is a generalization that encompasses several objects with similar methods. Since the Object Creation Process works from the more abstract to the less abstract, the generalized object is usually identified before its specific instances. Thus, the design of a drawing package will identify the abstraction of shapes before the design will identify specific shapes such as circles and squares. The specific instances of the generalized abstraction result from a need to handle each instance differently. To eliminate many tests that handle each instance differently, the developer should decompose each generalized type into its enumerated instances. The *Is-a-kind-of* relationship links each enumerated instance to the more generalized type.

Design Communication Media

Graphical design methods are well-suited to the one-dimensional view common to control-flow and data-flow design. A flow-chart quickly and easily explains the relationship between the steps in a process. Object-oriented designers, though, have difficulty expressing their designs in a graphical form.

This difficulty is a direct result of the many different types of relationships captured by an object-oriented design. Because the object-oriented design method uncovers many independent relationships, graphical representations quickly become overwhelming. Figure 4.1, for example, shows what happens if we try to extend the object-relationship diagram to encompass all these relationships. Even if we assign each relationship a different line type, the diagram quickly becomes too complex to be useful. Rather than pack all relationships into one diagram, one could produce separate drawings for each relationship (see Figure 4.2).

Separate diagrams keep the diagrams simple, but assimilating the many diagrams becomes cumbersome. Perhaps a better solution is to look for a communication medium that describes complex relationships tersely, yet understandably.

We prefer non-graphical representation called *pseudocode*. Pseudocode is a mixture of formal programming languages and natural language. There are no rigid rules for the syntax or constructs of pseudocode.

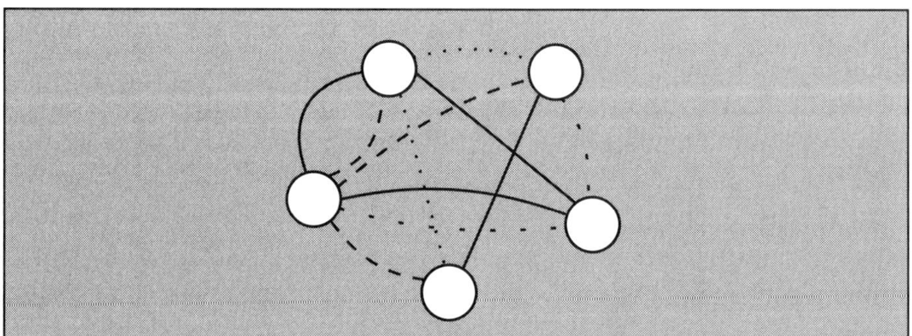

Figure 4.1 — An Example Object-Relationship Diagram

The lack of rigidity gives pseudocode its extensible expressive power. Any algorithm ever conceived can be expressed in some form of pseudocode.

Besides its extensible expressiveness, pseudocode has many other valuable traits. Most software engineers are comfortable using pseudocode since it is similar to a programming language. The familiarity of pseudocode eliminates the designer's need for special training. Since software developers understand programming language constructs, pseudocode is universally acceptable for communicating ideas.

Besides familiarity and comfort, pseudocode has the following strengths:

- ❑ Formality
- ❑ Expressiveness
- ❑ Terseness
- ❑ No special tools
- ❑ Non-compilable

Pseudocode is formal. With respect to methods, formality refers to the well-defined nature of the method. Formality reduces ambiguity in the design. Less ambiguous designs save development time and energy by making it easier to spot design flaws.

Pseudocode is expressive yet terse. Besides describing control flow and data flow, object-oriented developers can use pseudocode to describe

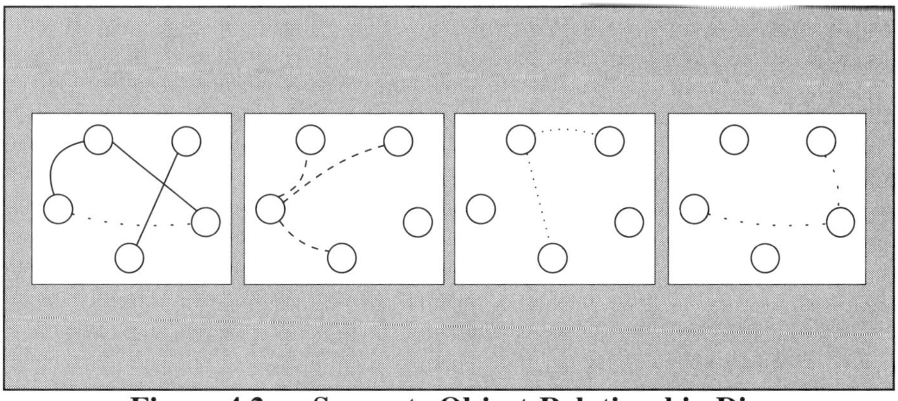

Figure 4.2 — Separate Object-Relationship Diagrams

the relationships between objects. Additionally, pseudocode is a compact tool for representing these aspects of software.

Pseudocode requires no special tools. One can easily create pseudocode using a standard text editor or even a pencil and paper. Text is also compatible with many standard support tools (e.g., word processors, E-mail, spelling programs, etc.).

Pseudocode cannot be compiled. During the implementation phase this restriction may seem like a disadvantage. During the design phase, however, this restriction is a strength. Since pseudocode cannot be compiled, there is no temptation to run a pseudocode program. The developer must actively engage in thinking through the operation of the code.

While pseudocode has an extensible free form, many patterns appear frequently. It is useful to categorize and identify these language patterns. The patterns include:

- Simple statements
- Conditionals
- Loops (both `while` and `until`)
- Convolution

The *simple statement*, the foundation of pseudocode, expresses a single operational idea. Although simple statements express only one idea, the idea may be an abstraction of many more detailed ideas. For example, a simple pseudocode statement might be, "Clear the screen." At one level of abstraction, clearing the screen is a single action, even though, at a lower level of abstraction, it implies iterating through each character position of the screen to fill the position with a blank and to disable the position's video attributes.

Simple statements change the state of data items. Statements may affect one or many data items, and the data items may be explicit or implicit. The following three statements are examples of how simple statements affect data item states:

- Increment the character count.
- Get the next character.
- Calculate the column totals.

The first statement is clearly changing the state of a single data item (i.e., the character count). The second statement does not explicitly refer to a data item. Implicitly the second statement changes the state of the target data item that holds the character. The third statement explicitly changes the states of many data items (one for each column).

Conditionals correspond to `if-then-else` branching statements. Conditionals use data item states to affect program control flow. Like simple statements, conditionals can use abstraction. For example

```
If the printer is ready,
  ...
```

might be an abstraction of the printer having toner, having paper, and being on line.

Loops are constructs that repeat simple statements based on the result of a conditional. `While` loops place the conditional at the beginning of the repetition. `Until` loops place the conditional at the end of the repetition. Middle conditional loops which place the loop conditional in the middle of the loop are useful because they eliminate the need for redundant code.

Convolution, a specific type of loop, addresses each member of a set. The phrases "For each . . .", "For every . . .", and "For all . . ." characterize convolution. Convolution applies the same operation to every member of a container set, such as an array or list. Typically, one would use a convolution operator to repaint graphics objects during a screen refresh:

```
For each graphics object on the screen . . .
  Paint the object
```

Inherent in pseudocode's simple statements and conditionals is the ability to express abstraction. Developers can "rewrite" both simple statements and conditionals in more detail at a lower level of abstraction by using other statements, conditionals, loops and convolution.

Designing with Pseudocode

Pseudocode lends itself to good top-down design. In the object-oriented world of design, top-down design means describing how an object works, and then using the description to identify the more detailed or subordinate objects. At each level of abstraction, objects become more detailed until the design yields existing objects (either in libraries or in the language itself).

To design a program using pseudocode, start by describing the program in pseudocode at the program's highest level of abstraction. Like the cartoon character at the beginning of the chapter, start with the general outline.

The Middle-Conditional Loop

The following example shows how middle conditional loops can be useful.

- *While* loop example:

```
Prompt for the command
Get the command
While the command is not valid
    Issue an error
    Prompt for the command
    Get the command
```

- *Until* loop example:

```
Do until the command is valid
    Prompt for the command
    Get the command
    If the command is not valid,
        Issue an error
```

- Middle conditional loop example:

```
Loop . . .
    Prompt for the command
    Get the command
    Quit the loop if
        the command is valid
    Issue an error
```

All three loops are semantically equivalent. But, the *While* loop requires "prompt" and input operations in two different places. The *Until* loop performs the same test twice. The middle conditional loop avoids both of these reduncancies.

While and *Until* loop maintenance is more likely to introduce errors because of the redundant code. When the redundant code needs to be changed, the maintenance programmer may erroneously change only one redundant code fragment. In addition, the *Until* loop requires an extra test operation. The loop with the conditional in the middle does not have these same exposures. The additional test is usually only significant in time-critical applications, but is easily avoided with the middle conditional loop.

Not all loops are created equal. When a loop is necessary, it is important to identify the appropriate loop construct. Experience teaches

The following guidelines can help you avoid too much detail in the first level design. Here are some guidelines to avoid excessive detail:

- ❑ Capture the algorithm in five to ten lines.
- ❑ Limit nesting to a single level.
- ❑ Use common sense to regulate the application of the previous two rules.

Typically, developers respond to these guidelines with, "This sounds good for simple programs, but it will never work for my sophisticated

programmers that loops are likely to be a source of errors. Programmers can eliminate many potential errors by approaching loops with caution. A common source of errors is to use a *While* loop when an *Until* loop is a better fit and vice versa. *Until* loops require at least one iteration. *While* loops require zero or more iterations. In this sense *While* loops are more general than *Until* loops. Since *While* loops are more general, they tend to avoid certain types of programming errors. Here is an example:

Until loop implementation:

```
Until the end of file . . .
    Get a character from the file
    ...
```

While loop implementation:

```
While not at end of file . . .
    Get a character from the file
    ...
```

Imagine entering both loops with a *True end of file* condition. When the *Until* loop executes, the *Get a character* line causes an error. The *While* loop will avoid the error since the *While* loop handles the more general case of zero iterations.

When it is confusing which loop type to use, first try designing the loop using the *While* construct. If the *While* loop does not seem to fit, try the *Until* construct. Reserve the use of middle conditional loops for only those cases where the middle conditional loop simplifies a *While* or *Until* loop.

program!" To prove that these guidelines work for sophisticated programs, think about designing a text editor. The highest level of abstraction for a complex text editor might look like this:

```
Initialize the edit buffer
Initialize the terminal
Until the command is a quit command...
    Get a command from the terminal
    Alter the edit buffer according to the command
Save the edit buffer
```

In this design description the statements are broad brush strokes, but are still descriptive of how the text editor works. *Initialize the edit buffer* describes the process of reading the file to edit into a buffer. *Initialize the terminal* implies clearing the screen and then displaying the top of the edit buffer on the screen. For some terminals, initialization might also imply putting the terminal in non-echo mode.

Staying On Track

Often, design errors result from starting in the middle of the program's abstraction hierarchy. If a developer's intuition suggests that a particularly interesting algorithm must be part of the design it is a temptation to begin with that algorithm.

To avoid starting in the middle of the program's abstraction, decide if the outline of the first algorithm completely describes the program's function. If the initial algorithm does not describe the complete function of the program, patiently move up a level of abstraction. The algorithm of interest will wait. It will be much easier to describe the lower level algorithm given a better understanding of the context of the algorithm.

The `Until` loop gets a command from the terminal until it receives the `quit` command. `Get a command from the terminal` means prompting for commands, receiving and translating commands, keystrokes, or mouse events. The `Alter the edit buffer according to the command` line performs the bulk of the work for the text editor. Here the user changes the edit file, and the terminal is updated accordingly. `Save the edit buffer` updates the file with the contents of the edit buffer.

Some developers object that such a broad description does little good. On the contrary, this simple design description anchors the design with a starting point and begins to shape the requirements for future objects.

Given a pseudocode algorithm, the next step is to identify the subordinate objects. Start by circling the noun phrases in each statement and condition.

```
Initialize the edit buffer
Initialize the terminal
Until the command is a quit command...
    Get a command from the terminal
    Alter the edit buffer according to the command
Save the edit buffer
```

Next, underline the verb phrases of each statement and condition.

```
Initialize the edit buffer
Initialize the terminal
Until the command is a quit command...
    Get a command from the terminal
    Alter the edit buffer according to the command
Save the edit buffer
```

The noun phrases represent the objects. Circled nouns not previously seen probably represent subordinates of the current object. The verb phrases represent methods associated with the objects. Simply organizing these items will produce a first draft description of the subordinate objects and their associated methods:

```
Edit buffer:
   Initialize
   Alter
   Save
Terminal:
   Initialize
   Get
Command:
   Is a quit
```

Before listing the objects and their methods, you may need to normalize the pseudocode terms. Developers frequently refer to the same object or method by different names. For example, the edit buffer might be called an edit buffer, a buffer or even a file. The same problem occurs with different verb phases that represent the same operations. This difference in terms can create confusion in the design if not recognized. You may also need to rewrite some statements to clarify the relationship between objects and methods. It is not always easy to identify the target object of a method. Rewriting statements in active voice pseudocode can help eliminate this problem. For example, instead of saying *`The edit buffer gets edited`* use the active voice *`Alter the edit buffer`*. Active voice makes the subjects and verbs stand out. There are several grammar checking software packages available to help developers in eliminating passive voice pseudocode.

A similar problem occurs when the object is not explicit in the pseudocode statement. The *`Get a command from the terminal`* line might have read *`Get a command`*. When a statement has an implied object, try to find a way to make the object explicit. Explicit objects make it easier to remember the methods associated with the objects.

Given the objects and their methods, list the information that each method needs (at this level) to do its job.

```
Edit buffer:
   Initialize(File name, Terminal)
   Alter(Command)
   Save(File name)
Terminal:
   Initialize(Edit buffer)
   Get(Target command)
Command:
   Is a quit
```

Finally, assume that each object requires a *constructor* and *destructor*. If several of an object's methods require the same information, the constructor can supply it. For example, the edit buffer's *Initialize* and *Save* methods both require the file name. Since the file name is the same for both methods, it makes sense to supply the information to the constructor:

```
Edit buffer:
   Constructor(File name, Terminal)
   Destructor
   Initialize
   Alter(Command)
   Save
Terminal:
   Constructor
   Destructor
   Initialize(Edit buffer)
   Get(Target command)
Command:
   Constructor
   Destructor
   Is a quit
```

The object name and its associated list of methods are the requirements for that object. The recursive Object Creation Process uses the requirements to create an object specification for each of the lower level objects. Lower level object specifications can be expressed as an annotated class specification. Use the pseudocode to annotate the specification.

```
class Editbuffer  {
public:
   // Construct an edit buffer
   EditBuffer(char *FileName);
   // Destroy the edit buffer
   ~EditBuffer();
   // Initialize the edit buffer
   Initialize();
   // Alter the edit buffer according to the command
   Alter(Command);
   // Save the edit buffer
   Save();
};

class Terminal  {
public:
   // Construct a terminal
   Terminal();
   // Destroy the terminal
   ~Terminal();
   Initialize(EditBuffer &EdBuf);
   // Get a command from the terminal
   Command &Get();
};

class Command  {
public:
   // Construct a command
   Command();
   // Destroy the command
   ~Command();
   // Is a quit command
   BOOLEAN  IsAQuit();
}
```

This first draft specification may not be complete. Developers commonly identify additional methods during the design of other objects. However, these class specifications are a good foundation to which you can add methods as they are identified. Similarly, the parameters of the methods may not be complete at first. Add parameters as their need is identified.

Designing the highest level of a program's abstraction yields requirements and specifications of lower level objects. Use the specifications of the lower level objects to design the methods of these objects in the same way.

Some popular object-oriented design approaches identify objects and their methods by recognizing nouns and verbs in the program's requirements. Two weaknesses result from using the program's requirements instead of each object's design. First, the program requirements are not likely to mention all the necessary objects used by the program. An incomplete list of objects leaves the developers guessing what might be missing. The second weakness results from having to work with all the program's objects at once. As the number of objects within a program increases, the number of interobject relationships will increase geometrically. By using an object's design instead of the program's requirements, objects and their relationships are introduced as necessary. This limits the general program design complexity.

Designing Classes in C++

Circling the nouns and noun phrases in the program's algorithm helps the developer identify the objects needed in the program, but not all identified objects are good class candidates. There are a few general guidelines that will help a developer design good classes in C++.

Real world concepts are good class candidates. These types of classes are most frequently found in graphics applications, embedded systems programming, and simulations. An algorithm that simulates the backup of a hard disk drive to a tape device might look like:

```
Initialize tape drive
Selected files to save
While there are files remaining
Read the file from the disk drive
Write the file to the tape drive
```

The noun phrases *tape drive*, *disk drive*, and *files* are all real world concepts and excellent candidates for classes.

The purpose of classes and of abstraction is to hide complexity. If an algorithm seems too complex it is highly probable that some instances of classes are missing. Search for any overlooked noun phrases and consider implementing them as classes.

Well-known algorithms and data structures such as lists, linked lists, stacks, and queues should be implemented as classes. Typically, these types of classes are at or near the "bottom" of the recursive design process. Some C++ compilers come with class libraries that implement many popular data structures as classes. It is in the best interest of every C++ programmer to become familiar with the classes contained in their compilers. Reusing "shrink-wrapped" class libraries significantly reduces development time. Shrink-wrapped class libraries that provide source code also present developers with an opportunity to learn class development by studying the designs of others.

Applying Inheritance Intelligently

Many popular object-oriented design techniques stress the importance of inheritance. A fixation on inheritance can produce a confusing design that lacks reusability. The purpose of inheritance is to maximize code reuse and to encourage generality in programs. However, inheritance must never be used to stretch the logical representation of a class. Stretching a class's logical representation eliminates the possibility of reusing the affected class in another application. Only apply the inheritance feature of the C++ language after establishing a class hierarchy and verifying that a class has the *Is-a-kind-of* relationship with another class.

The construct

```
class Car: public Vehicle {
 // ...
};
```

uses the inheritance feature of C++ to derive the class *Car* from the class *Vehicle*. This is an example of the proper use of inheritance in C++, since a *Car* is a kind of *Vehicle*. *Car* inherits all the member functions and variables of the class *Vehicle*. Inheritance is an extremely convenient and efficient way of relating classes when the power is not misused.

The construct

```
class Car:   public Vehicle, public Engine,
             public Transmission {
 // ...
};
```

misuses inheritance. A car is not a kind of engine or a kind of transmission; a car consists of an engine and a transmission. Do not use the inheritance feature of C++ to establish *Consists-of* relationships. The misuse of inheritance gives the `Car` all the member functions and variables of the `Engine` and the `Transmission`. Excessive inheritance destroys the abstract relationships between classes and creates too much complexity at a given level. The developer can better establish *Consists-of* relationships by creating objects inside client classes and by making pointers to objects inside client classes.

The construct

```
class Car:   public Vehicle {
   Engine my_engine;
   // ...
};
```

creates a class `Car` that contains the object `my_engine`, an instance of the class `Engine`. Class `Car` now contains instances of all of the member variables of `Engine`. However, the member functions of `Engine` are not automatically defined in `Car`. With this construct, the class designer must explicitly select the member functions of `Engine` that are to be available to `Car`:

```
class Car:   public Vehicle {
   Engine my_engine;
public:
   void      start()   {
      Engine.start();
   }
   // ...
};
```

At first, developers may find it difficult to identify *Is-a-kind-of* relationships. The following guidelines should help developers decide if inheritance is appropriate in a particular situation:

- ❑ If several classes have member variables in common or perform similar operations, look for a base class that groups the similarities. This use of inheritance allows you to reuse the variables and operations across derived classes.
- ❑ If groups of classes share a complex algorithm, a base class may implement the algorithm and allow the derived classes to share the algorithm through inheritance.
- ❑ Groups of classes that are special cases of a general concept are likely candidates for inheritance.

Do not use inheritance if:

- ❑ Doing so would cause the derived class to have access to unnecessary member variables or unnecessary member functions. A class with unnecessary data or operations suggests that the logical boundaries of the class have deteriorated.

Creating Member Functions

The verb phrases of the algorithm tell the developer what *action functions* an object must perform to do its job. Depending on their role, objects may require additional functions including *management functions* (constructors, destructors, copy constructors, and assignment operators), *access functions* (constant functions that return the value of member variables), and *internal operation functions* (private member functions and error handling routines). Most of the functions in a program should be member functions of some class. Making functions member functions will reduce the number of global names and reduce the chance of global name conflicts during reuse.

Virtual and Pure Virtual Member Functions

C++ allows developers to change the behavior of base classes by using *virtual functions*. A base class may contain critical member functions that should not be overridden by a derived class. Developers should be certain not to declare any critical member functions `virtual`. If a derived class cannot meaningfully override a member function, that member function should not be virtual.

Developers who have gone through the process of collecting common member variables and functions into a base class may discover a function that the base class cannot implement directly. In the chess game example, the base class `piece` contains the member function `move()`. `move()` is an undefined operation unless it refers to a specific instance of `piece` (such as queen or knight). Therefore, developers must not create instances of the class `piece`. Such a class is called an *abstract class.*

Developers generally implement abstract classes by using either pure virtual functions or impure virtual functions. Declaring undefined member functions as pure virtual member functions defers the implementation of the function to the derived class. If a derived class does not implement the pure virtual function, the C++ compiler generates an error. Developers implement impure virtual functions by supplying an implementation of the function that prints out an error message. Any erroneous calls to the abstract class are not detected until runtime. Pure virtual functions are preferable to impure virtual functions since they detect errors during compilation phase instead of the testing phase.

In-Line Member Functions

Functions that allow other classes to inspect the member variables of a class and other functions with very little code are ideal candidates for `inline` member functions. Sometimes, `inline` can improve the performance of a program. However, using `inline` in combination with `virtual` can make programs larger than necessary without improving performance. To determine the value of `virtual inline` function calls, developers should become familiar with their compiler's method for handling `virtual inline` functions.

Private and Protected Member Functions

If a member function could be easily misused by a client class, or if the member function is really only useful to other member functions, declare the member function as `private`. Make nonmember functions that need to use the private member function `friends` of the class. Avoid making modifications to existing classes to allow new classes or functions to be `friends`. Generally, this occurs when a new class is derived from an existing class. If this is the case, make the necessary private member functions `protected`. This allows the derived class to use them. If a protected member function needs to be disabled in the derived class, redefine it as private inside the derived class.

Member Variables and Accessibility

The member variables required by a class depend on what the class does. Abstract classes frequently have no member variables. Member variables declared `static` are shared as single instances by all instances of a class. A good example of the need for such a variable declaration is a window class in a GUI application that keeps track of how many windows are currently open. Consider making static member variables static *nonmember* variables and declaring them in the `.c` file with the member function definitions. This will limit the scope of a modification should the declaration of the variable need modification.

Designing for Object Reuse

Eventually the recursive design process identifies an object that can be completely or nearly completely fulfilled by existing objects. When an existing object fulfills the defined requirements, the object is considered *reusable*. Object reuse is a valuable concept because it saves development time and effort.

There are several attributes to consider when discussing object reuse. Some objects are completely reusable in their present form. Completely reusable objects require no alteration for reuse. While some objects are not completely reusable, it may be easier to reuse parts of the objects or extend the objects than to start from scratch. Consider partial object reuse to reduce software development effort.

Object reuse follows the 70/30 rule; 30 percent of all objects make up 70 percent of all programs. Unfortunately the 70 percent includes inherent types, such as integers, pointers, and strings. Beyond the inherent types provided in the language, the most reused objects include common container classes, such as lists, stacks, queues, and trees.

Another factor to consider in object reuse is the object's potential reuse *scope*. An object can potentially be reused in the same program, in a similar program, or in a dissimilar program. One can more easily develop objects which are reusable within a single program than in dissimilar programs. It is easier to visualize potential uses of an object within a single program, than to imagine how other unspecified programs might try to reuse an object. While the broader scope is harder to acheive, developers who create objects to reuse across dissimilar programs will improve their development process. The following guidelines help develop objects with the widest scope of reuse:

- ❑ Keep logically separate operations in separate methods.
- ❑ Keep logically separate data in separate data items.
- ❑ Eliminate implicit *Uses* dependencies of global data.
- ❑ Limit inheritance dependencies on other classes.

Logical separation means that each data element's or method's purpose is well-defined. When data items represent one thing in one situation and something else in another, the data is not logically separate. For example, a return value might represent the length of a string or an error value if the value is less than zero. Similarly, a method may perform multiple functions related only by the coincidental need to execute at the same point in time. Such a weak method might pop a stack and check the system time.

Logical separation of both methods and data is critical for software reuse. When data and methods are not logically separate, it is difficult to understand how to use the software. In addition, lack of logical separation requires users to carry along baggage that may not be helpful.

Reusable software limits its dependence on global data. The greatest strength of encapsulation is that it limits the scope of the encapsulated software's effects. Using global data within an object circumvents the object's encapsulation by relying upon and causing external side effects. Reusing an object that relies on global or external data requires the developers to understand enough about object's internal workings to know what global data must also be reused. In addition, reliance upon global data may even limit an object's reusability within the same program by preventing multiple instances of the same object.

Inheritance can also limit an object's reusability. Reusing a derived class of objects requires reusing the entire family of objects. It is reasonable to use inheritance if the inheritance represents a true *Is-a-kind-of* relationship. However, some developers have used inheritance as a short-sighted hack to extend the functionality of a class. While inheritance can be used as a quick-and-dirty means for extending a class's functionality, ultimately the results will make the class more difficult to understand and use (just like global data dependence).

Reviewing Designs

Object design reviews can be an effective way to shorten the software development cycle. Design reviews are more valuable than code reviews because design reviews help developers find oversights with a minimum investment in the software's development. Waiting to find design flaws until the software is coded and partially tested may force the developers to discard pieces of the software. The result is a significant waste of effort.

The structure of the design review should be appropriate to the project and comfortable for the design team. Reviews can be strictly formal and prescribe exactly how the review proceeds. Reviews can also be as informal as a few architects looking at a design during a break. Formality is usually a topic of concern for designers, but it is not the most important issue with respect to design reviews. Use a level of formality that is most comfortable for those involved in the review process.

Be Grateful for the Help

Before each flight, skydivers take time to inspect their parachutes. This is serious business for a skydiver since the slightest mistake could cost a human life. If you were a skydiver checking your chute and you overlooked a problem, would you be grateful if a colleague could point out the mistake before you actually used the chute?

Reviewing an object's design is analogous to a skydiver inspecting a parachute. Skydivers would not consider jumping without checking their parachutes. Similarly, software designers should not release a design for implementation without first inspecting the software. The purpose of a design review is to identify errors in the object's design. Yet many designers are offended when their colleagues point out flaws in the design. Effective software architects maintain a skydiving attitude when reviewing their designs with their colleagues.

Here are some guidelines for conducting design reviews:

- ❑ Maintain an egoless attitude.
- ❑ Concentrate on criticizing the design, not people.
- ❑ Assign roles for the reviewers.
- ❑ Allow time for review preparation.
- ❑ Keep review sessions short.
- ❑ Keep review metrics.

The single most important factor affecting design reviews is the attitude of those participating. If designers feel threatened, attacked, or intimidated the design review will produce little more than anxiety. However, if the reviewers can work with a cohesive attitude, all the participants will benefit and the design will be stronger.

Try to keep comments directed toward improving the design. Specific comments are more helpful than general comments. For example, "Moving this process before the previous process avoids an initialization error," is preferable to, "This design does not work."

Assign specific responsibilities to the review participants. Roles might include moderator, reader, scribe, and reviewer. The moderator sets up the review by scheduling the review, inviting the other participants, and assigning responsibilities. During the review the moderator makes sure the comments remain centered on the design and that the review stays on track. The reader leads the design review team through the design by explaining how the design works. The scribe makes notes of any comments that require further action. These action items include changes to the design, clarification of the designed object's context, or other necessary additional research.

Others may be invited to be part of the design review team to investigate and comment on the design. The designer usually participates as a reviewer and not as the moderator, scribe, or reader. This allows the designer to focus on and understand the comments of the other members of the review team.

Effective design reviews require preparation. When scheduling the review, the moderator should see that all members of the review team have access to the necessary materials well in advance. This allows the review team members to take the necessary time to understand the material before attending the review.

Limit the amount of time the review team spends in the review meeting. Design reviews that last more than an hour become ineffective. It is possible to keep the review meeting short only if review team members have taken the time in advance to understand the review material. If for some unforeseen reason the review meeting requires more time, consider scheduling a second meeting.

Keep metrics to help optimize design reviews. Ask each member of the review team to keep track of how much time he or she spends preparing for and participating in the review meeting. Keep track of the number of comments and issues that arise from the design review. Design reviews are a significant investment of development time. Use the design review metrics to help optimize the review process.

Be careful not to go overboard with the review metrics. Design teams must remain focused on the design and not focused on the metrics. If too much emphasis is placed on the metrics, design teams will generate pages of bogus issues to give the impression of progress. Overemphasizing the metrics will detract from design review effectiveness.

Design reviews can easily degenerate into a useless ritual. The keys to maintaining useful design reviews are attitude and preparation. If designers begrudgingly go through the motions of design reviews, they will derive much less benefit. Effective moderation and sufficient preparation time contribute significantly to keeping good morale in the design team.

The Example Chess Game's Design

We'll now present a complete design for the example chess game to illustrate the principles and techniques described in this chapter. The design process starts by considering the entire chess program as the top level object. The top level game object has only one method, one which runs the game. A pseudocode description of the top level object's method looks like this:

```
Chess game main entry point
 Until the user does not want to play again or quitting...
    Initialize the game
    Play the game
    If the user does not want to quit,
       Determine if the user wants to play again
 Clean up the game
```

The pseudocode outlines the major functions of the chess game. The loop allows users to play as many games as they wish. The lines inside the loop set up the game, play the game, and clean up the game. Game initialization amounts to arranging the board in its initial position and querying the user to select the white or black team. The *Play the game* line represents the alternation between white and black until the game ends. The final *Clean up the game* represents clearing the board.

Two additional lines inside the loop determine whether the user wants to continue. These two lines occur before the Clean up the game line, because the object's specification designates that the game asks the user before cleaning up the board. Otherwise, it might be possible to embed the user interaction in the loop conditional.

Investigation of the pseudocode identifies two objects. The most obvious, the *game*, must support three methods: *Initialize*, *Play*, and *Clean up*.

The second object, which is less obvious in the pseudocode, supplies interaction with the user. According to the specification, this object is the *User interaction line*. Based on this first level of pseudocode, the *User interaction line* object has only one requirement: to query the user to play again.

Both objects have implicit constructors and destructors. The *game* constructor creates an empty chess board. The *User interaction line* constructor initializes a clear line at the bottom of the screen. Thus, these objects and requirements are identified in the first level of pseudocode:

```
Game:
    Constructor
    Destructor
    Initialize
    Play to determine who wins
    Clean up
User interaction line:
    Constructor
    Destructor
    Query the user to play again
```

The next step of the object creation process is to translate the object requirements into specifications. For internal objects this is most easily accomplished by creating class definitions, as shown in Listing 4.0.

Creating the specification revealed the parameters that each method requires. The *game* object will need to display information on the screen and will also need to interact with the user. Therefore, the *game* class constructor requires a screen parameter and the user interaction line

Document 4.0 — The Design for Major Methods

Initialize the game
    Create a white **team**
    Create a black **team**
    If the **user** wants to be white,
        Tell white **team** to play manually
        Tell black **team** to play automatically
    Otherwise the user wants black,
        Tell white **team** to play automatically
        Tell black **team** to play manually

Play the game

    Initialize the current team to white
    While the current team is not in checkmate and
    The current **team** is not in stalemate and
    Not quitting...
        Have the current **team** make a move
        Change the current **team** to the other team
    If the user did not quit,
        Figure out who won

Clean up the game
    Clean up the **board**
    Destroy black **team**
    Destroy white **team**

Listing 4.0 — Specification for Internal Objects

```
class Game  {
public:
   // Create the game
   Game(
      Screen&,         // Screen handle
      Status&          // Status line handle
   );
   // Destroy the game
    ~Game();
    // Initialize the game
    void Initialize();
   // Play the game (return FALSE if the user quits)
   BOOLEAN  Play(
      Winner&          // Win-lose-draw inidiator
   );
   // Clean up the game
   void  CleanUp();
};

// game conclusion states
enum  Winner {
   WinUser,        // User wins
   WinComputer,    // Computer wins
   WinDraw         // Draw
};

// User interaction (status) line
class  Status {
public:
   // Create the user interaction line
   Status(Screen &);
   // Destroy the user interaction line
   ~Status();
   // Determine if the user wants to play again
   BOOLEAN  PlayAgain(const Winner);
};
```

parameter. Since the *user interaction line* will also interact with the user through the screen, the *User interaction line* constructor also requires a screen parameter.

The *Game* class's *Play* method must return an indicator telling who won the game. In addition, the specification shows us that any user interaction must allow the user to quit the game. Therefore, both the *Game* class's *Play* method and *Status*'s *PlayAgain* method must return a value indicating if the user wants to quit. The *PlayAgain* method also needs to know who won the game in order to display the appropriate prompt. The *Winner&* type parameter communicates this information from the *Play* method to the *PlayAgain* method.

Given the specification for the *Game* and *Status* objects, the Object Creation Process recurses to design each of these objects. First we will design the *Game* object's three major methods:

(Nouns that represent objects are in bold. Verbs that represent methods are underlines.)

The *Game* class's initialization method sets up the game by creating both chess teams, which also implies placing the teams' pieces in the appropriate places on the board. The initialization method also determines what color the user wants to be. Given the user's selection, the initialization method instructs each team to play manually or automatically as appropriate.

The *Game* class's *Play* method is a loop that lets each team alternate moving. The team whose turn it is to move is considered the *current* team. The current team alternates each time through the loop. The loop continues until the game is over or the user wants to quit. If the user does not quit, the *Play* method determines who won.

The *Game* object's *clean up* method is very simple. It clears the board of all pieces and destroys the two teams. If the user wants to play again, the board returns to its initial state.

It may be easiest to design an object's major methods before designing the constructor and destructor. The major methods help define key responsibilities of the constructor and destructor. The *Game* object constructor, for example, must create the empty board for the other *Game* object methods.

Once again, the next step is to identify the subordinate objects and methods. Here is a list of these objects and methods:

```
Team:
   Create
   Destroy
   Play manually
   Play automatically
   Is in checkmate
   Is in stalemate
   Make a move
User interaction line:
   Wants to be white
Board:
   Create
   Destroy
   Clean up
```

This pseudocode identifies two new objects, *Team* and *Board*, and an additional method for the existing *User interaction line* object. The *white* and *black* qualifiers indicate two instances of the *Team* object.

At this point in the design some of the constructs become simple enough that they need no further decomposition. For example, the *current team* from Document 4.0 is a simple variable that refers to either the black team or the white team, i.e., a pointer. Since a pointer type already exists, the pointer operations do not need to be explained with further design.

To design the remainder of the chess game, continue to recursively apply design, requirements, and specification. The design will gradually yield requirements for more and more existing object types. This recursive process ends when all objects subordinate to the program object exist or have been designed.

Document 4.1 is the entire pseudocode for the example chess game. The pseudocode shows the requirements and design for each object. The *class* specifications are the header files, which are included in Appendix B with the rest of the source for the chess game example.

Document 4.1 — Pseudocode for Chess Game

```
CHESS

Chess game main entry point

    Initialize the screen
    Create the user interaction line
    Create the game
    Until the user does not want to play again or quitting...
        Initialize the game
        Play the game
        If the user does not want to quit,
            Determine if the user wants to play again
        Clean up the game

GAME

Create the game

Initialize the game

    Create a white team
    Create a black team
    If the user wants to be white,
        Tell white team to play manually
        Tell black team to play automatically
    Otherwise the user wants black,
        Tell white team to play automatically
        Tell black team to play manually

Play the game

    Initialize the current team to white
    While the current team is not in checkmate and
      The current team is not in stalemate and
      Not quitting...
        Have the current team make a move
        Change the current team to the other team
    If the user did not quit,
        Figure out who won
```

Document 4.1 — *Cont'd*

Clean up the game

Clean up the board
Destroy black team
Destroy white team

BOARD

Create the board

Set the initial color to black
For each row on the board...
For each column in the row...
Create the square

Destroy the board
For each position on the board...
Destroy the square
Get the handle of the piece at the position
Place a piece on the board
Remove a piece from the square
Find the location of a specified piece
For each position on the board...
If this is the piece, return the piece's square
Try moving the piece to a new square on the board
Restore the piece to its original square
Select a position
While not done selecting and not quitting
Blink the current square as a prompt
Get a command from the terminal
Unblink the current square
Move the blinking square according to the command

Determine if there are pieces between the source and destination

Calculate the horizontal movement
Calculate the vertical movement
For each position between the start and end...
If there is a piece at the location,
There are pieces between the source and destination

Document 4.1 — *Cont'd*

Determine if the destination is a valid position

Clean up the board

    For each square on the board...
        Remove any piece from the square

Get the square associated with the row and column

Get the square associated with the coordinate

Create a square iterator (For each square on the board...)

Destroy the square iterator

Get the next square

SQUARE

Create a square

    Set the background for the square based upon its color
    Mark the square as containing no piece
    Draw the square

Draw the square

    Turn on the appropriate attributes
    For each line in the name buffer...
        Position at the beginning of the line
        Output the name buffer for the line

Destroy a square

    Remove the piece
    Set the attribute to none
    Draw the square

Get the coordinate for this square

Draw the square as bold

Document 4.1 — *Cont'd*

```
        Turn on the bold attribute
        Redraw the square

Draw the square as not bold

        Turn off the bold attribute
        Redraw the square

Draw the square as blinking

        Turn on the blink attribute
        Redraw the square

Draw the square as not blinking

        Turn off the blink attribute
        Redraw the square

Place the string in the center of the name buffer

Place a piece in the square

        Save the piece in the square
        Paint the piece's name
        Redraw the square;

Remove a piece from the square

Remove a piece from the square
Remove a piece from the square
        Remove the piece from this square
        Erase the piece's name
        Redraw the square

Try a piece in this location

        Save the original piece
        Use the try piece without updating the screen
        Return the piece that was in the square
Stop trying the piece in this location
```

Document 4.1 — *Cont'd*

Return the original piece to its square

STATUS

Create the user interaction line

Destroy the user interaction line

Cause a warning beep

Determine if the user wants to play again

Ask the user to play again
get the user's response

Get the color from the user

Prompt the user for the color
Get the user's response

Prompt for input

Show a status line

Clear the status line

Show the "Thinking" prompt

Show the "Select piece" prompt

Show the "Place piece" prompt

Show the "Illegal move" prompt

COMMAND

Create a command

Destroy the command
Create a command

Document 4.1 — *Cont'd*

Determine if the command is an up arrow

Determine if the command is a down arrow

Determine if the command is a left arrow

Determine if the command is a right arrow

Determine if the command is an arrow

Determine if the command is a quit command

Determine if the command is a white selection command

Determine if the command is a black selection command

Determine if the command is a yes command

Determine if the command is a no command

Determine if the command is an enter command

SCREEN

Initialize the screen

Close the screen

Clear the screen

Position the cursor

Output a string with the current attributes

Change the current attributes

Sound a warning beep

Get a command

Document 4.1 — *Cont'd*

TEAM

Create a team

Create a king
Create a queen
Create a bishop on the king's side
Create a bishop on the queen's side
Create a knight on the king's side
Create a knight on the queen's side
Create a castle on the king's side
Create a castle on the queen's side
For each pawn position...
    Create a pawn

Destroy the team

Destroy the king
Destroy the queen
Destroy the bishop on the king's side
Destroy the bishop on the queen's side
Destroy the knight on the king's side
Destroy the knight on the queen's side
Destroy the castle on the king's side
Destroy the castle on the queen's side
For each pawn position...
    Destroy a pawn

Tell the team to play automatically

Mark the team as an automatic player

Tell the team to play manually

Mark the team as a manual player

Determine if the team is a manual player

If so, the team plays manually.

Document 4.1 — *Cont'd*

```
Determine if the team is in check

      Find the king on the board
      For each square on the board...
           If the square contains a piece and
              The piece is not a team member and
              The piece can move to the king's square,
                 This is check

Determine if a specific piece has a legal move from this square
      For each square on the board...
           If this is a legal move for this piece,
                 This piece has a move

Determine if any legal moves exist

      For each square on the board...
           If the square contains a piece
              The piece is a team member and
              The piece has a move from this square,
                 Legal moves exist

Determine if the team is in checkmate

      The team is in checkmate if -
           The team is in check and
           No legal moves exist

Determine if the team is in stalemate

      The team is in stalemate if
           The team is not in checkmate and
           No legal moves exist

Select the source of the manual move

      Find the king on the board

      While a valid piece is not selected and not quitting...
           Select a square
Select the destination of the manual move
```

Document 4.1 — *Cont'd*

```
        Save the selected square
        Bold the starting square

        Select a square

        Unbold the starting square

Crown the pawn (convert it to a queen)

        For each pawn on the team...
            If this is the pawn,
                Destroy the pawn
                Create a queen

Make the move
        Remove any piece from the destination square
        Remove the piece from the source square
        If the piece is a pawn and
          The move is a final move,
            Crown the pawn
        Move the source piece to the destination
Determine if this is a valid destination
        The destination is valid if -
            The move is legal and
                The destination square contains no piece or
                The destination square contains a piece and
                The piece is not a member of this team
Make a manual move
        Until a piece makes a legal move or quitting...
            Select the board's source for the manual move
            Select the board's destination for the manual move
        If not quitting,
            Make the move
Calculate the best move from this square
        For each square on the board...
            If a move to this location is a valid move,
                Calculate the square's value
                If the square's value represents the best move,
                    Remember this move
```

Document 4.1 — *Cont'd*

Make an automatic move
    For each square on the board...
        If the square contains a piece and
          The piece is a member of this team,
            Calculate the best move for this square
            If this move is better than the best so far,
                Remember this move as the best
    Make the move
Have the team make a move
    If this team is a manual player,
        Make manual move
    Otherwise the team is an automatic player
        Make automatic move
Determine if a move causes checkmate
    Try moving the piece to the new square
    See if this puts the king in check
    Restore the piece to its original location

PIECE

Create a piece
Destroy the piece
Determine if the piece is a member of the team
Mark the piece as having moved
Determine if the piece has moved
Determine if the piece is the same color as that specified
Determine if the piece is white
Determine if this move causes checkmate

KING

Create a king
Destroy the king
Return the name of the piece
Return the value of this type of piece
Return the type of the piece

Document 4.1 — *Cont'd*

Determine if this is a legal move
    The move is legal if -
        The new square is not the old one and
            The destination is less than one row/column away or
            The new position is a legal castle move
        And
        The destination does not contain the same team and
        The move does not cause (self-inflicted) checkmate

QUEEN

Create a queen
Destroy the queen
Return the name of the piece
Return the value of this type of piece
Return the type of the piece
Determine if this is a legal move
    The move is legal if -
        The source is not the destination and
        The move is
            Horizontal or
            Vertical or
            Diagonal
        And
        There is no piece between source and destination and
        The destination does not contain the same team and
        The move does not cause (self-inflicted) checkmate

BISHOP

Create a bishop

Destroy the bishop

Return the name of the piece

Return the value of this type of piece

Return the type of the piece

Determine if this is a legal move

Document 4.1 — *Cont'd*

The move is legal if -
    The source is not the destination and
    The move is diagonal and
    There is no piece between the source and destination and
    The destination does not contain the same team and
    The move does not cause (self-inflicted) checkmate

KNIGHT

Create a knight

Destroy the knight

Return the name of the piece

Return the value of this type of piece

Return the type of the piece

Determine if this is a legal move

The move is legal if -
    The source is not the destination and
    The move is
        A move up or
        A move down or
        A move left or
        A move right
    And
    The destination does not contain the same team and
    The move does not cause (self-inflicted) checkmate

CASTLE

Create a castle

Destroy the castle

Return the name of the piece

Document 4.1 — *Cont'd*

Return the value of this type of piece

Return the type of the piece

Determine if this is a legal move

The move is legal if -
- The source is not the destination and
- The move is
  - Horizontal or
  - Vertical
- And
- There is no piece between the source and destination and
- The destination does not contain the same team and
- The move does not cause (self-inflicted) checkmate

PAWN

Create a pawn

Destroy the pawn

Return the name of the piece

Return the value of this type of piece

Return the type of the piece

Determine if this is a legal move

The move is legal if -
- The source is not the destination and
- The move is
  - An initial move or
  - A striking move or
  - A normal move
- And
- The move does not cause (self-inflicted) checkmate

Summary

This chapter described some important aspects of object-oriented design as it applies to the Object Creation Process. Abstraction is fundamental to our stepwise design process. Design identifies and describes the relationships between objects. Pseudocode is used to capture and describe the interobject relationships. Remember that design reviews are critical. This chapter points out some helpful ideas to maintain effective design reviews.

With this additional detail, we can now give a fully developed pseudocode description of the design process within the Object Creation Process.

The *DesignObject* function consists of four major steps: creating a pseudocode description of how the object works in terms of its subordinate objects, identifying the subordinate objects, identifying the subordinate object's methods, and creating the requirements of the subordinate objects.

The *DescribeHowTheObjectWorks* stresses the importance of design reviews. An object must iterate until all design review issues are resolved. Before reviewing a pseudocode description, work to minimize the length and nesting of the design.

IdentifySubordinateObjects and *IdentifySubordinateMethods* represent the steps of circling the noun phrases and underlining the verb phrases. The work from these functions feeds the final design function, *CreateSubordinateRequirements*. The final step lists each of the subordinate objects with its associated methods.

Document 4.2 — The Design Process

```
DesignObject(ObjectSpec) {
    // Describe the specified object in terms of its subordinates
    PseudoCode = DescribeHowObjectWorks(ObjectSpec);
    // Circle the noun phrases
    IdentifySubordinateObjects(PseudoCode);
    // Underline the verb phrases
    IdentifySubordinateMethods(PseudoCode);
    // List the subordinate objects and methods
    CreateSubordinateRequirements(PseudoCode);
    // The PseudoCode is the design artifact
    Return PesudoCode
}

DescribeHowObjectWorks(ObjectSpec) {
    Until all review issues are resolved... {
        While the PseudoCode does not tell how the object works and
            the PseudoCode is long ( 10 lines) and
            the PseudoCode has too much indentation... {
            Edit the PseudoCode
        }
        Review the PseudoCode
    }
}

IdentifySubordinateObjects(PseudoCode) {
    For each line in the PseudoCode... {
        Identify the noun phrase of the line
    }
}

IdentifySubordinateMethods(PseudoCode) {
    For each line in the PseudoCode... {
        Identify the verb phrase of the line
    }
}
```

Document 4.2 — *Cont'd*

```
CreateSubordinateRequirements(PseudoCode) {
    For each line in the PseudoCode... {
        If the noun phrase has not yet been seen
            Add the noun phrase to the list of subordinate objects
        If the verb phrase has not yet been seen
            Add the verb phrase to the list of methods
                associated with the object
    }
}
```

Exercises

0. List the four interobject relationships and give an example of each relationship.
1. List the various roles of design review team members.
2. Use abstraction to describe the components of a personal computer system.
3. List five strengths of pseudocode as a design media.
4. List the four major pseudocode constructs and tell when to use each.

Code = CodeObject(ObjectDesign, Subordina

Chapter 5

Object Implementation

The Object Creation Process works from high levels of abstraction to lower levels; identifying objects requirements, creating objects specifications, and developing object designs. After designing all the objects within a program, the Object Creation Process changes direction; implementing and testing each object, starting at the lowest levels of abstraction and working toward the highest level. This chapter discusses the implementation phase of the Object Creation Process.

Design and Implementation

Some software developers believe that all the real work of software development occurs during the design phase. While design is an important and creative process, it is no more creative or important than the other phases of development. The implementation phase of the Object Creation Process requires tremendous amounts of creativity and skill. The ability to implement reliable objects is an important part of software development. Without reliable objects, software developers will not achieve their goal of dependable, high quality software.

Implementation is the act of taking an object's design and reducing it to executable code. Creating executable code from an object's design is analogous to a musician playing an instrument to create composed music. A musician and a composer rely on each other to create music. A composer describes the sound of the music, but a musician creates the melody.

The quality of music depends on the skill and expertise of both the composer and the musician. The musicians playing in an orchestra must be highly skilled or the audience cannot fully appreciate the efforts of the composer. Conversely, even the most talented musicians cannot rescue a poor composer.

This analogy exemplifies the relationship between the object designer and the object implementor. Software implementors' skills are every bit as important as the designers' skills. Implementors must learn their skills through practice and study. To be effective, implementors must develop expertise with a given language and development environment. This chapter suggests how implementors can improve their skills.

Attributes of Good Software Implementation

The process of translating ideas into computer instructions is computer programming. Since many people have some form of programming experience, many people also believe they are programmers. However, there is a significant difference between translating ideas into computer instructions and being a great programmer.

Great programmers produce programs that exhibit the following five attributes:

- ❑ Functionality
- ❑ Competency
- ❑ Efficiency
- ❑ Consistency
- ❑ Moderation

Functionality

The most critical aspect of an object's code is its *functionality*. If the object does not function properly, its other attributes are of little concern. An object's code functions properly when it follows its design. If the object's methods execute according to the design, yet the object exhibits undesirable behavior, the object's design or specification may be at fault.

Developers should not try to correct design or specification errors in the implementation phase. If the implementation process uncovers specification or design errors, developers must revert to the specification or design phases and correct the errors at the source. A design or specification error may affect objects at lower levels of abstraction. Attempting to correct these types of errors by changing the implementation will result in unreliable objects with weak foundations.

Competency

Competency refers to the programmer's ability to use the programming language with good form. To us, good form means using the language constructs that most appropriately represent the design concepts. For example, a competent programmer will use an array to represent a collection of similar data items and separate variables for a collection of dissimilar data items.

Competency requires a thorough understanding of the target language's syntax and semantics. Some programmers discount the importance of prior experience with a specific language and argue that all programming languages are alike. These programmers believe that knowing one language makes it easy to learn any language. While it's true that learning one language makes it easier to learn a second, understanding the subtle nuances of one language doesn't automatically make one appreciate the subtleties of a second language. As languages become more expressive, it becomes even more important to spend time studying the language. Sometimes programmers attempt to demonstrate their competency by using many language features, even if using the feature obfuscates the code. Others, enthusiastic about a new language, may overuse or misuse exciting features. Object-oriented languages such as C++ give programmers great power and flexibility, but exciting features like operator overloading and multiple inheritance must be used appropriately. The temptation to be clever must be tempered with the realization of the maintenance effects of obfuscated code.

Improving Your Competence

You can improve your language competency by reviewing code created by different competent programmers. Extract the constructs and approaches that seem clear and concise and incorporate these into your own programming style. To ensure a well-rounded perspective, take time to review the work of many different programmers. Code listings are easy to obtain; programmer's trade journals, computer book stores, and object libraries are excellent sources of code listings.

For example, the following three lines of C++ show three different expressions of the same concept:

```
X = Y + Y + Y + Y;
X = Y << 2;
X = 4 * Y;
```

Each of these statements has the same effect. The first statement displays a lack of understanding of the language; the programmer is unaware of the multiplication operator. The second statement is an excessively clever approach where the programmer is showing off an understanding of the more obscure bitwise operators. The third statement clearly states the conceptual effects of the operation.

While it's healthy for programmers to get excited about new language features, good programmers resist the temptation to use a language feature in a situation where it obfuscates the code.

Efficiency

Efficient programs perform the necessary work while minimizing resource utilization (where resources include wall time, processor cycles, main memory, extended memory, and disk space). Though an object's design greatly affects its efficiency, implementation also has a significant impact. It's important to consider how an object's implementation affects its efficiency.

The goal of software efficiency may conflict with the software's goal of clarity. For example, the statement

```
X = Y << 2;
```

may execute more efficiently than the statement

```
X = 4 * Y;
```

In these situations programmers must use their expertise to decide if efficiency is more important than program clarity. When in doubt, select clarity. It is easier to make clear (but inefficient) code run faster than it is to understand obfuscated (but efficient) code.

Competency and experience clearly affect a programmer's ability to create efficient programs. If a programmer only knows one way of expressing a concept, the programmer has no implementation choice.

Familiarity with three or four ways of representing an operation allows the programmer to choose an approach that yields the necessary efficiency and clarity.

The tradeoff between efficiency and clarity need not be an all-or-nothing decision. Documenting the code listing is a simple but effective method for clarifying necessarily obfuscated, but efficient, code. For example:

```
// Read the next assignment as X = 4 * Y;
// (Implemented for efficiency purposes)
X = Y << 2;
```

The simple comment clarifies the intent of the obfuscated code, thus minimizing the negative impact of the optimization.

Consistency

Consistency, meaning like expression of like constructs, is also important to software clarity. Consistency allows programmers to focus on program's general semantics, rather than on the program's detailed syntax. Programs that exhibit a high degree of consistency are easier to read, test, debug, and maintain.

Consistency is not limited to a single function or file; its scope may extend throughout a project, or even an entire organization. With large programming teams, choosing a standard style can consume an enormous amount of time and energy — especially if individual programmers lobby adamantly for their favorite style.

In many cases, commercially available code "beautifiers" can avert a deadlock over style by allowing individuals to reformat the code they are working with in their preferred style. The same beautifier is then used to return the code to a standard style for group access.

Despite the political hazards, a broadly-practiced, consistent style is worth seeking. The efficiency of a development effort is proportional to the scope of the consistency. Programmers will increase their efficiency as a team more through consistency than through personal style.

Moderation

The final critical aspect of good object implementation is moderation. *Moderation* is a subjective aspect that refers to the use of common sense in implementing an object. Moderation is probably the most difficult implementation aspect to master. One can easily go overboard with

How Important Is Consistency

Time yourself while you evaluate the following code fragment. Try to describe in one or two short sentences the function performed by the code fragment

```
int funcA(int a) {
        int x;
    if (a < 0)
    {
        x = 1;
        } else x = (a < 10)? 2: 3;
    return x;
    }
```

While *funcA* is syntactically correct, it demonstrates several common types of inconsistency. The most obvious inconsistency is the misuse of indentation and white space. Indentation and white space are pseudo-graphical mechanisms that help describe how the software works. Inconsistent use of white space and indentation is extremely misleading.

This example also uses braces inconsistently. Both the *if* and the *else* conditions have only one statement, but only the *if* condition has braces around its statement.

Consistency affects function as well as style. *funcA* uses different constructs for similar conditional assignments. The first conditional assignment is by way of the *if* statement. The second conditional assignment is by way of the ternarg operator *()?:*. Readers of *funcA* notice the different implementations of conditional assignment and waste effort trying to find a reason for the difference. Consistent usage of constructs helps the reader avoid expending energy in the wrong places.

In a similar fashion, time yourself as you review the following function:

```
int funcB(int b) {
    int n;

    if (b < 0) {
        n = 0;
    } else if (b < 10) {
        n = 1;
    } else
        n = 2;
    }
    return n;
}
```

funcB is semantically similar to *funcA*. Empirical tests indicate that programmers understand *funcB* in roughly half the time of *funcA*, even though *funcB* takes up 40 percent more space. The subjects tested understood *funcB* faster because *funcB* is consistent. *funcB* may not adhere to your familiar coding style; but that is not the point. The style in *funcB* is consistent throughout, and the consistency helps clarify the operation of the function. Within reason, consistency of style is more important than "correctness" of style.

concerns about consistency, efficiency, competency, and even functionality. The essence of moderation is knowing how to balance usefulness with effort.

Defensive Implementation Techniques

A quality implementation involves more than just the code necessary to support the required functionality. By using defensive techniques, the implementor can equip the software to defend itself against inadvertent implementation errors.

Listing 5.0 — A Class with Implicit Assumptions

```
class          String {
   char        *Buffer;
   int         BufLen;
public:
   String(char *str);
   ~String();
   String    &operator=(char *str);
};

String::String(char *str) {
   BufLen = strlen(str) + 1;
   Buffer = new char[BufLen];
   strcpy(Buffer, str);
}

String::~String() {
   delete[] Buffer;
}

String &String::operator=(char *str) {
   if (strlen(str) >= BufLen) {
      delete[] Buffer;
      BufLen = strlen(str)+1;
      Buffer = new char[BufLen];
   }
   strcpy(Buffer, str);
   return *this;
}
```

Defensive techniques allow programmers to explicitly describe attributes, assumptions and beliefs about their software. This self-policing facility alerts the programmer whenever something does not work as expected. When used rigorously, defensive techniques make it easy to identify errors and locate the error's cause.

One class of defensive techniques, called *assertions*, explicitly describes and tests assumptions and beliefs about the software. Assertions describe states or relations that must always be true.

Moderation Please!

The prologue (a section at the beginning of a file or function that serves as an introduction) in the listing at right shows how easily one can get carried away.

```
//*************************************************************
//
//    FILE:         stack.cpp
//    AUTHOR:       Fred Programmer
//    DEPT.:        Software Development
//    PROJECT:      Mars Orbital Rocket Control Panel
//    DATE
//    CREATED:      June 19, 1991
//
//    REVISION INFO:
//        Dec. 10, 1992- Increased capacity
//                       to handle 20 items
//        July 2, 1992-  Updated the pseudocode to
//                       reflect bug fixes
//        June 28, 1992- Added function prologues
//        June 25, 1992- Fixed overflow condition bug
//        June 23, 1992- Fixed empty stack condition bug
//
//    DESCRIPTION:
//        The stack class is a LIFO queue that stores
//        pointers of an unspecified type (i.e., void*).
//        The stack class provides methods to
//        construct, destruct, push, pop
//        and determine if the stack is empty.
//
//    PSEUDOCODE:
//        Constructor (Create a stack):
//            Initialize top-of-stack index to zero
//        Destroy (Destroy the stack):
```

To function properly, the *string* class in Listing 5.0 must observe certain implicit assumptions. Neither the constructor nor the *operator=* methods should ever receive a *NULL* character pointer. When a *NULL* pointer is passed to these methods, the results are undefined.

Methods that assume a pointer is not *NULL* should make the assumption explicit by asserting that the pointer has a value. The methods in Listing 5.1 show how explicit assumptions strengthen the class.

```
//            Do nothing
//        Push (Push an item onto the stack):
//            Check for overflow
//            Assign input pointer to top of stack array
//            Increment top-of-stack index
//        Pop (Pop an item off stack):
//            Check for underflow
//            Decrement top-of-stack index
//            Return the pointer at top of stack
//        IsEmpty (Determine if stack is empty):
//            The stack is empty if -
//            The top-of-stack index is zero
//
//    DEPENDENT CLASSES:
//        Array
//        Index
//
//    USING CLASSES:
//        Button
//        Tree
//        DialogBoxList
//        CommandParser
//
//    KNOWN BUGS:
//        None
//
//*****************************************************
```

This elaborate prologue is a valiant effort to keep track of important information but will soon be out-of-date. Updating such an elaborate prologue becomes a minor bureaucratic annoyance that some programmers will likely overlook. Moreover, there are more efficient ways to maintain the same information. Rather than relying upon a *USING CLASSES* list in the prologue, developers can use a search utility like *grep* to identify *current* instances of the *stack* class.

There are more efficient ways of handling most of the information in the example prologue. A revision control system, like UNIX's SCCS, can efficiently manage the fields that deal with file revisions and updates. A software defect database can handle the *KNOWN BUGS* field. Rather than build catch-all file prologues, developers should migrate information to places where the

In this version the constructor and the *operator=* contain additional code that will generate an error message and terminate the program if the string pointer (*str*) is equal to *NULL*.

Functions and methods should not limit themselves to checking for *NULL* pointers. A totally defensive function examines every parameter for possible errors. A function that accepts an integer should verify that the integer's value is within reasonable limits. If a function uses an integer value as the denominator in an equation, the function should assert that the integer is not equal to zero. Explicitly identifying these assumptions makes it obvious when a parameter violates an assumption.

What About Design Documentation?

Our approach to keeping the design documentation up-to-date with the software is to embed the design documentation into the software but *not* in a *proglogue*. If the design documentation is in the form of pseudocode, the design can be scattered through the source code in the form of comments. Embedding the design pseudocode in the source code has several advantages. With the pseudocode and source code in close proximity, it is clear when the two are not consistent. Pseudocode mixed in with the source is easy to maintain because the pseudocode can be updated at the same time the source is updated. Pseudocode is also a good way to document and explain what the source code does.

We might have embedded the pseudocode from the overly elaborate file prologue (see "Moderation, Please!") like this:

```
//* Push (Push an item
//* onto the stack):
Stack::Push(void *p) {
    //* Check for overflow
    assert(Top < StackSize-1);
    //* Assign the input pointer to
    //* the top of the stack array
    Array[Top] = p;
    //* Increment the
    //* top-of-stack index
    Top++;
}
```

The pseudocode forms a good outline for the source code. Notice that each pseudocode comment begins with an asterisk (*). The asterisk helps identify pseudocode lines and differentiate them from other comments. The pseudocode lines describing the design are easy to extract from the source code using a simple utility like UNIX's *AWK*. In fact, the design shown in the previous chapter was extracted from the code. The complete program design and code appears in Appendix B.

Expect the Unexpected

The *string* class of Listing 5.1 assumes that *new* will always be successful. In an application that requires large amounts of heap space, *new* may fail. A defensively coded function should perform exception handling to ensure a safe recovery should *new* fail. Until C++ compilers provide exception handling mechanisms, programmers should at least explicitly check *new*'s *return* status.

Listing 5.1 — A Class with Explicit Assumptions

```
String::String(char *str) {
   if (str == NULL) {
      fprintf(stderr, "Error: %s %d\n",
                               __FILE__, __LINE__);
      exit(-1);
   }
   BufLen = strlen(str) + 1;
   Buffer = new char[BufLen];
   for (int i = 0; i < BufLen; i++)
      Buffer[i] = '\0';
   strcpy(Buffer, str);
}

String &String::operator=(char *str) {
   if (str == NULL) {
      fprintf(stderr, "Error: %s %d\n",
                               __FILE__,   LINE__);
      exit(-1);
   }
   if (strlen(str) >= BufLen) {
      delete[] Buffer;
      BufLen = strlen(str)+1;
      Buffer = new char[BufLen];
   }
   strcpy(Buffer, str);
   return *this;
}
```

Loops are another likely source of errors. The following string constructor contains an initialization loop that illustrates the potential danger of loops:

```
String::String(char *str) {
  assert(str != NULL);
  BufLen = strlen(str) + 1;
  Buffer = new char[BufLen];
  assert(Buffer != NULL);
  for (int i = 0; i <= BufLen; i++) {
     Buffer[i] = '\0';
  }
  strcpy(Buffer, str);
}
```

The loop is not really necessary, but it illustrates a point. The loop has an error; it initializes one too many array elements. Inserting a *loop*

Listing 5.2 — A Class with Exception Handling

```
String::String(char *str) {
   assert(str != NULL);
   BufLen = strlen(str) + 1;
   Buffer = new char[BufLen];
   assert(Buffer != NULL);
   strcpy(Buffer, str);
}

String &String::operator=(char *str) {
   assert(str != NULL);
   if (strlen(str) >= BufLen) {
      delete[] Buffer;
      BufLen = strlen(str)+1;
      Buffer = new char[BufLen];
      assert(Buffer != NULL);
   }
   strcpy(Buffer, str);
   return *this;
}
```

invariant, i.e., a condition that remains true during the life of the loop, will enable automatic detection of such errors. The previous loop could include an invariant in the form of the following assertion:

```
for (int i = 0; i <= BufLen; i++) {
    assert((i >= 0) && (i < BufLen));
    Buffer[i] = '\0';
}
```

The loop invariant assertion would catch the error on the final iteration. Classes also have *invariants* — conditions that remain true during the life of a class instance. For example, in a *String* class the buffer must always be big enough to hold the *string*, since by definition the class invariant is true throughout the life of the class instance, all class invariant assumptions must be collected into a single, conveniently-maintained private method, as in Listing 5.3.

The *assert()* Macro

Most C and C++ compilers provide an *assert()* macro that simplifies the development of explicit assumptions. The *assert()* macro takes one Boolean expression as an argument. If the Boolean expression is false, *assert()* prints to *stderr* the object expression, the file name, and line number where the test appears. *assert()* then calls *abort()* to terminate program execution. To use *assert()*, specify a condition that must be true for the method to function properly. In the following listing, the *string* class constructor and *operator=* methods contain *assert()* macros that replace the test used to make the valid pointer assumption explicit:

```
String::String(char *str) {
    assert(str != NULL);
    BufLen = strlen(str) + 1;
    Buffer = new char[BufLen];
    strcpy(Buffer, str);
}

String      &String::operator=
                (char *str) {
    assert(str != NULL);
    if (strlen(str) >= BufLen) {
        delete[] Buffer;
        BufLen = strlen(str)+1;
        Buffer = new char[BufLen];
    }
    strcpy(Buffer, str);
    return *this;
}
```

Listing 5.3 — A Class with Invariants

```
class       String {
    char        *Buffer;
    int         BufLen;
    void        Invariant();
public:
    String(char *str);
    ~String();
    String      &operator=(char *str);
};

inline void     String::Invariant() {
    assert(strlen(Buffer) < BufLen);
}

String::String(char *str) {
    assert(str != NULL);
    BufLen = strlen(str) + 1;
    Buffer = new char[BufLen];
    assert(Buffer != NULL);
    strcpy(Buffer, str);
    Invariant();
}

String::~String() {
    Invariant();
    delete[] Buffer;
}

String &String::operator=(char *str) {
    Invariant();
    assert(str != NULL);
    if (strlen(str) >= BufLen) {
        delete[] Buffer;
        BufLen = strlen(str)+1;
        Buffer = new char[BufLen];
        assert(Buffer != NULL);
    }
    strcpy(Buffer, str);
    return *this;
}
```

C++ passes an implicit parameter, the *this* pointer, to all class methods. Even though it is normally hidden, the *this* pointer can be modified (usually inadvertantly), resulting in errors that are difficult to identify. These errors can be detected automatically by using an assertion to test the implicit assumption that *this* points to a valid object instance.

Listing 5.4 — A Class that Uses a Magic Number

```
class                String {
   static char  MagicValue;
   char              *Magic;
   char              *Buffer;
   int               BufLen;
   void              MagicOn() { Magic = &MagicValue; }
   void              MagicOff() { Magic = NULL; }
   void              Invariant();
public:
   String(char *str);
   ~String();
   String            &operator=(char *str);
};

char                 String::MagicValue = '\0';

inline void     String::Invariant() {
   assert(this != NULL);
   assert(Magic == &MagicValue);
   assert(strlen(Buffer) < BufLen);
}

String::String(char *str) {
   assert(str != NULL);
   BufLen = strlen(str) + 1;
   Buffer = new char[BufLen];
   assert(Buffer != NULL);
   strcpy(Buffer, str);
   MagicOn();
   Invariant();
}
```

Programmers can validate this assumption with a special type of assertion, one based upon a *magic number*.

A magic number is a class variable that holds an arbitrary, class-specific value during the life span of the object. Any arbitrary value will do as long as each class has a different value. (The address of a class's static member works, and is always conveniently available.) Listing 5.4 shows an implementation of a magic number in the `String` class.

A valid magic number guarantees to the member function that it is operating on a valid instance of the object. Magic number checks can catch errors such as unconstructed object references, deleted object references, and mismatches between an object's type and its methods.

If an application is so time-sensitive that it can't tolerate the small overhead associated with testing magic numbers, the magic number code can be excluded from the production class using conditional compilation. Conditional compilation allows the programmer to build, test, and integrate the class with the magic number safety net, and then eliminate the magic number code for the production software.

Listing 5.4 — *Cont'd*

```
String::~String() {
   Invariant();
   MagicOff();
   delete[] Buffer;
}

String &String::operator=(char *str) {
   Invariant();
   assert(str != NULL);
   if (strlen(str) >= BufLen) {
      delete[] Buffer;
      BufLen = strlen(str)+1;
      Buffer = new char[BufLen];
      assert(Buffer != NULL);
   }
   strcpy(Buffer, str);
   return *this;
}
```

Defensive Facilities in C++

C++ provides many defensive facilities to programmers, including rigorous type checking, the *const* keyword, and detection of illegally implemented abstract classes. C++ requires that parameter types, return value types, and assignment types be consistent. This rigorous type checking helps identify possible errors. The assignment of a character pointer to a pointer, or an enumerated type to an integer, usually indicates

Listing 5.5 — A Class with *const* Parameters

```
class String {
   static char  MagicValue;
   char         *Magic;
   char         *Buffer;
   int          BufLen;
   void         MagicOn() { Magic = &MagicValue; }
   void         MagicOff() { Magic = NULL; }
   void         Invariant() const;
public:
   String(const char *str);
   ~String();
   String       &operator=(const char *str);
   int          Length() const;
};

char              String::MagicValue = '\0';

inline void  String::Invariant() const {
   assert(this != NULL);
   assert(Magic == &MagicValue);
   assert(strlen(Buffer) < BufLen);
}

int          String::Length() const {
   Invariant();
   for (int i =0; Buffer[i]; i++);
   return i;
}
```

a typographical or logical error. Programmers can circumvent the compiler's type checking by casting variables to other types, but casting opens the door to all the problems that strict type checking is trying to prevent. Casting can and usually should be avoided.

Another safety feature of C++ is the *const* declaration modifier. Adding a *const* modifier to a variable's function parameter's declaration notifies the compiler that the variable's value cannot be changed. Beyond adding safety, *const* also helps document the intended purpose of a parameter.

Listing 5.5 — *Cont'd*

```
String::String(const char *str) {
    assert(str != NULL);
    BufLen = strlen(str) + 1;
    Buffer = new char[BufLen];
    assert(Buffer != NULL);
    strcpy(Buffer, str);
    MagicOn();
    Invariant();
}

String::~String() {
    Invariant();
    MagicOff();
    delete[] Buffer;
}

String &String::operator=(const char *str) {
    Invariant();
    assert(str != NULL);
    if (strlen(str) >= BufLen) {
        delete[] Buffer;
        BufLen = strlen(str)+1;
        Buffer = new char[BufLen];
        assert(Buffer != NULL);
    }
    strcpy(Buffer, str);
    return *this;
}
```

The `const` keyword can also be used to describe methods that do not modify their object's contents. If a `const` method attempts to modify the object's values, the compiler will generate an error. A `String` class that uses `const` parameters and methods appears in Listing 5.5.

Classes that encapsulate data and operations common to other classes are called *abstract classes*. Abstract classes contribute no stand-alone functionality; they are meaningful only as base classes. For example, the abstract class `fruit` contains data and operations common to the concrete classes `apple`, `banana`, and `pineapple` (see Listing 5.6). All three concrete classes share the method `color` which is, therefore, placed in

Listing 5.6 — A Class with Pure Virtual Methods

```
class    Fruit {
public:
   virtual const char *Color() = 0;
};

class    Apple:public Fruit {
public:
   const char   *Color() {
      return "Red";
   }
};

class    Banana:public Fruit {
public:
   const char   *Color() {
      return "Yellow";
   }
};

class Orange:public Fruit {
public:
   const char   *Color() {
      return "Orange";
   }
};
```

the base class *fruit*, allowing the concrete classes to access *color* through inheritance. Because there is no default fruit color, the *color* method has no meaningful implementation in the *fruit* class — *color* is a *virtual* method. To enable automatic detection of illegal implementations of abstract classes, C++ allows programmers to distinguish *pure virtual methods* from other virtual methods by adding *=0* to the end of

Listing 5.7 — The *Screen* Class

```
// Interactive terminal class
class    Screen {
   MAGIC                 // Magic number macro
   // Assert the class invariants
   void  Invariant() const;
public:
   // Initialize the screen
   Screen();
   // Close the screen
   ~Screen();
   // Clear the screen
   void  Clear() const;
   // Position the cursor
   void  GoToXY(
      const int,         // Cursor X position value
      const int          // Cursor Y position value
   ) const;
   // Output a string with the current attributes
   void  PutString(
      const char*        // String to output
   ) const;
   // Change the current attributes
   void  Attribute(
      const Att          // The target attribute(s)
   ) const;
   // Sound a warning beep
   void  Beep() const;
   // Get a character
   UCommand     GetCommand() const;
};
```

the method declaration. Listing 5.6 shows the *fruit* class using pure virtual methods.

These defensive techniques not only improve the actual compiler's error checking but also force the programmer to adopt a more precision-oriented mindset. Features like *const*, assertions, and pure virtual methods require programmers to make their assumptions explicit. Precision thinking requires more time and effort than sloppy thinking, but *only* precision thinking can produce quality software.

Implementation of the Chess Game Example

Until now, because we were *designing*, our work on the chess game has proceeded top-down. Because the design identifies the lowest level objects, the implementation can proceed bottom-up. Working bottom-up allows higher level objects to use lower level objects for testing purposes. This section presents the implementation of only part of the chess game example. The entire implementation of the chess game example is in Appendix B.

Our implementation begins with the lowest level classes, namely *Screen*, *Coord*, and *Piece*. The *Screen* class (Listing 5.7) handles all the lowest level details about the game's interface. Because the *Screen*

Listing 5.8 — The *Coord* Class

```
class     Coord {
   int    R;            // Row index
   int    C;            // Column index
public:
   // Create a coordinate from a row and column
   Coord(
      const int r = 0, // Row value
      const int c = 0  // Column value
   ): R(r), C(c) {}
   // Create a coordinate as a duplicate
   Coord(
      const Coord &c   // Coordinate to duplicate
   ): R(c.Row()), C(c.Col()) {}
   // Get the coordinate's row
   int    Row() const {return R;}
```

class hides all the interface details, the game could be ported to another platform by rewriting only the `Screen` class. Because the compiler's runtime library directly provides most of `Screen`'s functionality, we implement it as a *wrapper* class. Wrappers combine related non-OOP functions into a common abstraction or class.

Listing 5.8 — *Cont'd*

```
    // Get the coordinate's column
    int    Col() const {return C;}
    // Set the coordinate's row to the specific value
    void   SetRow(
       const int row        // Row value
    ) { R = row; }
    // Set the coordinate's column to the specific value
    void   SetCol(
       const int col     // Column value
    ) { C = col; }
    // Determine if two coordinates have the same value
    BOOLEAN       operator == (
       const Coord &c       // Comparison Coordinate
    ) const {
       return ((R==c.R)&&(C==c.C));
    }
    // Determine if two coordinates do not have
    // the same value
    BOOLEAN       operator != (
       const Coord &c       // Comparison Coordinate
    ) const {
       return ((R!=c.R)||(C!=c.C));
    }
    // Copy the contents of one coordinate to another
    Coord& operator = (
       const Coord &c       // Coordinate to copy
    ) {
       R = c.R;
       C = c.C;
       return *this;
    }
};
```

The *Coord* class (Listing 5.8) is an abstraction that represents a *Square*'s coordinate location on the chess board. *Coord* is a very simple class with all of its methods implemented *inline*.

The purpose of the *Piece* class is to maintain the data and methods common to concrete classes that are *a-kind-of* piece. Concrete classes make use of the *Piece* class data and methods through inheritance. Because it has no meaningful instantiation, *Piece* is an abstract base class pure virtual functions. Because *Piece* is an abstract base class, its derived classes: *King*, *Queen*, *Bishop*, *Knight*, *Castle* and *Pawn* — should be studied as part of *Piece*'s implementation process.

Like the *Coord* class, many of the *Piece* related methods are extremely simple. Even simple functions, however, can benefit from defensive techniques. We present *Piece*, together with its derived classes, in Listing 5.9.

Listing 5.9 — The *Piece* Class and its Derived Classes

```
class           Piece {
   MAGIC                       // Magic number macro
   BOOLEAN      White;         // Is this piece white?
   BOOLEAN      Moved;         // Has this piece moved?
   Team         *team;         // Piece's team handle
   // Assert the class invariants
   void         Invariant() const;
public:
   // Create a piece
   Piece(
      Team*,                // Piece's team handle
      BOOLEAN               // True if the piece is white
   );
   // Destroy a piece
   virtual      ~Piece() = 0;
   // Determine if the piece is a member of the team
   BOOLEAN      IsMember(
      const Team*           // Team in question
   ) const;
   // Mark the piece as having moved
   void         Move();
   // Determine if the piece has moved
   BOOLEAN      HasMoved() const;
```

To properly implement certain chess pieces the program must know whether the piece has ever moved. For example, knowing if a pawn has moved helps determine if the pawn is allowed to move forward two squares or only one. The *Piece* class provides two methods to help identify pieces that have not moved. The first method, *Piece::Move*, is called when a piece is moved. *Piece::Move* sets a flag indicating the piece has moved. The second related method, *Piece::HasMoved*, returns the value of the piece's move flag. Since *Piece::HasMoved* should never change the piece's internals, this method function is declared as *const*. This prevents the implementor from inadvertently changing the object's contents.

Listing 5.9 — *Cont'd*

```
     // Determine the piece type
     virtual      PieceType    GetType() const = 0;
     // Get the name of the piece
     virtual      char         *Name() const = 0;
     // Return the value of this piece
     virtual      int          Value() const = 0;
     // Determine if the piece is the same color
     // as that specified
     BOOLEAN      IsSameColor(
        const BOOLEAN    // Color indicator (true if white)
     ) const;
     // Determine if the piece is white
     BOOLEAN      IsWhite() const;
     // Determine if this is a legal move for this piece
     virtual      BOOLEAN      IsLegalMove(
        const Coord&,    // Source location
        const Coord&     // Destination location
     ) const = 0;
     // Determine if this move causes checkmate
     BOOLEAN   CausesCheckmate(
        const Coord&,    // Source location
        const Coord&     // Destination location
     ) const;
};
```

If the chess program has the opportunity to attack more than one piece, it attacks the piece with the highest value. The *Piece::Value* method helps the program select a target by returning the value of a piece. Since the value of each kind of piece is different and there is no default value, the *Piece::Value* method is a pure virtual function. Declaring *Piece::Value* as purely virtual forces each class derived from *Piece* to create a specific *Value* method.

The main chore of implementation is to translate the pseudocode design into executable code. Listing 5.10 contains an example method from the *Pawn* class.

This method determines if a move from the source coordinate to the destination coordinate is a legal move for a pawn. The pseudocode design

Listing 5.10 — The *IsLegalMove* Method from the *Pawn* Class

```
//* Determine if this is a legal move
BOOLEAN      Pawn::IsLegalMove(const Coord &src,
                               const Coord &dest) const {

    Invariant();
    //* The move is legal if -
    return(
        //* The source is not the destination and
        (src != dest) &&
        //* The move is
        (
            //* An initial move or
            IsInitial(src, dest) ||
            //* A striking move or
            IsStriking(src, dest) ||
            //* A normal move
            IsNormal(src, dest)
        //* And
        ) &&
        //* The move does not cause
        //* (self-inflicted) checkmate
        (!CausesCheckmate(src, dest))
    );
}
```

is embedded in the implementation in the form of comments. The design comments have the additional asterisk (*) indicator to allow the design to be pulled from the implementation automatically.

Thoroughly designing *Pawn::IsLegalMove* simplifies the translation of design statements into code. As the design indicates, many of the code statements are abstractions of more detailed concepts. The code statement that compares the source location with the destination location, however, needs no further decomposition.

Compare the *Pawn::IsLegalMove* method with the *Pawn::IsInitial* method in Listing 5.11.

Many of the design statements of *Pawn::IsInitial* translate directly into code statements that require no further decomposition. For example, determining that the move has no vertical component translates into

Listing 5.11 — The *IsInitial* Method from *Pawn* Class

```
//* Determine if this is an initial move
BOOLEAN      Pawn::IsInitial(const Coord &src,
                             const Coord &dest) const {

    Invariant();
    int       Delta = dest.Col() - src.Col();
    //* The move is a legal initial move if -
    return(
        //* The pawn is in the initial position and
        !HasMoved() &&
        //* The move has no vertical component and
        (src.Row() == dest.Row()) &&
        //* Move's horizontal component is < 2 and
        ((abs(Delta) > 0) && (abs(Delta) <= 2)) &&
        //* Horizontal component is in right direction and
        ((IsWhite() && (Delta  0))
            || ((!IsWhite()) && (Delta  0))) &&
        //* The destination is not occupied and
        (board.GetPiece(dest) == NULL) &&
        //* There is no piece between source and dest.
        (!board.PiecesBetween(src, dest))
    );
}
```

making sure the source coordinate row and the destination coordinate row are equal.

The Object Creation Process uses abstraction at every level to prevent objects from becoming too complex. Subordinate objects are identified at every level of abstraction. The design phase identifies the subordinate objects *Board* and *Team* midway through the design of the chess game program. Pseudocode is used to describe the methods supported by each object, and abstraction keeps the methods simple. The pseudocode descriptions identify *Board* and *Team*'s subordinate objects. Later, the implementation phase translates each line of design pseudocode into its corresponding line(s) of source code.

While implementing the *Board* class, it became apparent that a routine method for traversing *Board*'s squares was needed. The result was the container iterator *BoardIterator* of Listing 5.12. (An *Iterator* traverses

Listing 5.12 — A Container Iterator (*BoardIterator*)

```
// Class for iterating through the squares on a board
class     BoardIterator{
   MAGIC                  // Magic number macro
   Board  &board;         // Board handle
   int    row;            // Current row
   int    col;            // Current column
   int    SquareNo;       // Number of squares iterated
   // Assert the class invariants
   void   Invariant() const;
public:
   // Create a square iterator (For each board square)
   BoardIterator(
      Board&,             // Board for iteration
                          // Start at a random location
      BOOLEAN UseRandom = FALSE
   );
   ~BoardIterator();
   // Get the next square
   Square*   operator++(int);
};
```

a container, sequentially accessing each stored object to perform a test or action.)

BoardIterator traverses each square on the game board. The *BoardIterator* class is capable of starting the iteration at random locations on the board. Since the program selects pieces and movements based on the iteration, this feature introduces a randomness that makes it difficult for the program's opponent to predict its moves.

The *BoardIterator* class has two major methods (Listing 5.13); the constructor and the incrementor. The *constructor* selects a random starting location on the board and initializes the square count to zero. The

Listing 5.13 — Details of the Iterator's Methods

```
//* Create a square iterator
//* (For each square on the board...)
BoardIterator::BoardIterator(Board &b,
                                        BOOLEAN UseRandom):
    board(b),
    row(UseRandom? rand() % BoardRows: 0),
    col(UseRandom? rand() % BoardCols: 0),
    SquareNo(0)
{
    MagicOn();
    Invariant();
}

//* Get the next square
Square*   BoardIterator::operator ++ (int) {

    Invariant();
    Square    *S = (SquareNo++ < BoardSquares)?
        board.GetSquare(row++, col): NULL;
    if (row >= BoardRows) {
        row = 0;
        col++;
        if (col >= BoardCols) col = 0;
    }
    return S;
}
```

incrementor returns each successive square on the board until it has returned each square once. The *BoardIterator* class uses the public *Board::GetSquare* function and the global *BoardCols*, *BoardRows*, and *BoardSquares* constants. These data items and functions provide all the necessary access to the *Board* class without using *friends*. Using *friend* members can cause tighter coupling between classes, and tighter coupling makes object development and support more difficult.

As the implementation process moves up the levels of abstraction, it encounters more powerful classes and methods. The use of abstraction during the design process simplifies the implementation of the powerful methods located at the highest levels of abstraction. In the chess program the highest level classes are the *Game* class and the chess program itself. *Game*'s *Play* method shows how using abstraction during the design process simplifies the implementation of powerful methods in Listing 5.14.

Listing 5.14 — The *Play* Method

```
//* Play the game
BOOLEAN          Game::Play(Winner &WinResult) {

    Invariant();
    BOOLEAN      Quitting = FALSE;
    BOOLEAN      Checkmate;
    BOOLEAN      Stalemate;

    // set the default result in case of a quit
    WinResult = WinDraw;
    //* Initialize the current team to white
    Team *Current = White;
    //* While the current team is not in checkmate and
    while ((!(Checkmate = Current->IsCheckmate())) &&
         //* The current team is not in stalemate and
         (!(Stalemate = Current->IsStalemate())) &&
         //* Not quitting...
         (!Quitting)) {
        //* Have the current team make a move
        Quitting = Current->Move();
```

Most of the design statements in *Game::Play* translate into simple implementation statements. The *Game::Play* method is a high-level method, but its implementation is no more difficult than the methods at the lower levels. A good design makes the implementation effort consistent for all levels of abstraction. If the implementation requires significantly different levels of effort at different levels of abstraction you should question the design; it may be incomplete. The best way to address an incomplete design is to return to the design phases and look for missing abstractions.

There is one somewhat complex section in the *Game::Play* method that determines who won the game. The chess game can result in one of four conditions; the user quit, the game was a stalemate, the computer won, or the user won. The section that determines who won simply sets a flag to indicate which condition ended the game.

Listing 5.14. — *Cont'd*

```
        //* Change the current team to the other team
        Current = (Current == White)? Black: White;
    }
    //* If the user did not quit,
    if (!Quitting) {
        //* Figure out who won
        if (Stalemate) {
            WinResult = WinDraw;
        } else {
            assert(Checkmate);
            if (Current->IsManual()) {
                WinResult = WinComputer;
            } else {
                WinResult = WinUser;
            }
        }
    }
    return(Quitting);
}
```

Summary

This chapter discussed the process of implementation using the pseudocode design. The chapter stressed the importance of good implementation skills. The important aspects of implementation include proper function, competency, efficiency, consistency, and moderation. This chapter also introduced some general defensive programming techniques and some defensive techniques specific to C++.

Document 5.0 presents a pseudocode description of implementation as described by the Object Creation Process. In this description, the `CodeObject` function prepares for implementation by creating a file and adding the magic number definitions to the `class` definition. The next step in implementation is to translate the design pseudocode into target source code. The function `TranslateDesign` performs the translation. The final step of the `CodeObject` is to add the defensive mechanisms. These mechanisms include `class` invariants, parameter assertions, loop invariants, and C++ specific features.

`AddClassInvariant` adds the necessary class-wide assertions. These assertions explicitly identify the possible legal values of a class's data members. After deciding what values the `class invariant` checks, `AddClassInvariant` implements each method with a call to the invariant function. Notice that the constructor must call the invariant after it initializes all the data members (including the magic number). When an object is deleted the destructor must turn off the magic number.

Both the `CheckParameters` and `CheckLoops` functions add assertions as appropriate. The `CheckParameters` function adds assertions to bound the legal values of the parameters. `CheckLoops` adds assertions to guarantee the loop invariants.

Finally, `AddC++Features` adds any appropriate C++ defensive facilities. These facilities include the constant declaration of parameters, non-modifying functions, and pure virtual function declarations.

Document 5.0 — The Implementation Phase

```
Code = CodeObject(ObjectDesign, Subordinates) {

    // Create a new source code file
    SourceFile = new file;
    Add magic number data members to the class definition

    TranslateDesign(SourceFile, ObjectDesign, Subordinates);

    AddClassInvariant(SourceFile);
    CheckParameter(SourceFile);
    CheckLoops(SourceFile);
    If the SourceFile contains C++,
        AddC++Features(SourceFile);

    Return SourceFile
}

TranslateDesign(Source, Design, Subordinates) {

    For each method in the design... {
        Create an empty method body
        For each design line in the method... {
            Make a comment of the design line
            Create source lines to implement the design line
        }
    }
}

AddClassInvariant(Source) {

    Create an invariant method
    For each data member of the class {
        Add assertions to the invariant
            to bound the member's values
    }
    Add the magic number assertion

    For each method in the source... {
        If the method is a constructor,
            Add code to turn on the magic number
```

Document 5.0 — *Cont'd*

```
                Add code at end of method to check invariant
           Otherwise if the method is a destructor,
                Add code to check invariant at beginning of method
                Add code to turn off magic at end of the method
           Otherwise
                Add code to check invariant at beginning of method
      }
}

CheckParameter(Source) {

      For each method in the source... {
           For each parameter of the method... {
L               add assertions to bound the parameter's values
           }
      }
}

CheckLoops(Source) {
      For each method in the source... {
           For each loop in the method... {
                Add assertions to loop describing loop invariants
           }
      }
}

AddC++Features(Source) {

      For each constant parameter in the source... {
           Add const declarative to the parameter declaration
      }
      For each non-modifying method... {
           add const declarative to the method declaration
      }


      For each pure virtual function... {
           Add the "=0" to the function declaration
      }
}
```

Exercises

0. List and describe the five important aspects of implementation presented in this chapter.
1. Give an example of each of the five aspects of implementation presented in this chapter.
2. Describe what a magic number is and tell what types of errors magic numbers prevent.
3. List areas in which assertions can be especially useful.
4. List some specific defensive facilities provided by C++ that are not provided by C.

TestSet = CreateBlackBoxTests(ObjectSp

Chapter 6

Object Verification

Once implemented, the object must be verified. During object verification, a developer assumes the role of referee. In this role, the developer devises experiments which test whether the object's external behavior matches that described by the object specification. As referee, the developer tests only *external* behaviors.

Object verification is analogous to what the software industry calls testing. Good software testing strategies are critical to developing high quality software. To achieve the goals of software reliability and reusability, software engineers must become better software testers. Many of the testing techniques described in this chapter are derived from *The Art of Software Testing*, by Glenford Myers. We recommend Myers's book to for all students of software development.

An Overview of Object Verification

Object-oriented programming holds great possibilities for software testing. Each object, because it is fully encapsulated, is essentially a complete program with a defined scope of operations and inputs. The object specification describes the desired result of each operation. Therefore, the process of verifying the object is a matter of comparing the results of an operation with the desired result contained in the object specification.

Object verification seeks to find an object's deviation from its specification. As Chapter 1 pointed out, the object's specification acts as a rule book for the referee's perspective. During object verification the referee tests everything that the object's specification describes.

Programmers often rationalize that the operational goals of the object are perfectly clear, so creating a specification is a waste of time. The stack object is a good example of why this rationalization is incorrect. Any novice programmer knows what should happen when they push something onto a stack. Still, even the clean stack object has some fuzzy edges to its definition. What happens when a program pops an empty stack? What happens if the program tries to destroy a nonexistent stack? How many concurrent stacks can a program create? How many items can a program push onto a stack? Developers need to answer these types of questions before they can verify objects. The object's specification provides the answers to these questions.

Object verification has four major steps, each of which produces a different artifact:

- ❑ Building the verification plan.
- ❑ Building the verification driver.
- ❑ Building verification cases.
- ❑ Building valid verification benchmarks.

When it Works!

Several years ago, one author helped a small start-up company develop a text retrieval system. This system read unformatted text documents such as magazine articles, reports, or books, and then, using an artificial intelligence algorithm, classified the articles based on their subject matter. Users of the text retrieval system could issue ordinary English queries of the documents the system had read. The system would find and retrieve documents relevant to the user's request and present the documents to the user in rank order based on their relevance to the request.

Because the company was small, and could devote only limited resources to development work, the project proceeded slowly. But eventually the developers completed a prototype and began showing it to potential customers. Sometimes the results of retrieval did not seem quite right. To complicate matters, the artificial intelligence algorithm in the system made it difficult to determine exactly which documents should be retrieved and in

The next four sections describe each of the object verification steps in detail.

Building the Verification Plan

The verification plan describes how to test an object. It is the design document for the testing process. To create an effective plan, the developers must design tests from the referee's perspective, i.e., they must strive to police deviations and violations of the rule book (i.e., the object's specification). Using the referee's perspective, the developers brainstorm ways to verify that the object meets the specification and capture these ideas in the verification plan.

Designing an effective verification plan involves more than creating a myriad of tests. The plan must include the right number of the right tests. Too few tests, and the plan may not verify all aspects of the object or detect all the defects. On the other hand, too many tests may be redundant and simply waste testing time. To identify useful tests, referees employ a test strategy. Test strategies differ by whether they test the software's external or internal behavior.

As in other branches of science and engineering, tests based on external views of the object are *black-box* tests because the implementation details of the object are not visible. Conversely, tests developed using

what order. Still, the system did retrieve documents and since some documents did seem relevant, the developers were certain the system worked as advertised.

After showing the prototype system to potential customers for about a year, one developer decided to investigate these strange retrieval results. This testing revealed a simple but significant error which, in effect, was causing the system to select and retrieve random documents. Neither the customers nor the developers of the text retrieval system realized that the system was producing random results.

Unfortunately, the defective text retrieval system is not an isolated incident. Defective software stories plague the software industry. The secret to keeping embarrassing and potentially deadly errors out of software lies in the object verification phase of the Object Creation Process.

an internal view of the object are called *white-box*. Experience shows that combining both black-box and white-box testing strategies forms a powerful assault on software defects. The referee's perspective considers only the black-box test strategies. The inspector's perspective (discussed in Chapter 7) uses white-box tests.

Exhaustively testing an object as though it were a black box could be overwhelming. Consider black-box testing a simple string comparison function like *strcmp*. It is impossible to try comparing all combinations of strings. Even restricting the string length to three and the number of possible characters to 26 gives over three million possible test combinations. As a result, developers must find a limited, reasonable approach to selecting tests.

Empirically, a useful approach to identifying object tests is to group the object's inputs into similar categories. For the *strcmp* example, this means grouping equal strings into one set, greater first parameter strings into another set, and greater second parameter strings into a third set. After grouping inputs into sets, developers can select just a few from each set as representative.

Next, the test designer must decide how to select appropriate inputs to represent the entire set. Most input sets have an implicit ordering. For example, the input strings to *strcmp* are ordered by the ASCII values of the characters in the string. This ordering is key to knowing which members of the set to select as representative inputs. Members on or around the extremes of the set order are primary targets to represent the set. Extremes of an input set are called *boundaries*. The members of the set with values at or near the boundaries of the set are called *boundary*

Nobody, Indeed!

Because invalid inputs can greatly affect software, developers often become defensive about these tests and may accuse the tester of adding meaningless overhead, since "nobody would do that." Testers who receive this abuse from the developers should find solace in knowing that they are probably doing a good job. Testers can defend themselves by asking the developers to point out in the object's specification where it says that these types of inputs are illegal. These appeals to the referee point out the importance of a complete object specification.

values. For example, string inputs range from short strings with low values to the large strings with high values. The shortest string might be the empty string (*""*) and the longest high value string might be a long repeating high value like *ZZZ ....* These values *on* the boundary should be selected as inputs to represent the set.

Values *near* the boundaries are also effective in revealing defects. Besides the empty string, a representative subset of inputs might include the next string in the list, *A*, and the next to last string (i.e., *ZZZ...Y*). Besides the boundary values, consider a point midway on the range. For the *strcmp* example this might be a string like *THISISASTRING*.

When identifying values to use in testing, consider inputs with unique attributes. What happens to the *strcmp* function if the input strings consist of digits like *12572*, symbols like *<>#$&* or control characters like *^G^C^N^F^A*?

In addition to identifying inputs the object should handle, consider inputs the object should *not* handle. Examples of invalid inputs for the *strcmp* function might include a *NULL* character pointer, a pointer to an integer, or a floating point number.

In addition to varying the inputs, testers should also try calling member functions in various sequences. What happens if a test calls an object's data manipulation function before giving the object data? In the stack example, what happens if a test calls the *pop* function more often than the *push* function?

To identify the important calling sequences, separate the member functions into three groups. Place all the constructors and destructors in one group. Place functions which alter the externally visible state of the object in a second group. Place all remaining functions in a third group. The stack example might be grouped as follows:

```
Constructors/Destructors
   Stack
   ~Stack
State Changing Functions
   Push
   Pop
Non-State Changing Functions
   IsEmpty
```

Tests for functions in the first group should use each constructor with all permutations of its parameters' boundary values, and should use the destructor with each constructor. Tests for the state changing functions should attempt to change the state of the object from every state to every other possible state. At each state, consider using each of the non-state changing functions to be certain that they work in all states. Any combination or sequence which is declared illegal in the object's specification may be eliminated.

The object verification plan should also explore object *concurrency*, i.e., the verification should answer the question, "How independent are multiple instances of an object?" Concurrency tests reveal an object's reliance on static or global data. Imagine a stack object that relies on a global variable to identify the top of the stack. Multiple instances of the stack would rely on the same global variable and would get very confused. Thus, whenever an implementation allows instances of an object, it is important to verify that the objects can operate independently.

In addition to describing the inputs, testers must describe what they expect as outputs. Simply calling a function gives no guarantee that the function really performed as specified. For example, tests of the *strcmp* function should investigate the return value of the function to be certain that the function behaved appropriately. Sometimes testers can only see the result of a test indirectly. For example, the only way to know if an item is successfully pushed onto a stack is to pop the stack. Finding ways to investigate the results of a test may require ingenuity and can often lead to more test ideas.

Once developers have used the referee's perspective to identify the desired tests, they document the test ideas in the verification plan. The actual format of the verification plan may vary depending upon the developer's individual preference, but some useful items to include would be:

- ❑ The name of the target class.
- ❑ The name of the target member function.
- ❑ A test ID.
- ❑ A description of what the test is doing.
- ❑ A description of the expected results of the test.
- ❑ The test's strategy type.

Document 6.0 — A Verification Plan for the Stack Object

Object Verification Plan

Object: STK

Function: STK

Test case name:	StkCon01	Test type:	BB Valid
Description:	Create a single stack		
Verification:	The stack handle is non-null		
Test case name:	StkCon02	Test type:	BB Valid
Description:	Create many stacks		
Verification:	The stack handles are non-null		

Function: ~STK

Test case name:	StkDes01	Test type:	BB Valid
Description:	Destroy a single stack		
Verification:	Member function completes normally		
Test case name:	StkDes02	Test type:	BB Valid
Description:	Destroy many stacks		
Verification:	Member function completes normally		
Test case name:	StkDes03	Test type:	BB Valid
Description:	Destroy many stacks (in different orders)		
Verification:	Member function completes normally		
Test case name:	StkDes04	Test type:	BB Invalid
Description:	Try to destroy a null pointer		
Verification:	Member function terminates program		
Test case name:	StkDes05	Test type:	BB Invalid
Description:	Try to destroy a stack twice		
Verification:	Member function terminates program on second call		
Test case name:	StkDes06	Test type:	BB Invalid
Description:	Try to destroy a non-stack, but valid pointer		
Verification:	Member function terminates program		

Function: Push

Test case name:	StkPus01	Test type:	BB Valid
Description:	Push an item onto a stack		
Verification:	Item can be popped off the stack		
Test case name:	StkPus02	Test type:	BB Valid
Description:	Push many (10) items on the stack		
Verification:	Items can be popped off the stack in reverse order		

The name of the target object identifies which object the verification plan is testing. In addition to the target object, each test description targets an associated member function. Giving each test description a unique ID helps developers distinctly identify tests during later phases of verification and defect tracking. The test descriptions and the expected test results are the basis of the verification plan. Test descriptions and results are the actual designs for the test. A test strategy describes the principles guiding the test idea, for example, black-box versus white-box, and valid inputs versus invalid inputs. Document 6.0 gives an example verification plan for the stack object from Chapter 0.

The final step of building the object verification plan is to review the plan to assure it covers all aspects of the object's specification. During this review the developer examines each statement and idea in the specification to see how it is tested in the verification plan. If the verification plan doesn't verify all statements and ideas in the specification, then the plan must be amended. A simple verification plan review quickly determines the effectiveness of the testing plan.

Document 6.0 — *Cont'd*

Test case name:	StkPus03	Test type:	BB Valid
Description:	Push many (10) items on many (>1) stacks		
Verification:	Items can be popped off each stack in reverse order		
Test case name:	StkPus04	Test type:	BB Valid
Description:	Push a null pointer on the stack in various positions		
Verification:	The null pointer can be popped of the stack		
Test case name:	StkPus05	Test type:	BB Invalid
Description:	Try to push something with a null stack handle		
Verification:	Member function terminates program		
Test case name:	StkPus06	Test type:	BB Invalid
Description:	Try to push something with a non-stack handle		
Verification:	Member function terminates program		
Test case name:	StkPus07	Test type:	BB Invalid
Description:	Try to push something on a destroyed stack handle		
Verification:	Member function terminates program		
Test case name:	StkPus08	Test type:	BB Invalid
Description:	Try to push too many (>10) items on the stack		
Verification:	Member function terminates program		

Document 6.0 — *Cont'd*

Function: Pop

Test case name: StkPop01 Test type: BB Valid
Description: Pop a single item from a stack
Verification: Item can be popped off the stack

Test case name: StkPop02 Test type: BB Valid
Description: Pop many (10) items from a stack
Verification: Items can be popped off the stack in reverse order

Test case name: StkPop03 Test type: BB Valid
Description: Pop many (10) items from many (>1) stacks
Verification: Items can be popped off the stacks in reverse order

Test case name: StkPop04 Test type: BB Valid
Description: Pop a null pointer from a stack
Verification: Null pointer can be popped from stack

Test case name: StkPop05 Test type: BB Invalid
Description: Try to pop something with a null stack handle
Verification: Member function terminates program

Test case name: StkPop06 Test type: BB Invalid
Description: Try to pop something with a non-stack handle
Verification: Member function terminates program

Test case name: StkPop07 Test type: BB Invalid
Description: Try to pop something with a destroyed stack handle
Verification: Member function terminates program

Test case name: StkPop08 Test type: BB Invalid
Description: Try to pop from an empty stack
Verification: Member function terminates program

Function: IsEmpty

Test case name: StkIsE01 Test type: BB Valid
Description: Test a newly created stack
Verification: Stack is empty

Test case name: StkIsE02 Test type: BB Valid
Description: Test a stack that has had one push and one pop
Verification: Stack is empty

Test case name: StkIsE03 Test type: BB Valid
Description: Test a stack using many (10) pushes and (10) pops
Verification: Stack is empty

Building the Verification Driver

Once the verification plan is complete, the developers can begin building a framework to exercise the object. This testing framework, called a *verification driver*, can take any of several forms. Developers might build a separate program for each test or one large program that performs all the tests in the verification plan. Another approach that works well for many types of objects is to build a user interface that allows developers to interactively exercise the object's functions.

Interactive drivers offer several distinct advantages. Interactive verification drivers can support many different testing exercises with a limited amount of maintenance.

Document 6.0 — *Cont'd*

Test case name:	StkIsE04	Test type:	BB Valid
Description:	Test a stack after a push-pop push-pop sequence		
Verification:	Stack is empty		
Test case name:	StkIsE05	Test type:	BB Valid
Description:	Test a stack after a single push		
Verification:	Stack is not empty		
Test case name:	StkIsE06	Test type:	BB Valid
Description:	Test a stack after many (10) pushes		
Verification:	Stack is not empty		
Test case name:	StkIsE07	Test type:	BB Invalid
Description:	Test a null stack handle		
Verification:	Member function terminates the program		
Test case name:	StkIsE08	Test type:	BB Invalid
Description:	Test a non-stack handle		
Verification:	Member function terminates the program		
Test case name:	StkIsE09	Test type:	BB Invalid
Description:	Test a destroyed stack handle		
Verification:	Member function terminates the program		

Low maintenance drivers are less apt to introduce errors into the testing process. Simple interactive drivers also create opportunities for less experienced programmers to contribute to the testing process. Finally, interactive drivers also assist developers in their search for reusable objects. Developers can quickly explore the capabilities and limitations of an unfamiliar object by exercising the object's interactive driver. The interactive driver becomes a laboratory for conducting experiments on the object. The interactive driver is not a replacement for a good specification, but a good driver supplements an object and helps others quickly comprehend it.

A test driver should allow a user to interactively exercise every parameter of every function. In addition, test drivers must also display member function outputs. It is important that the functions' outputs be as complete and clear as possible. Complete and clear function outputs simplify the process of finding and fixing defects.

Listing 6.0 gives an example verification driver for the stack object. The driver's main loop fetches commands from the user and prompts for parameters as needed. The driver maintains an array of stack handles so that the user can create several stacks concurrently. Only one handle can be the *current* handle at any given time. The user can change the current handle by using the *H)andle* command. Besides the legitimate handles, the handle array contains a *NULL* handle and a wild pointer. These illegal handles support the invalid tests.

Listing 6.0 — A Verification Driver

```
#include <ctype.h>
#include <assert.h>
#include "stack.hpp"
#define   NHANDLES  5      // number of stack handles
#define   MAXBUF    256    // maximum input buffer size
static    char   *SomeString = "Some String";

// Determine if the number is in the range
static int   InRange(int n, int low, int high) {
   return((n >= low) && (n <= high));
}
```

Listing 6.0 — *Cont'd*

```
// Determine if the line is a comment
static int   IsComment(char *line) {
char      c;

   istrstream   ins(line, strlen(line));
   ins >> c >> ws;
   return c == '#';
}

// Get the next int
static int   NextI(char *Prompt, ofstream *Log) {
char         line[MAXBUF];
int    i;

   cout << Prompt;
   do {
      cin.getline(line, MAXBUF);
      if (Log) {
         *Log << line << endl;
      }
   } while (IsComment(line));

   istrstream   ins(line, strlen(line));
   ins >> i;
   return i;
}
// Get the next character
static char  NextC(char *Prompt, ofstream *Log) {
char         line[MAXBUF];
char         c;

   cout << Prompt;
   do {
      cin.getline(line, MAXBUF);
      if (Log) {
         *Log << line << endl;
      }
   } while (IsComment(line));
```

Listing 6.0 — *Cont'd*

```
    istrstream   ins(line, strlen(line));
    ins >> c;
    return c;
}

// Class driver
int     main(int argc, char *argv[]) {
STK     *handles[NHANDLES+2];
int     current;
int     done;
char    resp;
char    buf[MAXBUF];
int     value;

    // check command line for a recording file
    switch (argc) {
    case 1:
        Recording = NULL;
        break;
    case 2:
        Recording = new ofstream(argv[1]);
        break;


    default:
        cout << "USAGE: " << argv[0] << " [RECORD_FILE]" << endl;
        return(-1);
    }

    // initialize the handles
    for (current = 0; current < NHANDLES; current++) {
        handles[current] = NULL;
    }
    // create a couple of bogus pointers
    handles[current++] = NULL;
    handles[current] = (STK*) SomeString;
    current = 0;
```

Listing 6.0 — *Cont'd*

```
    // interact with the user
    for (done = 0; !done; ) {
        resp = NextC("STK => ", Recording);
        switch (toupper(resp)) {
        case 'C': // construct a stack
            cout << "Constructing stack " << current << endl;
            handles[current] = new STK;
            if (handles[current] == NULL) {
                cout << "Construct returned a NULL pointer" <<
                    endl;
            }
            break;
        case 'D': // destroy a stack
            cout << "Destroying stack " << current << endl;
            delete handles[current];
            break;
        case 'P': // push an item on a stack
            value = NextI("Enter a push value => ", Recording);
            cout << "Pushing " << value <<
                " onto stack " << current << endl;
            handles[current]->Push(value);
            break;
        case 'O': // pop an item off a stack
            value = handles[current]->Pop();
            cout << "Popped " << value << " from stack " <<
                current << endl;
            break;
        case 'I': // determine if the stack is empty
            cout << "Stack " << current << " is " <<
                (handles[current]->IsEmpty()?"":"NOT ") <<
                "empty" << endl;
            break;
        case 'H': // change the current handle index
            cout << "The current stack handle is " <<
                current << endl;
            do {
                cout << "Enter the number of the new handle"
                     << endl;
```

Building the Verification Cases

After creating the verification plan and designing a verification driver to exercise the object, developers can implement the verification plan as a series of verification cases. Each case implements a specific idea in the verification plan.

To make it easier to build verification cases, our example driver includes a logging feature. When given a file name as a command line argument, the driver will log all its inputs to the named file.

To build a verification case, the developer runs the driver with inputs that correspond to a test idea in the verification plan. For example, the *StkPus01* test idea described in the verification plan suggests pushing an item onto the stack and then popping the item to see if the stack works. To carry out this test idea, the tester runs the driver, constructing a stack

Listing 6.0 — *Cont'd*

```
                cout << "0-" << NHANDLES-1 << ", " <<
                    NHANDLES << "=NULL " <<
                    NHANDLES+1 << "=non-stack" << endl;
                current = NextI(" => ", Recording);
            } while (!InRange(current,0,NHANDLES+1));
            break;
        case 'Q': // quit program
            done = 1;
            break;
        default:
            cout << "Valid commands are: C)onstruct D)estroy"
                 << endl;
            cout << "P)ush p(O)p I)sempty H)andle Q)uit\n"
                 << endl;
            break;
        }
    }
    return(0);
}
```

using the *C* driver command. The tester then pushes an arbitrary value onto the stack using the *P* driver command. Finally, the tester pops the stack (using the *O* driver command) to see if the stack returns the pushed value. To complete the test, the tester destroys the stack (with the *D* command) and quits the driver program (with the *Q* command). If the tester has supplied the optional recording file name as a command line parameter, the recorded input is the verification case. The stack push test case might look like Document 6.1.

To rerun the test, the tester runs the driver and redirects the driver's input from the verification case. The verification case is a simple text file that developers can edit with a text editor. (Lines that begin with # are comments and have no effect on the operation of the verification case. Comments are especially important when the test turns up a defect. The verification comments help the developers understand the verification case, just like comments help developers understand the program's source code.)

The example verification driver for the stack object accepts commands that are longer than a single character. The first character of the command is the only significant part of the command, but using the entire word as the command makes the verification case less cryptic. For most

Document 6.1 — A Stack Push Test

```
#
#     StkPus01 - Push an item onto a stack
#
# Create a stack
Construct
# Push an arbitrary value onto the stack
Push
12345
# Pop the stack to see if we get the same value back
O(pop)
# Destroy the stack
Destroy
# End the program
Quit
```

of the driver commands, the command character corresponds to the first letter of the command's word, such as *P* for *push*. Conflicts with duplicate first letters can be resolved by choosing an obvious alternate, such as *O* for *pop*. As the number of verification cases proliferates, it is useful to correlate each verification case with its test idea in the verification plan. One simple way to do this is to use the test idea's ID as the file name of the verification case. By linking the verification plan to each of the verification cases, the plan becomes a synopsis and a table of contents for the test cases.

Test Independence

Verification cases should also be as independent as possible. Verification cases become dependent on one another when one verification case relies on side effects of a previous case. A verification case that uses a file created by another test depends on the results of that test. A dependent verification case forces some restrictions on how and when to run the verification case. Changing the order in which dependent verification cases run can quickly render the cases useless.

A Useful Side Effect

A ready library of verification cases also supports regression testing, making it easier to find any defects that might be introduced into the object by future modifications.

Good programmers verify that the changes they have made do not damage the software. Having a collection of verification cases associated with an object simplifies the task of validating a change. The developer can perform regression testing on a modified object by rerunning the object's verification cases.

Building Valid Verification Benchmarks

Capturing test input in verification cases makes running regression tests easier, but testers must always remember that a running verification case does not guarantee correctness. Checking a running verification case for correctness is *validation*. To support automated regression testing, developers need to automate the validation process. As developers run the verification cases against the object, they capture the output and measure its accuracy. The captured output is called a benchmark. After creating a benchmark, developers can rerun a test case and know if the test case ran correctly by comparing its output with the benchmark. Here is the benchmark associated with the previous stack object verification case:

```
STK => Constructing stack 0
STK => Enter a push value => Pushing 12345 onto stack 0
STK => Popped 12345 from stack 0
STK => Destroying stack 0
STK =>
```

Benchmarks, like verification cases, are simple text files. There is a one-to-one correlation between benchmarks and verification cases. Developers can use a file naming scheme to tie the benchmark back to the verification case and the verification plan. For example, the verification case associated with test idea *ID StkPus01* is named *StkPus01.tst.* The corresponding benchmark is named *StkPus01.bmk.*

Given the verification cases and benchmarks, developers can build batch files or scripts that can run large regression test suites overnight or on the weekend. Utilities like *diff* and *cmp* can compare test output with the corresponding benchmarks. Developers can automatically search the results from *diff* to find those tests that identified defects. The only necessary human intervention occurs when the regression tests identify defects in the software.

Automatic screening can determine if the verification case output contains transient information such as time stamps or pointer values. Developers planning to use *diff*, *cmp*, or *fc* should avoid embedding time stamps and other forms of transient information in the test case outputs. Some commercial testing products are intelligent enough to handle these types of variances between the benchmarks and verification case outputs.

Managing Object Verification Artifacts

Because it seems more natural, the Object Creation Process places verification after design and implementation. In practice, developers can begin building the verification plan and drivers as soon as the specification is complete. This flexibility allows the early stages of verification to proceed in parallel with design and implementation, potentially accelerating the development schedule.

Managing the Process

Figure 6.0 shows the relationships between the various verification related artifacts.

To minimize development effort, the test artifacts should be managed carefully and maintained with the same care shown the source code. Since test artifacts will be revised at least as often as the source code, they too should be managed by a *revision control system*. Such carefully structured testing may appear to require significantly more effort than traditional seat-of-the-pants approaches. While thorough verification has drawbacks, additional effort is not one of them. Our approach does not require more effort — it simply moves the effort to the earlier stages of the software development cycle (i.e., *before the product gets to the customer*). Ultimately, careful verification should reduce effort and improve quality.

A readily available and easily understood set of regression tests also facilitates the development of reusable software. Most developers would like to reuse software in other applications. Existing software, however, rarely fits precisely and generally requires some modification. Programmers

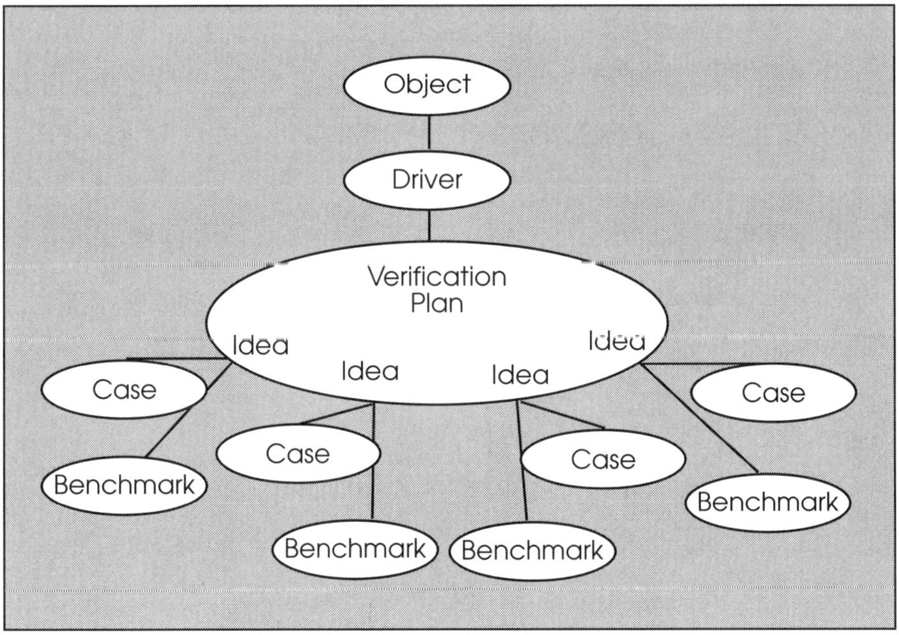

Figure 6.0 — Verification Artifacts and Their Relationships

are usually wary of making modifications to a piece of software unless they completely understand it. If a test scaffolding accompanies the reusable object, programmers can fearlessly change the software and verify that the software still works. This safety net approach provides for verifiable software integrity and increases the potential for software reuse.

Testing the Chess Game Object

While all our previous verification examples tested member functions (i.e., *internal* objects), the same principles apply to higher level objects (*external* objects — not to be confused with the external *view* of an object). This section shows how to apply object verification to a high-level object, namely, the example chess game object.

The chess game example does not have member functions like internal objects. However, the chess game does require stimulus and input for its functioning. A good verification plan for the chess game example should be organized according to these inputs, as in Document 6.2, the verification

Document 6.2 — Verification Plan for Chess Game

Object Verification Plan

Object: Example Chess Game

Function: Color selection

Test case name:	SelClr00	Test type:	BB Valid
Description:	Verify display as per spec		
Verification:	Correct squares, correct piece names & positions, color prompt		
Test case name:	SelClr01	Test type:	BB Valid
Description:	Select white using W		
Verification:	White is the user's color, white moves first		
Test case name:	SelClr02	Test type:	BB Valid
Description:	Select white using w		
Verification:	Black is the user's color, white moves first		

Document 6.2 — *Cont'd*

Test case name: SelClr03 Test type: BB Valid
Description: Select black using B
Verification: Black is the user's color, white moves first

Test case name: SelClr04 Test type: BB Valid
Description: Select black using b
Verification: White is the user's color, white moves first

Test case name: SelClr05 Test type: BB Invalid
Description: Select an invalid color (R, 1, <)
Verification: Each invalid input is rejected with a beep (no state change)

Function: Move state (Program)

Test case name: MovPrg00 Test type: BB Valid
Description: Select user color black and watch first move
Verification: Status is "blinking", piece makes legal move

Test case name: MovPrg01 Test type: BB Valid
Description: Check piece movements (Give away pieces to make others move)
Verification: Each piece moves legally

Function: Move state (User)

Test case name: MovUsr00 Test type: BB Valid
Description: Verify initial state
Verification: User king is blinking, status = Select piece prompt

Test case name: MovUsr01 Test type: BB Valid
Description: Verify arrow keys (move all four directions, include wrap)
Verification: Blinking square moves according to spec

Test case name: MovUsr02 Test type: BB Invalid
Description: Press non-arrow, non-enter keys
Verification: Beep occurs

Test case name: MovUsr03 Test type: BB Invalid
Description: Try to select a non-piece
Verification: Beep occurs

Document 6.2 — *Cont'd*

Test case name:	MovUsr04	Test type:	BB Invalid
Description:	Try to select a program piece		
Verification:	Beep occurs		
Test case name:	MovUsr05	Test type:	BB Invalid
Description:	Move into checkmate		
Verification:	Invalid move status		

Function: Move state (Pawn)

Test case name:	MovPwn00	Test type:	BB Valid
Description:	Move a pawn one position		
Verification:	Legal move accepted		
Test case name:	MovPwn01	Test type:	BB Valid
Description:	Move pawn 2 places on first move		
Verification:	Legal move accepted		
Test case name:	MovPwn02	Test type:	BB Valid
Description:	Move diagonally to take another piece		
Verification:	Legal move accepted, piece taken		
Test case name:	MovPwn03	Test type:	BB Valid
Description:	Make final move to opposite side		
Verification:	Legal move accepted, pawn becomes queen		
Test case name:	MovPwn04	Test type:	BB Invalid
Description:	Move diagonally, backwards and sideways illegally		
Verification:	Illegal move status		
Test case name:	MovPwn05	Test type:	BB Invalid
Description:	Move 3 positions forward		
Verification:	Illegal move status		
Test case name:	MovPwn06	Test type:	BB Invalid
Description:	Move zero positions		
Verification:	illegal move status		
Test case name:	MovPwn07	Test type:	BB Invalid
Description:	Move over a piece on first move		
Verification:	illegal move status		
Test case name:	MovPwn08	Test type:	BB Invalid
Description:	Try to take a piece without moving diagonally		
Verification:	illegal move status		

Document 6.2 — *Cont'd*

Test case name: MovPwn09 Test type: BB Invalid
Description: Try to take piece of the same color
Verification: illegal move status

Function: Move state (Castle)

Test case name: MovCsl00 Test type: BB Valid
Description: Move horizontally one position
Verification: Legal move accepted

Test case name: MovCsl01 Test type: BB Valid
Description: Move horizontally many positions
Verification: Legal move accepted

Test case name: MovCsl02 Test type: BB Valid
Description: Move vertically one position
Verification: Legal move accepted

Test case name: MovCsl03 Test type: BB Valid
Description: Move vertically many positions
Verification: Legal move accepted

Test case name: MovCsl04 Test type: BB Valid
Description: Move legally to take another piece
Verification: Legal move accepted, piece taken

Test case name: MovCsl05 Test type: BB Invalid
Description: Move diagonally
Verification: Illegal move status

Test case name: MovCsl06 Test type: BB Invalid
Description: Move past another piece in path
Verification: Illegal move status

Test case name: MovCsl07 Test type: BB Invalid
Description: Try to take piece of the same color
Verification: Illegal move status

Test case name: MovCsl08 Test type: BB Invalid
Description: Move zero positions
Verification: Illegal move status

Function: Move state (Knight)

Test case name: MovKnt00 Test type: BB Valid
Description: Move legally on first move
Verification: Legal move accepted

Test case name: MovKnt01 Test type: BB Valid
Description: Try all eight legal moves in sequence
Verification: Legal move accepted

Document 6.2 — *Cont'd*

Test case name: MovKnt02 Test type: BB Valid
Description: Move legally and take a piece
Verification: Legal move accepted, piece taken
Test case name: MovKnt03 Test type: BB Invalid
Description: Move in an illegal manner to an open position
Verification: Illegal move status
Test case name: MovKnt04 Test type: BB Invalid
Description: Move zero positions
Verification: Illegal move status
Test case name: MovKnt05 Test type: BB invalid
Description: Try to take a piece of the same color
Verification: Illegal move status
Test case name: MovKnt06 Test type: BB invalid
Description: Try to take a piece with an illegal move
Verification: Illegal move status

Function: Move state (Bishop)
Test case name: MovBsh00 Test type: BB Valid
Description: Move vertically one position in each of the four directions
Verification: Legal move accepted
Test case name: MovBsh01 Test type: BB Valid
Description: Move vertically many positions in each of the four directions
Verification: Legal move accepted
Test case name: MovBsh02 Test type: BB Valid
Description: Take a piece with a legal move
Verification: Legal move accepted, piece taken
Test case name: MovBsh03 Test type: BB Invalid
Description: Move in an illegal manner to an open position
Verification: Illegal move status
Test case name: MovBsh04 Test type: BB Invalid
Description: Move past another piece in path
Verification: Illegal move status
Test case name: MovBsh05 Test type: BB Invalid
Description: Move zero positions
Verification: Illegal move status

Document 6.2 — *Cont'd*

Test case name: MovBsh06 Test type: BB Invalid
Description: Try to take a piece of the same color
Verification: Illegal move status

Function: Move state (Queen)

Test case name: MovQun00 Test type: BB Valid
Description: Move one position all four horizontal/vertical directions
Verification: Legal move accepted

Test case name: MovQun01 Test type: BB Valid
Description: Move one position all four diagonal directions
Verification: Legal move accepted

Test case name: MovQun02 Test type: BB Valid
Description: Move many positions all four horizontal/vertical directions
Verification: Legal move accepted

Test case name: MovQun03 Test type: BB Valid
Description: Move many positions all four diagonal directions
Verification: Legal move accepted

Test case name: MovQun04 Test type: BB Valid
Description: Take a piece with a legal move
Verification: Legal move accepted, piece taken

Test case name: MovQun05 Test type: BB Invalid
Description: Move non-diagonally, non-Horizontally/vertically
Verification: Illegal move status

Test case name: MovQun06 Test type: BB Invalid
Description: Take a piece of the same color
Verification: Illegal move status

Test case name: MovQun07 Test type: BB Invalid
Description: Move past a piece in the path
Verification: Illegal move status

Test case name: MovQun08 Test type: BB Invalid
Description: Move zero positions
Verification: Illegal move statue

Document 6.2 — *Cont'd*

Function: Move state (King)

Test case name: MovKin00 Test type: BB Valid
Description: Move one position in all directions
Verification: Legal move accepted

Test case name: MovKin01 Test type: BB Valid
Description: Take a piece with a legal move
Verification: Legal move accepted, piece taken

Test case name: MovKin02 Test type: BB Valid
Description: Make a legal castle move
Verification: Illegal move status

Test case name: MovKin03 Test type: BB Invalid
Description: Try to move more than one position
Verification: Illegal move status

Test case name: MovKin04 Test type: BB Invalid
Description: Move zero positions
Verification: Illegal move status

Test case name: MovKin05 Test type: BB Invalid
Description: Perform an illegal castle (knight has moved)
Verification: Illegal status

Test case name: MovKin06 Test type: BB Invalid
Description: Perform an illegal castle (knight not in position)
Verification: Illegal move status

Function: Game result

Test case name: GamRes00 Test type: BB Valid
Description: Computer wins
Verification: Game over status

Test case name: GamRes01 Test type: BB Valid
Description: User wins
Verification: Game over status

Test case name: GamRes02 Test type: BB Valid
Description: Draw
Verification: Game over status

Test case name: GamRes03 Test type: BB Valid
Description: Play again with Y and/or y
Verification: New game

plan for the chess game example. The tests in the chess game verification plan are black-box tests, focused on the boundaries of the input.

Since the chess game object is an external object, its driver cannot call functions directly as internal object drivers do. The game itself provides some driver functionality, because the chess game is already interactive. The game does not provide all the necessary test driver processes. For example, the game interface does not perform comment processing or log input; also, the chess game output is not as easy to capture in a file as was internal driver output.

Some sophisticated commercial products provide the full spectrum of test driver functionality for external objects such as the chess game. Commercial test drivers often run as TSR (Terminate and Stay Resident) programs that intercept and record all key strokes and capture all screen changes. The only real drawback of commercial verification drivers is, perhaps, portability. Many commercial drivers operate only in DOS or Windows. This is only a significant limitation if the target object must run on several platforms.

Developers can also provide test driver functionality by creating *wrapper/stub* software. The wrapper/stub software replaces *main* with a new *main*, and replaces the necessary I/O functions with customized intercept functions. Unfortunately, wrapper/stub drivers cannot test the object in its final form. Wrapper and stub functions must be conditionally compiled into the program. Once testing completes, the developer must remove the wrapper and stub functions. This recompilation is a potential

Document 6.2 — *Cont'd*

Test case name:	GamRes04	Test type:	BB Valid
Description:	Play again with Y and/or y		
Verification:	New game		
Test case name:	GamRes05	Test type:	BB Valid
Description:	Do not play again with N and/or n		
Verification:	Program terminates		
Test case name:	GamRes06	Test type:	BB Invalid
Description:	Invalid play again response (R, 1, <)		
Verification:	Program terminates		

Listing 6.1 — A Low-Level Class

```
//
// screen.hpp - low level terminal interface
//

class     Screen;

#ifndef   SCREEN_HPP
#define   SCREEN_HPP

#include  <conio.h>
#include  <dos.h>
#include  "global.hpp"
#include  "magic.hpp"

// Screen video attributes
typedef   int Att;
const     AttNone   =  0; // No attributes
const     AttBold   =  1; // Bold attribute
const     AttBlink  =  2; // Blink attribute
const     AttRevid  =  4; // Reverse video attribute

// Interactive terminal class
class     Screen {
   MAGIC        // Magic number macro
   // Assert the class invariants
   void  Invariant() const;
public:
   // Initialize the screen
   Screen();
   // Close the screen
   ~Screen();
   // Clear the screen
   void  Clear() const;
   // Position the cursor
   void  GoToXY(
      const int,       // Cursor X position value
      const int        // Cursor Y position value
   ) const;
```

source of errors. However, the likelihood of introducing serious errors is small. The test driver for the chess game example is of the wrapper/stub type.

To understand how wrapper/stub drivers work, it is sometimes necessary to understand something about the internals of the object. Listing 6.3 shows the low level class that controls the computer's screen and key board for the chess game.

Notice the inclusion of *wrapper.hpp* near the end of Listing 6.1. The file *wrapper.hpp* (in Listing 6.2) defines an interceptor class that inserts itself between the *screen* class and its callers.

When the macro *VERIFICATION* is defined, the *NewScreen* class intercepts calls to the display and echoes the command to *cout*. The *cout* information can be stored in a file for benchmark purposes. *NewScreen* also intercepts input from the keyboard. The file *wrapper.cpp* (Listing 6.3) contains the keyboard intercept function and the *main* wrapper.

The *main* wrapper function opens the recording file (if there is one) and calls the regular *main*. Both the wrapper *main* function and the *NewScreen* class insert themselves by means of the renaming macros at the end of *wrapper.hpp*. The *GetChIntercept* function handles input recording and comment stripping for *Screen::GetCh*. By default, the wrapper and stubs are not compiled into the chess game. To add the

Listing 6.1 — *Cont'd*

```
    // Output a string with the current attributes
    void   PutString(
       const char*      // String to output
    ) const;
    // Change the current attributes
    void   Attribute(
       const Att     // The target attribute(s)
    ) const;
    // Sound a warning beep
    void   Beep() const;
    // Get a character command
    int    GetCh() const;
};

#include "wrapper.hpp" // verification driver
#endif    // SCREEN_HPP
```

Listing 6.2 — An Interceptor Class

```
// wrapper.hpp -chess game wrapper/stub class
//                  for the verification driver

#ifndef      WRAPPER_HPP
#define      WRAPPER_HPP

#ifdef    VERIFICATION // definition turns on the driver

#include  <fstream.h>
#include  "magic.hpp"

// NewScreen class intercepts
// calls to screen for verification purposes
class        NewScreen {
   MAGIC                    // Magic number macro
   Screen    screen;
   // Assert the class invariants
   void      Invariant() const {
                            // Check the magic number
      MagicCheck();
   }
public:
   // Create the screen interceptor
   NewScreen() {
      MagicOn();
      Invariant();
   }
   // Destroy the interceptor
   ~NewScreen() {
      Invariant();
      MagicOff();
   }
   // Clear the screen (with echo)
   void      Clear() const {
      Invariant();
      cout < "clear()" < endl;
      screen.Clear();
   }
```

Listing 6.2 — *Cont'd*

```
// Position the cursor (with echo)
void  GoToXY(
   const int x,
   const int y
) const {
   Invariant();
   cout << "GoToXY(" << x << "," << y << ")" << endl;
   screen.GoToXY(x, y);
}
// Output a string with the
// current attributes (with echo)
void  PutString(
   const char *str
) const {
   Invariant();
   cout << "PutString(" << str << ")" << endl;
   screen.PutString(str);
}
// Change the current attributes (with echo)
void  Attribute(
   const Att att
) const {
   Invariant();
   cout << "Attribute(";
   if (att == AttNone) cout << "AttNone";
   if (att & AttBold)  cout << "AttBold";
   if (att & AttBlink) cout << "AttBlink";
   if (att & AttRevid) cout << "AttRevid";
   cout << ")" << endl;
   screen.Attribute(att);
}
// Sound a warning beep
void  Beep() const {
   Invariant();
   cout << "Beep()" << endl;
   screen.Beep();
}
```

Listing 6.2 — *Cont'd*

```
    // Get a character
    int GetCh() const {
        Invariant();
        int c = screen.GetCh();
        return c;
    }
};

// Redirect the old function calls to the new ones
#define   Screen NewScreen
#define   main       OldMain
#define   getch  GetChIntercept
int       GetChIntercept();

#endif    // VERIFICATION
#endif    // WRAPPER_HPP
```

Listing 6.3 — Keyboard Intercept Function and *main* Wrapper

```
//      wrapper.cpp - Verification wrapper/stub
//      code for the chess game
//
#include <stdio.h>
#include <string.h>
#include <ctype.h>
#include "screen.hpp"

#ifdef VERIFICATION

// Undo the redefinitions
#ifdef    main
#undef    main
#undef    Screen
#undef    getch
#endif    // main

char          NewScreen::MagicValue = '\0';
extern void   OldMain();          //the chess main
```

Listing 6.3 — *Cont'd*

```
static        FILE   *Recording;  //recording stream handle
const char    *ProcOn = "Processing_On";
const         MAXLINE = 128;

// Get a line of input
void          GetLine(char buffer[]) {

   int i = 0;
   int c;
   while (((c = getch()) != '\r') && (c != '\n')) {
      // Truncate lines that are too long
      if (i < (MAXLINE-1)) {
         buffer[i++] = c;
      }
   }
   // Strip the newline
   if (c == '\r') c = getch();
   buffer[i] = '\0';
}

// intercepting char getting routine
// records input and process comments
int        GetChIntercept() {

   int    c;
   char   buffer[MAXLINE];
   static BOOLEAN   Processing = FALSE;

   // get a character and eat all the comment lines
   while ((c = getch()) == '#') {
      // Put the comment into a buffer
      GetLine(buffer);
      // Turn on processing if necessary
      if (strcmp(buffer, ProcOn) == 0) Processing = TRUE;
      // Echo the comment
      if (Recording != NULL) {
         fprintf(Recording, "#%s\n", buffer);
      }
   }
```

Listing 6.3 — *Cont'd*

```
    // If processing has been turned on
    if (Processing) {
        // Get the whole line
        buffer[0] = c;
        GetLine(&buffer[1]);
        // Convert processed input to non-processed form
        sscanf(buffer, "%d", &c);
        // Echo the line if necessary
        if (Recording != NULL)
            fprintf(Recording, "%s\n", buffer);
    } else {
        // Record the input if necessary
        if (Recording != NULL) {
            // Mark recorded input as processed
            static    BOOLEAN   FirstTime = TRUE;
            if (FirstTime) {
                FirstTime = FALSE;
                fprintf(Recording, "#%s\n", ProcOn);
            }
            fprintf(Recording, "%d c\n",c,
                                    isalnum(c)?(char)c:'!');
        }
    }

    return c;
}

// This is the driver main (wrapper)
void      main(int argc, char *argv[]) {
    // if there is a recording file, open it
    Recording = (argc==2)? fopen(argv[1],"w"): NULL;
    // call the chess game's main
    OldMain();
}

#endif // Verification
```

wrapper and stubs to the game, recompile the program with the *VERIFICATION* macro defined. The wrapper and verification scaffolding makes it easy to implement the verification plan. For example, verification case *MovUsr03* might look like:

```
# MovUsr03 - Try to select a non-piece
#
# Select White
87 W
# Move right
0 !
77 M
# Move right
0 !
77 M
# Select square
13 !
# Quit
81 Q
```

The first line indicates that the verification case requires special processing. The wrapper's character intercept function created the verification case in a processed (i.e., human readable) form. Thus, when the character intercept function reads this file as input, it must "unprocess" the input so that the input looks like it came directly from the keyboard. While this additional processing adds some overhead, the processed file is more readable and can be perused in a standard text editor.

The comments on the second, third, and fourth lines identify this verification case and describe what it does. The remaining comment lines, one for each of the chess game commands, were added with a text editor to clarify each step of the verification case. This verification case selects white (with the *W* command), moves right twice (by using two right arrow keys), tries to select the empty square (with the *Enter* key), and quits the program (with the *Q* command). The case should generate output that agrees with the benchmark file (Document 6.3).

The benchmark file starts with a prompt to select a piece. After the prompt, the program blinks the king's square, the pawn's square, and the empty square. When the program tries to change the empty square to reverse video, it notices the square is empty and turns off the reverse video. Finally, the program outputs the warning beep, all in accordance with the specification. Verification generally does not require the testers to manually review the benchmark files. Testers can instead monitor the screen display directly. The benchmark file will be used instead to automatically verify that regression tests ran correctly.

Document 6.3 — The Benchmark File

```
...
GoToXY(2,24)
PutString(Select the piece to move (use arrow keys to
     position or enter key to select))
Attribute(AttBlink)
GoToXY(0,12)
PutString. Whit. )
GoToXY(0,13)
PutString.  Kin.  )
GoToXY(0,14)
PutString. . .  )
Attribute(AttNone)
GoToXY(0,12)
PutString. Whit. )
GoToXY(0,13)
PutString.  Kin.  )
GoToXY(0,14)
PutString. . .  )
Attribute(AttBlinkAttRevid)
GoToXY(10,12)
PutString. Whit. )
GoToXY(10,13)
PutString.  Paw.  )
GoToXY(10,14)
PutString. . .  )
Attribute(AttRevid)
GoToXY(10,12)
PutString. Whit. )
GoToXY(10,13)
PutString.  Paw.  )
GoToXY(10,14)
```

Summary

The four steps in the Object Verification Process —

- ❏ building the verification plan,
- ❏ building the verification driver,
- ❏ building the verification cases,
- ❏ and building valid verification benchmarks,

produce a testing regimen which assures that the final object's external behavior will conform to the design specification. Disciplined testing using this process produces additional, important benefits:

- ❏ Ready-made regression tasks.
- ❏ Less bug-related maintenance after release.
- ❏ Better support for code reusability.
- ❏ Better understanding of individual objects.
- ❏ Support for automated testing.

Document 6.3 — *Cont'd*

```
PutString. . .  )
Attribute(AttBlinkAttRevid)
GoToXY(20,12)
PutString([[[[[[[[[)
GoToXY(20,13)
PutString([[[[[[[[[)
GoToXY(20,14)
PutString([[[[[[[[[)
Attribute(AttRevid)
GoToXY(20,12)
PutString([[[[[[[[[)
GoToXY(20,13)
PutString([[[[[[[[[)
GoToXY(20,14)
PutString([[[[[[[[[)
Beep()
...
```

The effectiveness of this process depends upon the completeness of the object specifications and upon the developer's commitment to the referee's perspective. Incomplete specification can only produce incomplete tests. Only when testers *seek* the system's *failures* will they find them.

These black-box tests determine only whether the system produces results that conform to the specification. The white-box tests in the next chapter test whether these results are being produced *for the right reasons*.

Refining the Pseudocode

Verification planning occurs within the *CreateBlackBoxTests* section of the Object Creation Process. Document 6.4 gives the pseudocode for this section. *CreateBlackBoxTests* starts by considering the functions' parameters. The first loop in *CreateBlackBoxTests* creates the boundary value tests and the invalid value tests for each parameter. The second major loop within *CreateBlackBoxTests* adds the state transition tests and the concurrency test.

The final phase of *CreateBlackBoxTests* reviews the verification plan to make sure it covers everything in the object's specification.

Both black-box and white-box tests (see Document 6.5) are implemented in the test of the Object Creation Process's *while* loop.

Given an object, the process next creates a driver that can completely exercise the object and show the results of the object's functions. Finally, the process creates verification cases and benchmarks that exercise the driver according to the verification plan. If all the verification cases behave as specified, the object passes the tests.

Document 6.4 — Test Planning

```
CreateBlackBoxTests(TestSet) {
    For each of the objects functions... {
        For each parameter of the function... {
            Identify the groups of input
            For each group of input... {
                Select values on or near the boundaries
                // Add tests for the boundary values
                TestSet += boundary value tests
            }
            Identify invalid values for the parameter
            // Add tests for the invalid values
            TestSet += invalid value tests
        }
        TestSet += case
    }
    // Test state transitions and concurrency
    For each externally visible state of the function... {
        Call this state the source state
        For each externally visible state of the function... {
            Call this state the destination state
            // Add state transition tests
            Identify functions to move from source to destination
            TestSet += function sequence tests
            // Add concurrency tests
            Identify tests with an object in each state
            TestSet += concurrency tests
        }
    }
    // Review the verification plan
    For each statement/idea in the object's specification {
        StatementSupported = FALSE
        For each test idea in the verification plan... {
            If the test idea verifies the statement
                StatementSupported = TRUE
        }
        If the Statement is not supported {
            // Add tests to verify the statement
            TestSet += tests to verify the statement
        }
```

Document 6.5 — Test Implementation

```
DoesPassTest(TestSet) {
    // Build the verification driver
    For each of the object's input stimulus... {
        If the driver does not support the stimulus
            Make the driver supports access to the stimulus
    }
    For each of the object's outputs... {
        If the driver does not represent the output
            Make sure the driver represents the output
    }
    // Build the verification cases and benchmarks
    PassTest = TRUE
    For each test in the test set... {
        Run the driver
            Create the recorded input to implement the test
            Capture the output from the driver
        If the captured output is correct
            Make the captured output the verification benchmark
        Otherwise captured output is not correct
            PassTest = FALSE
    }
    return PassTest
}
```

Exercises

0. Describe how to identify boundary values.
1. Describe the difference between valid and invalid parameter values.
2. Create a verification plan for the standard C *printf* function.
3. Explain how to use state transition diagrams for black-box testing.
4. Describe when and how to verify object concurrency.
5. Build a verification driver for the following class:

```
class Set{
   ...
public:
   Set();
   ~Set();
   void  Add(void*);
   void  Remove(void*);
   int Count();
   void  Show();
};
```

AddWhiteBoxTest(ObjectDesign, Test

Chapter 7

White-Box Testing

White-box testing, the final step of the Object Creation Process, differs from black-box object verification because it uses the investigator's *internal* view rather than the referee's *external* view. The investigator's internal view considers how well the object implements the design. Both black-box and white-box testing are important for good quality software. This chapter shows how to use white-box testing to supplement black-box tests.

Why White-Box Tests?

The program described in Document 7.0 and Listing 7.0 illustrates why black-box tests must be supplemented with white-box tests. This program, which reverses the characters in a null-terminated string, contains a bug that black-box testing would probably not find.

This program is designed to efficiently reverse long strings. It divides the string into pages, and pushes each page onto a stack. As the pages are popped from the stack, the characters of the page are output in reverse order.

(The pseudocode identifies two subordinate objects: the *stack* and the *page*. The *page* is an object that contains a character buffer and a length. Normally the *page* object would be a separate class, but to simplify the illustration, our routine does not encapsulate the *page*.)

Black-box tests for this program would probably include a suite of varying length commands: an empty string, a short string (i.e., one character), a medium string (i.e., a string of length 10), and a long string (i.e., a string of length 100). All of these black-box tests would execute correctly — even though the program is incorrect! Black-box testing is unlikely to expose the bug in this program, because the bug is very implementation-specific.

Notice that *pages* can contain either a complete buffer string segment or a partially full buffer string segment. The reversal routine pushes and pops pages on and off of the stack in a reasonable manner. However, the implementor assumes that a partial page buffer is always the last page in the string. Thus, the program appends the *null* terminating character only when the last page buffer is partially full. While partially full page buffers always indicate the last page in the string, it is not true that the last page buffer is always partially full. If the string length is an even multiple of the buffer length, the string never gets a null termination character.

Because the string reversal routine interface hides the design and implementation details, black-box testers might never guess that the routine uses a paging mechanism. Only chance would lead a black-box tester to find the page boundary condition that causes the software to fail. The odds of a tester finding this condition with black-box testing are a grim 16 to 1.

Because some bugs are very implementation-specific, developers must do more than black-box testing. Black-box testing is important because it proves that the software meets its functionality requirements, but white-box testing is necessary to assure the developers know exactly

Document 7.0 — Pseudocode for a String Reversing Program

```
Reverse the input character string and place it in the output buffer
    While there are characters left...
        Allocate a page
        Load the page
        Push the page on the stack

    While the stack is not empty...
        Pop a page from the stack
        Unload the page in reverse order
        Deallocate the page
```

how the software will operate. The remainder of this chapter will show how to supplement the object's quality assurance with white-box testing.

White-Box Test Strategies

Except for a difference in strategies, white-box tests are developed with the same four-step process used to develop black-box tests: build a test plan, build a test driver, build test cases, and build benchmarks. White-box tests, however, are derived from the object's code, rather than from its specifications. All white-box strategies focus on trying to exercise all of the object's code. The simplest strategy (statement coverage) does just that — it exercises every line of code at least once. The more sophisticated strategies (decision coverage and condition coverage) exercise all the code, but they also try to exercise all important *combinations* of code.

There are several strategies for exercising the object's code. The most obvious approach is to create tests that execute every statement in the

Listing 7.0 — Implementation of the String Program

```
const     BufLen = 16;

struct Page   {
   char   Buf[BufLen]; // Character buffer
   int    BufSiz;      // Length of the character buffer
};

//* Reverse the input character string
//* and place it in the output buffer
void  Reverse(
   char *input, // Input character string
   char *output // Output buffer
) {
   Stack  Stk;

   *output = '\0';
   //* While there are characters left...
   char *cp = input;
   char *last = &input[strlen(input)];
   while (cp < last) {
      //* Allocate a page
      Page *p = new Page;
      //* Load the page
```

object's methods. Exercising all of an object's statements is called *statement coverage*.

Consider the following code fragment:

```
i = j + 1;
if (A && B) {
   x = y + z;
}
n = p + 1;
```

To exercise every statement of this code fragment requires only that *A* and *B* both be *TRUE*. If either *A* or *B* is *FALSE*, the statement inside the *if* will not get executed. Thus, simple statement coverage would generate only one test case for this fragment.

Listing7.0 — *Cont'd*

```
            p->BufSiz = min(BufLen, strlen(cp));
            for (int i = 0; i < p->BufSiz; i++) {
               p->Buf[i] = *cp++;
            }
            //* Push the page on the stack
            Stk.Push((void*) p);
        }

        //* While the stack is not empty...
        while (!Stk.IsEmpty()) {
            //* Pop a page from the stack
            Page *p = (Page*) Stk.Pop();
            //* Unload the page in reverse order
            int Size = p->BufSiz == BufLen? BufLen: p->BufSiz;
            for (int i = Size-1; i >= 0; i--) {
               *output++ = p->Buf[i];
            }
            if (Size < BufLen) {
               *output = '\0';
            }
            //* Deallocate the page
            delete p;
        }
    }
```

Statement coverage will uncover many software problems, but may leave some implicit paths untried. A control flow diagram (see Figure 7.0) of the previous code segment shows that statement coverage leaves a path through the code completely untested. Statement coverage requires only that both *A* and *B* be *true*. All the *statements* are exercised, but the *FALSE branch* of the *if* test is not exercised. Consider the effectiveness of statement coverage testing if the code segment is modified slightly:

```
i = 0;
if (A && B) {
    i = 1;
}
x = y / i;
```

Now, the *FALSE* branch of the *if* will result in a divide by zero error. A statement coverage test strategy may not uncover this defect. Even though the *FALSE* branch from the *if* test executes no additional statements, the *FALSE* branch needs to be tested.

To make sure every *path* through the code gets exercised, every *decision* in the code must be executed so as to be *TRUE* and *FALSE*.

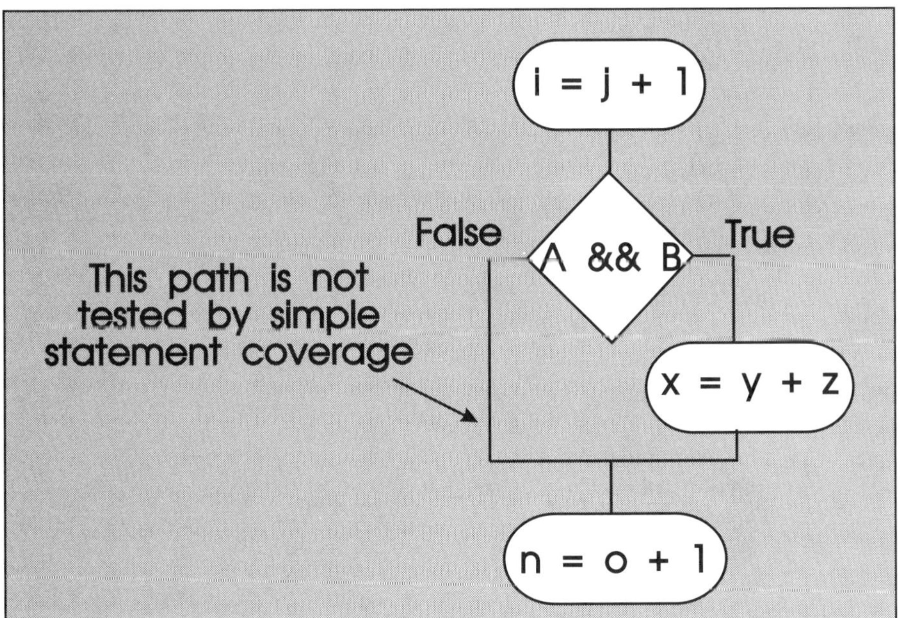

Figure 7.0 — Flow Diagram Showing Statement Coverage

The white-box testing strategy that checks both outcomes of every decision is called *decision coverage*. For the example code segment, decision coverage requires that the *A && B* condition result in a *TRUE* value in at least one test and a *FALSE* value in at least one other test.

Decision coverage will find the division-by-zero defect in the previous code segment, but decision coverage does not guarantee that all possible code sequences get executed.

For example, in the code fragment of Listing 7.1, *A* and *B* are Boolean functions with return values dependent on *Flag1* and *Flag2* respectively. When *Flag1* and *Flag2* are both *TRUE,* the code segment's *if* test takes the *TRUE* branch. When *Flag1* is *FALSE*, the code segment's *if* test

Listing 7.1 — An Error Not Detected by Decision Coverage

```
intQ;

...
i = j + 1;
if (A() && B()) {
    x = y + z;
}
n = p + 1;
...

BOOLEAN   A() {
    if (Flag1) {
        Q = 0;
        return TRUE;
    } else {
        return FALSE;
    }
}

BOOLEAN   B() {
    if (Flag2) {
        return TRUE;
    } else {
        int x = 10 / Q;
        return FALSE;
    }
}
```

takes the *FALSE* branch. These two tests are sufficient for decision coverage, but these two tests alone do not uncover the defect that results when *Flag1* is *TRUE* and *Flag2* is *FALSE*. When *Flag1* is *TRUE* and *Flag2* is *FALSE*, the side effects of the functions have a disastrous effect that causes division by zero in function *B*.

Finding defects as exemplified by this code segment requires a different white-box strategy, one that exercises all decision *combinations*. This white-box test strategy is called *condition coverage*. For the previous code segment, condition coverage requires three tests; *A()* returning *TRUE* and *B()* returning *TRUE*, *A()* returning *TRUE* and *B()* returning *FALSE*, *A()* returning *FALSE*. (When *A()* returns *FALSE*, *B()* is not executed.) Condition coverage requires the most testing, but is also the most effective of the white-box strategies.

To add condition coverage to an object's test suite, start by identifying every condition in each of the object's methods. Next, for each of the object's conditions, review the existing black-box tests to see if they already force the necessary conditions. If the existing tests do not cause the condition to have both a *TRUE* and *FALSE* value, supplement the test suite by adding tests to perform condition coverage.

It is important to avoid adding white-box tests that are redundant with black-box tests. Redundant tests add no real value to the test suite, but can add significant cost, both in test design time and in test run-time. In some cases, there could be extensive overlap between white-box and black-box tests. For example, a review of the methods and conditions in the *STK* stack class example of the previous chapter will show that the black-box tests leave only one condition untested. Thus, the test plan only needs one supplemental white-box verification case:

```
Object Verification Plan
Object:   STK

Function: STK
      ...
Test case name:   StkCon03          Test type:    WB Invalid
      Description:   Cause the STK memory allocation to fail
      Verification:  The last stack handle is null
```

This test checks the condition that may occur if there is insufficient memory to create the stack. The black-box tests handle all the other conditions in the *STK* class.

White-Box Testing of the Chess Game

In a program with many objects, such as the example chess game, it is important to use white-box testing to exercise each method of every object. The Object Verification Phase creates a verification plan and a verification driver for each object. White-box testing supplements each object's verification plan with white-box tests, and uses the object's verification driver to implement the tests.

As an example of how to create white-box tests within the chess game, consider the *main()* function. The Object Creation Process sees *main()* as a single method of the highest level program object. White-box testing for other objects follows the same process, but applies it to lower level objects.

We will employ the strongest of the white-box strategies, namely, condition coverage. Examining *main()* for decisions/branches produces only two decision/branches: the *if (!Quitting)* test, and the *while (PlayAgain && !Quitting)* loop test. (See the boldface lines in Listing 7.2.)

Condition coverage for the *if* test requires that the software exercise *Quitting* with both *TRUE* and *FALSE* values. A *FALSE* value for *Quitting* results when the user plays the entire chess game without prematurely giving up. When the user does not give up and *Quitting* becomes *FALSE*, the *if* test is *TRUE* and the user is prompted to play again. If the user decides to quit the game prematurely, *Quitting* will have a *TRUE* value, which will by-pass prompting the user to play again. These two cases represent potential white-box tests:

Test case name:	main01	Test type:	WB Valid
Description:	Play entire game without quitting		
Verification:	Program prompts to play again		
Test case name:	main02	Test type:	WB Valid
Description:	Quit game prematurely		
Verification:	Program does not prompt to play again		

The *do...while* test is more complex than the *if* test, because it is a compound conditional involving two Boolean variables. The first variable,

PlayAgain, represents the result of querying the user to play the chess game again. If the user wants to play the game again, *PlayAgain* will be *TRUE*, otherwise *PlayAgain* will be *FALSE*. The *Quitting* variable is the same variable used in the *if* test.

At first glance, it seems that exercising all possible states of the *do...while* conditional will require four tests. Further investigation shows it is only possible to test three of the condition's states. Notice that when *Quitting* is *TRUE*, *PlayAgain* is undefined (i.e., *Quitting* is not deterministically *TRUE* or *FALSE*). Is this an error? Because the two

Listing 7.2 — A Candidate for Condition Coverage

```
//* Chess game main entry point
void         main() {

    //* Initialize the screen
    Screen     screen;
    //* Create the user interaction line
    Status     status(screen);
    //* Create the game
    Game       game(screen, status);
    BOOLEAN    Quitting;
    BOOLEAN    PlayAgain;
    Winner     Result;

    //* Until the user does not want
    //* to play again or quitting...
    do {
        //* Initialize the game
        game.Initialize();
        //* Play the game
        Quitting = game.Play(Result);
        //* If the user does not want to quit,
        if (!Quitting) {
            //* Determine if the user wants to play again
            PlayAgain = status.PlayAgain(Result);
        }
        //* Clean up the game
        game.CleanUp();
    } while (PlayAgain && !Quitting);
}
```

variables of the condition are joined by a logical *and* (i.e., *&&*), when one of the variables is *FALSE*, the value of the other is unimportant. Therefore, when *Quitting* is *TRUE* and *!Quitting* is *FALSE*, the value of *PlayAgain* does not matter. The resultant *FALSE* condition will end the loop and game. In the verification plan this test looks as follows:

Test case name:	main03	Test type:	WB Valid
Description:	Quit game prematurely		
Verification:	Program does not prompt to play again		

This is exactly the same test as *main02*. Redundant tests waste time and effort with no additional value. Therefore, test *main03* should not be added to the verification plan.

When *Quitting* is *FALSE*, the value of *PlayAgain* is significant, because its value determines the outcome of the condition. If *Quitting* is *FALSE* and *PlayAgain* is *TRUE*, the condition is *TRUE* and the user begins another game. If *PlayAgain* is *FALSE*, the condition is *FALSE* regardless of *Quitting*'s value, and the program terminates. Both of these conditions require a test case.

Test case name:	main04	Test type:	WB Valid
Description:	Do not quit and play again		
Verification:	Program starts a new game		
Test case name:	main05	Test type:	WB Valid
Description:	Do not quit and do not play again		
Verification:	Program terminates		

Either of these tests make test *main01* redundant, because they both test the condition of not quitting the game prematurely. Thus, the three tests — *main02*, *main04*, and *main05* — are a complete set of white-box tests for *main()*.

Test case name:	GamRes03	Test type:	BB Valid
Description:	Play again with Y and/or y		
Verification:	New game		
Test case name:	GamRes04	Test type:	BB Valid
Description:	Do not play again with N and/or n		
Verification:	Program terminates		

The next step is to eliminate white-box tests that are the same as black-box tests. Reviewing the black-box verification plan identifies the following tests:

These tests from the black-box verification plan are the same as *main04* and *main05*. The test cases *main04* and *main05* can, therefore, be eliminated. This leaves *main02* as the only necessary additional test. It may be useful to add the other tests to the plan documentation, i.e., *main01*, *main03*, *main04*, and *main05*, but mark these tests as redundant. Adding redundant tests to the test plan can help those reviewing the white-box tests to make sure they are complete.

Given the updated verification plan, use the original driver to create the additional necessary verification cases. The verification cases are simply recorded inputs to the verification driver, just like their black-box counterparts. The verification case for *main02* is:

```
#Processing_On
119 w
113 q
```

The remainder of the white-box testing process is identical to the black-box verification process.

Some white-box tests are difficult to validate externally. It may be difficult to know that a white-box test case caused the specific conditions required by the test plan. Under these circumstances it may be important to run the test case using a debugger to verify that the software achieved the specific values and conditions.

The remainder of the white-box testing of the chess game objects work like the example *main()*. Inspect each method of each object to be certain that the tests exercise all possible conditions.

Summary

This chapter has described how to use white-box testing to supplement object verification. There are three white-box strategies: statement coverage, decision coverage, and condition coverage. This chapter explains the difference between these three strategies and suggests condition coverage as the optimal strategy.

Document 7.1 gives the algorithmic description for applying white-box testing.

The *CreateObject* process calls the *AddWhiteBoxTests* function directly. *AddWhiteBoxTests* is a simple function that finds each of a class's conditions and makes sure the class's test suite exercises both of the conditions's outcomes. Checking for existing tests can eliminate redundant testing.

Document 7.1 — Psuedocode for White Box Tests

```
AddWhiteBoxTests(TestSet) {
      For each method in the class... {
            For condition in the method... {
                  If no existing tests force a true condition,
                        Create a true condition test
                  If no existing tests force a false condition,
                        Create a false condition test
            }
      }
}
```

Exercises

0. List the three white-box test strategies discussed in this chapter and describe each.
1. Create a defective code segment that can only be detected by condition coverage.
2. Enumerate the possible tests for a three-conditional decision.
3. Explain the limitations of exclusively using white-box testing or black-box testing.

```
ject(Requirements
scribe the objects externals
tSpec = CreateSpec(Requiremen
the object until it passes
all veri     tests
Do {
    // Describe how th
    ObjectDesign = DesignO
    // Find or build subordina
    Subordinates = CreateSu
    // Implement this objec
    Code = CodeObject(O
    // Create boundary v
    TestSet = CreateBla
    // Create condition
    WhiteBoxTes
```

Chapter 8

Concluding Topics

The previous chapters described the Object Creation Process in detail. This chapter addresses additional software development issues that affect the Object Creation Process: event-driven software development, software maintenance, software reuse, project planning, development metrics, and improving the development process.

Modern Graphical User Interfaces (GUIs) are *event-driven* applications. In event-driven programs, the user dictates the types and order of interactions. In conventional non-event-driven programs, the application controls the sequence of the user interface operations. Event-driven programs are built around an *event loop* that processes an event, such as a mouse click or key press, and routes the event to the appropriate menu, panel, or dialog box. The event loop is the top level of control for an event-driven program. Developers accustomed to building non-event-driven applications must alter their way of thinking. Programmers no longer dictate the interaction sequence. Now programmers must design interfaces that respond to user requests using an event-driven model.

Application frameworks can simplify the creation of event-driven user interfaces. An application framework is a package created by a third party that supplies the program with many of the GUI constructs, such as menus, buttons, fields, and list boxes. Application frameworks also provide the main event loop manager to route messages and handle mouse and keyboard interaction.

Application frameworks are an attractive alternative to developing an application from scratch. Frameworks tout all the benefits of reusable software. Reusing the framework relieves the developer from redesigning, implementing, and testing common functions. Additionally, many frameworks support the Common User Access (CUA) standard.

Application Frameworks and Event-Driven Programs

Since an application framework predefines a program's top-level structures, one might be tempted to abandon the top-down approach of the Object Creation Process. In fact, the Object Creation Process can, and *should*, be applied to framework-generated programs.

Even though frameworks supply much of the necessary interface design and code, developers must guard against overlooking the application's requirements and specification phases. Event-driven programs still need a requirements phase as described in Chapter 2.

Framework-based applications also need an external specification as described in Chapter 3. In addition to other external interfaces, the specification must include a complete user interface description. A complete description includes what the interface looks like and how the interface interacts with the user.

Many application framework products include a prototyping tool that allows developers to create a description of the interface interactively.

The CUA Interface Standard

Most windowing interfaces comply with the Common User Access (CUA) interface standard. This standard defines objects such as menu bars, pull-down menus, dialog boxes and the mouse/keyboard interaction. Microsoft Windows and OS/2 Presentation Manager are both CUA-compliant environments.

Applications that conform to the CUA standard share a common look and feel. Users appreciate this consistency. Similar interfaces make an application's behavior more predictable. Predictable behavior reduces the time it takes to learn new applications.

The prototype becomes the user interface specification. While a prototype is always stronger than a written interface description, prototypes are not complete external specifications. The prototype describes *only* the user interface.

When first learning to work with an application framework, enumerate the events handled by lower level software (developer supplied software). List each event with a description of the response to the event. These descriptions are similar to the requirements descriptions in the Object Creation Process. Group similar events together and normalize the descriptions of the events. The descriptions should use the same words to describe the same objects and operations. Next, eliminate redundant descriptions. Finally, for each object that the descriptions identify, create a specification. The specification should include a method for each unique event description. At this point the framework-oriented development process merges back into the normal flow of the Object Creation Process.

Some Notable Similarities

The functions of software generators and the Object Creation Process are remarkably similar. Frameworks automatically generate the application's software skeleton. Usually the developer must supply lower level functions and objects to the software generated by the framework. A software generator uses the top level object's specification to design and implement the first few levels of abstraction. Using the generated software as a starting point the developer creates specifications for each of the lower level functions and objects.

Lower level functions required by the generated software intuitively group into methods that form an object. For example, a GUI might display a list and allow the user to add to, edit, or delete items from the list. The add, edit, and delete operations require three functions to manipulate the list. The list becomes the class with *add*, *edit*, and *delete* methods.

Selecting an Application Framework

There are a few issues to consider when selecting an application framework. To help identify potential strengths and weaknesses of an application framework, ask yourself the following questions:

- ❑ Does the framework provide useful components for all the user interface constructs (or constructs to build) as defined by the top level object's specification?
- ❑ Does the framework have a design tool?
- ❑ How much software will the framework provide?
- ❑ How easy is it to learn and use the framework?
- ❑ If the framework generates code, does the code require any modification?
- ❑ If the generated code requires modification, how does the framework retrofit your modifications if you need to regenerate the code?
- ❑ What constraints does the framework impose upon how you develop software?

While most frameworks supply the standard GUI constructs, the set of constructs supported in a particular framework may not satisfy your application's specification. Many frameworks supply tools to extend the framework, but these extensions take time. It may be advantageous to select a framework that contains all necessary GUI constructs.

While the right design tool can reduce the tedium in the specification effort and yield a more understandable specification, a tool that is hard to learn, hard to use, or incomplete, can quickly become a costly burden. Before committing to a design tool, make sure that it can configure all the GUI constructs and that the tool is intuitive.

The amount of software that a framework supplies or generates also varies. Some framework packages supply only a simple main event loop, while other packages may generate function skeletons. More is usually better, but be careful that the framework-generated code is easily extended.

Many framework packages generate code that requires modification. For example, a generated event loop may need to be modified to handle each event. With such a tool, if the interface needs to be changed slightly, the modifications that handle various events may be lost when the code generator regenerates the event loop code. When evaluating a framework, take time to consider this likely scenario.

The purpose for using a framework is to reduce cost and shorten development time. If the framework is useful for several projects, it may warrant a significant learning investment; otherwise it must be easy to learn. Beware of frameworks that supply "the source" but offer limited documentation or support. Unsupported, poorly documented framework packages may require an enormous amount of time to learn.

Finally, beware of frameworks that impose undesirable constraints on your programming style or environment. For example, a framework may require an unfamiliar compiler or language. A less obvious, but similarly disruptive, constraint might be the impact of inheritance or exception handling. The framework may only work with objects that have a common undesirable base class, or the framework may impose constraints on exception handling that are not feasible for a given application. Take time to understand all of a framework's constraints and requirements.

Maintenance and the Object Creation Process

Experienced developers create software with an eye toward the software's eventual evolution. Highly adaptive software will have a longer and more useful life. Ultimately, software that is easy to maintain yields a better return on the development investment.

Software maintenance can involve defect resolution or software enhancement. Software defects result from inconsistencies between steps of the Object Creation Process. The specification may not fulfill the requirements. The design does not meet the specification, or the implementation is not consistent with the design.

Software enhancements result when the requirements change. Enhancements may include additional functionality, a changed interface, or better response time.

Traditionally, developers use weak maintenance techniques. Most programmers perform maintenance by changing only the source code, which results in out-of-date and useless designs and specifications. Because this approach to maintenance undermines the integrity of the program's supporting artifacts, the artifacts can no longer be used to navigate or understand the program.

As traditional maintenance proceeds, the difference between the actual software and its artifacts increases. Reverse engineering tools try to close the gap between the software and its artifacts, but current reverse engineering technology only recovers some design descriptions.

The Object Creation Process reduces the cost of maintenance by preparing for the maintenance phase. The requirements, specification and design artifacts help the developer quickly identify the source of defects. Regression tests keep maintenance programmers from propagating defects by easily identifying defects introduced during the maintenance process. Without these resources, maintenance efforts are risky. To fix software defects, start at the top of the Object Creation Process and review each of the steps. Identify the source of the defect by identifying the inconsistency between the steps. Then address the defect based upon the identified inconsistency.

Be careful to understand the real source of the defect. Attempting to fix a defect at the wrong level is a frustrating exercise. Imagine trying to fix a design level defect by changing the implementation, or a specification defect by changing the design.

Once you have identified the source of the defect, every artifact affected by a modification must be brought into compliance. If the defect is a result of an incorrect specification, the specification must be corrected to fulfill the requirements. The design must be changed to satisfy the specification, and the implementation must be changed to satisfy the design. Specification defects have more impact on the development process, and therefore are the most costly defects. Conversely, implementation defects have less impact on the development process, and are thus less costly.

To add an enhancement (i.e., a changed requirement) using the Object Creation Process, change the object's requirements, specification, design, and implementation as necessary. These changes will have a rippling effect into lower level objects. The breadth and depth of the objects affected by both enhancements and defects is a function of the size of the change or inconsistency.

Performance Enhancement

Making software run faster is an art that sometimes requires creative genius. There are, however, some generally useful rules of thumb:

- ❑ Implementation changes can increase performance by roughly a factor of two or three.
- ❑ Design changes can yield orders of magnitude performance improvements.
- ❑ Understand where an object is spending time before attempting to optimize the object.

The first step to enhancing software performance is to understand the magnitude of the required improvement. Changing the implementation can probably make the software run in half the time. Greater improvements will likely require design changes.

Enhancing a program's performance can be an emotionally charged event. Before redesigning the entire application, take time to understand what operations are consuming the majority of the execution time. The answer to this question is not always intuitive. Profiling tools can show exactly where an application is spending its time. Once you know where to focus, brainstorm ways to improve the performance.

Software Reuse

Potentially, software reuse can save both development time and resources. Unfortunately, three obstacles impede software reuse: environmental coupling, uncertain quality, and inaccessibility.

Developers can seldom simply copy software from one application to another because most software relies upon a specific context (i.e., global variables and procedures). Objects that rely heavily on their context are said to be tightly coupled to their environment and are difficult to reuse. Encapsulation reduces tight coupling. In turn, encapsulated objects are easier to successfully copy from one application to another.

Developers are often unwilling to reuse existing software because they are uncertain of its quality. Poorly documented objects, built by anonymous developers might prove to be riddled with defects. The Object

Creation Process artifacts serve as an "owner's manual" for the objects. These artifacts address quality and integrity problems by presenting the objects' requirements, specifications, designs, and regression tests along with the objects' source code. A developer wishing to reuse an object can verify the object's quality by running regression tests and comparing the results with the object's specification.

The last obstacle to reusable software is finding appropriate software. One of the first steps to increasing software reuse is to create a software depository. As developers add reusable software to the depository, the number of different classes can become unwieldy. If developers are to find software with a specific function, they must organize and catalog the software. The objects' specifications form the basis for this organization.

Project Planning and Development Metrics

Software development scheduling estimates have the reputation of being grossly inaccurate. Since development costs are directly proportional to development time, inaccuracies in estimating development schedules make development costs difficult to project.

Reliable estimates require more than pure guesswork. Since an object is the atomic building block of object-oriented-based software development,

Building a Wall

Imagine estimating the time it takes to build a brick wall. It's impossible to make an accurate estimate without knowing anything about the wall. However, knowing some important details about the wall makes it easier to produce a reasonably accurate estimate. For example, the brick wall is 6 feet high and 10 feet long. If bricks are roughly 4 inches high and 9 inches long, the wall will require approximately 234 bricks (60 square feet at 3.9 bricks per square foot) laid in 18 courses (18 courses at 4 inches/course is 6 feet). At the edges of the wall, every other brick is a half-size brick. Therefore, the wall will require 18 half-sized bricks, or nine bricks cut in half.

Because each brick laid represents a task of uniform size and complexity, you can easily and accurately estimate the time required to build the wall if you have an accurate estimate of the time needed to lay one brick. Someone

total development effort will be directly proportional to the number of objects the application contains. Early, accurate estimates of the number of objects in the application and the time required to develop an object enable the developer to accurately forecast development schedules.

The secret to accurate estimates is to create an accurate model of the project. The more accurately the model represents the process, the more accurate the estimate will be.

A good starting point for a development model is to assume that each object is of uniform size and complexity. Armed with this assumption, developers need only determine how long it takes to create an object and how many objects the application contains to accurately estimate total development effort.

Some may argue that this model does not reasonably represent the development process because of the differences in objects. Admittedly, some objects are very complex and require much more development effort, and other objects are very simple and require very little effort. Overall, though, these variations don't affect the accuracy of the estimate for two important reasons.

First, the adept use of abstraction in identifying objects will drastically limit the deviation in complexity between objects. A large difference in complexity between objects usually indicates a poor or incomplete

who has never laid bricks before might try putting two or three of them in place and timing themselves. If it takes 2 minutes to position a brick, it will probably take 7 hours and 48 minutes to build the wall.

Once you've started building the wall, you may discover the tasks aren't quite as uniform as you thought. For example, you might learn that bricks in the middle of a course only take 1 minute and 45 seconds to position, while bricks at the ends of a course take 4 minutes to place. (The bricks at the end must be carefully placed without the aid of a guide string.) Reducing the time it takes to position a brick to 1 minute 45 seconds changes the estimated time to build the wall to 6 hours and 50 minutes. However, adding time to place the end bricks increases the estimate to 7 hours and 29 minutes. Thus, the revised estimate remains very close to the original.

decomposition of the objects. As developers gain experience with abstraction, the level of object complexity becomes much more uniform.

Second, object complexity tends to even out. Within an application there may be objects that are slightly larger or more complex than others, but there are also some objects that are slightly simpler and smaller. These differences tend to offset each other with respect to estimating development effort.

Project planners must answer two questions in order to develop a project planning model:

- ❑ How many objects will the project require?
- ❑ How much effort will each phase of an object's development require?

To answer the first question, project planners must complete initial program requirements and specifications because it is impossible to accurately determine how many objects the project requires until the software's functions are well-defined.

Armed with the initial program specification, project planners can use *rapid decomposition* to determine the number of objects in the system. Rapid decomposition means quickly and informally proposing a design for the specified software. During rapid decomposition, planners work quickly from higher levels of abstraction to lower levels in a way that mimics the recursive requirements, specification, and design steps of the Object Creation Process. The intent is not to define a complete design; rapid decomposition quickly enumerates possible objects.

As an example, the rapid decomposition of the chess game took approximately five minutes. The decomposition amounted to reading through the specification and then scratching some object names on a note pad with a cursory explanation about the intended use of the object.

There are two rules to keep in mind when using rapid decomposition. First, work quickly. Do not allow the rapid decomposition effort to become stalled on a technical detail or a difference of opinion. When these stumbling blocks occur, make a quick decision and move on. It may be helpful to set a time limit for the rapid decomposition effort. Setting a time limit encourages you to keep moving.

The second rule is to not enforce any of the design decisions made during rapid decomposition. Rapid decomposition is used only to get a feel for the number of objects in a project. Enforcing design decisions made during rapid decomposition will cause the estimation effort to bog down and will impact the quality of the design.

Rapid decomposition is simply an intuitive "roller brush" design. The accuracy of rapid decomposition depends upon the level of expertise of the estimator and the level of complexity of the project. Estimators with strong design and decomposition skills will estimate relatively simple projects with ease. As the level of a project's complexity grows, there are more opportunities to make mistakes in estimation. Therefore, the amount of time required for rapid decomposition is proportional to the level of complexity of the project.

As developers learn more about the software project and as the actual software design emerges, project planners can reiterate rapid decomposition with greater accuracy. It is unreasonable to trust a project plan based on one single rapid decomposition early in the project. The project plan should be a living model of the anticipated project. The development effort will be easier to track if the model is updated frequently.

One approach to updating the model of the project plan is to schedule periodic rapid decomposition sessions. As the project's design emerges, it affects the rapid decomposition. The parts of the design that are complete serve as anchor points to yield greater accuracy during rapid decomposition. As the project proceeds, the number of objects identified by the design and the number of objects estimated by rapid prototyping will converge. Figure 8.0 shows how rapid decomposition estimates may converge with the actual design.

Note that this convergence occurs exclusively in the *design* phase of the project. If the design follows the method outlined by the Object Creation Process, the number of required objects should not change as a result of implementation or verification. Thus, planners can be certain of the number of objects in a project once all the objects are designed. In the example of the chess program, planners knew how many objects the project would contain when all the objects had been identified, specified, and designed (roughly 40 percent into the project). While the object count wasn't *fixed* until the design was finished, the object count was stable enough to produce highly accurate estimates once one-third of the objects had been designed (roughly 20 percent into the project).

Once a project-planner knows how many objects are required, he or she must find an answer for the second question: how long does it take to perform each phase of development for each object. The estimates of effort for each phase of object development will vary significantly (i.e., by as much as an order of magnitude) from one developer to another because of differences in training and experience.

For this reason, historical data (by developers) from previous projects is the most accurate basis for estimates of the effort required. If such data does not exist, it may be useful to measure a developer while building a prototypical object such as a linked list, stack, or binary tree.

Development metrics are most useful if they measure each development phase separately. Thus, before gathering development metrics, define exactly when one phase of development ends and the next one begins. The artifacts of the Object Creation Process help delineate development phases. For example, a complete external specification delineates the beginning of design. A crisp definition of the bounds of each development phase will give meaning to the development metrics. Once planners know how long it will take developers during each phase of an object's development and how many objects a project requires, planning and tracking the project is a straightforward process (see the spreadsheet in Figure 8.1). Project planners should adjust their estimates as more information becomes available to help them hone the object counts or phase metrics. Planners must ground their plans on a rational model of development. It is common for planners to build a development model only to find the total estimated effort unbelievable. Do not abandon the results of the model in favor of intuition. When it comes to estimating and planning development efforts, intuition can be very deceptive. Work

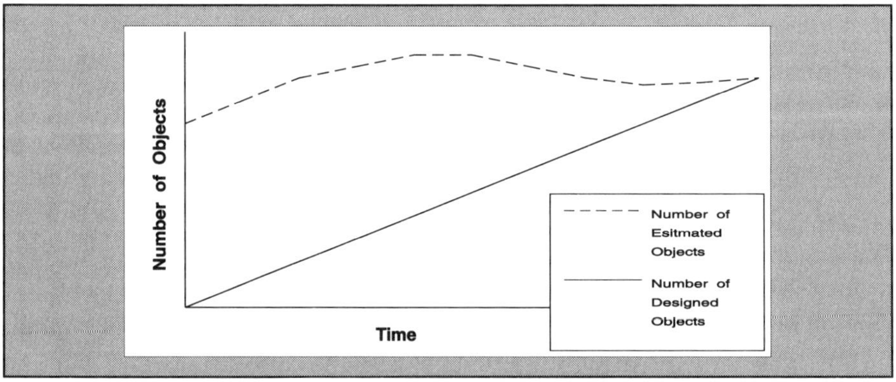

Figure 8.0 — Convergence of the Number of Objects Estimated and the Number of Objects Designed

Updating the Estimate

We like to keep our estimating model in a spreadsheet where each row of the spreadsheet represents an object, and each column represents a phase in the Object Creation Process. (Black-box and white-box verification phases are grouped together as the "Verification" phase.) The cells of the spreadsheet represent estimates of the amount of effort (in hours) of each phase of each object's development. Figure 8.1 shows the planning spreadsheet for the chess game example. Notice that the totals on the right side of the spreadsheet estimate the effort required to develop each object. The totals along the bottom show how much estimated effort each phase of the project requires. The number in the bottom-right corner of the spreadsheet represents the estimated total effort for the development of the chess game.

The spreadsheet helps us track progress by making changes more convenient and by providing an accurate picture of "where we are." We can easily update the list of objects as we identify new objects. As we complete each phase of an object's development, we can replace the estimated effort value with actual measured values. Dividing the total measured effort by the total estimated effort gives a measure of completion.

Object Name	Requirements	Specification	Deisgn	Implementation	Verification	Total
Chess	1.00	4.00	0.50	1.00	1.00	7.5
Game	0.25	0.50	0.50	1.00	1.00	3.25
Status	0.25	0.50	0.50	1.00	1.00	3.25
Screen	0.25	0.50	0.50	1.00	1.00	3.25
Board	0.25	0.50	0.50	1.00	1.00	3.25
Square	0.25	0.50	0.50	1.00	1.00	3.25
Coord	0.25	0.50	0.50	1.00	1.00	3.25
Team	0.25	0.50	0.50	1.00	1.00	3.25
Piece	0.25	0.50	0.50	1.00	1.00	3.25
King	0.25	0.50	0.50	1.00	1.00	3.25
Queen	0.25	0.50	0.50	1.00	1.00	3.25
Bishop	0.25	0.50	0.50	1.00	1.00	3.25
Knight	0.25	0.50	0.50	1.00	1.00	3.25
Castle	0.25	0.50	0.50	1.00	1.00	3.25
Pawn	0.25	0.50	0.50	1.00	1.00	3.25
Command	0.25	0.50	0.50	1.00	1.00	3.25
Total	4.75	11.50	8.00	16.00	16.00	56.25

(Times shown in hours.)

Figure 8.1 — Project Planning Model for the Chess Game Example

with the model to try to find any flaws or fallacies. Once a rational model exists, it will help plan and track the project with minimal disappointment and frustration.

Evolving the Object Creation Process

The Object Creation Process is an empirical process that has evolved over time. As new techniques proved useful, they were incorporated into the process. As useless traditions or obsolete mechanisms were discovered, they were removed. We believe the Object Creation Process should continue to evolve. Even so, this change must be carefully managed. Two considerations — understanding and timeliness — are particularly important.

First, before dramatically changing the Object Creation Process methodology, take time to understand the rationale for the methodology. Experiment with changes on a small scale before attempting wide-reaching changes with significant impact. Limited experiments can reveal the value of changes with minimal risk. Some methodological changes that seem good in theory (e.g., header files) can cause significant problems in practice.

Second, be careful about the timing of changes. Changing the methodology in midstream can be very dangerous. Changes in methodology may result in inconsistent development artifacts that are difficult to understand and maintain. Before making methodological changes, take time to project the effects and ramifications of the changes.

There are two modes of operation for software development. One mode is to use a methodology religiously to create software. The other mode is to experiment with changes, striving to continuously improve the methodology. Wise developers will balance the two modes, thus ensuring reliable progress on today's project while preparing for better results on tomorrow's.

Exercises

0. Discuss how to use the Object Creation Process with a third party application framework. Identify possible points of confusion and describe how to avoid them.
1. List five evaluation criteria for application frameworks.
2. Identify the two main reasons for performing software maintenance. Discuss the difference between these two reasons.
3. Outline the steps for defect maintenance and show how these steps relate to the Object Creation Process.
4. Describe the two dimensions of scheduling an application development effort. Tell how to assess the size of each dimension.
5. Discuss if and when the Object Creation Process should evolve.

```
ject(Requiremen
scribe the objects externals
tSpec = CreateSpec(Requiremen
the object until it passes
tests
all veri
Do {
    // Describe how th
    ObjectDesign = Design
    // Find or build subordina
    Subordinates = CreateSu
    // Implement this objec
    Code = CodeObject(O
    // Create boundary v
    TestSet = CreateBlac
    // Create condition
    WhiteBoxTest
    ject d
```

Appendix A

The Object Creation Process Algorithmic Summary

This appendix is an algorithmic summary of the entire Object Creation Process. The algorithmic summary can be a ready reference to quickly remind developers of the Object Creation Process steps.

Appendix A

```
StartingPoint() {
    // Identify the program requirements
    ProgramRequirements = IdentifyRequirements();
    // Create the program
    CreateObject(ProgramRequirements)
}

CreateObject(Requirements) {

    // Describe the objects externals
    ObjectSpec = CreateSpec(Requirements)
    // Work on the object until it passes all verification tests
    Do {
        // Describe how the object works
        ObjectDesign = DesignObject(ObjectSpec)
        // Find or build subordinates
        Subordinates = CreateSubObjects(ObjectDesign)
        // Implement this object
        Code = CodeObject(ObjectDesign, Subordinates)
        // Create boundary value analysis tests
        TestSet = CreateBlackBoxTests(ObjectSpec)
        // Create condition coverage tests
        AddWhiteBoxTests(ObjectDesign, TestSet)
    } While the object does not pass the tests (TestSet, Code)
}

CreateSubObjects(Design) {

    // Identify the objects within the design
    ObjectRequirementsList = IdentifyObject(Design)
    For each of the ObjectRequirements in the list...
        If no object exists that meets the requirements
            // Create the object
            CreateObject(ObjectRequirements)
}
```

Appendix A — *Cont'd*

```
IdentifyRequirements() {

    // Create an empty requirements set
    new Requirements
    // Identify the functions and preferences
    IdentifyFunctions(Requirements);
    // Identify the attributes
    AddAttributes(Requirements);
    // Identify the constraints
    AddConstraints(Requirements);
}

IdentifyFunctions(Requirements) {

    // Brainstorm functions
    While customers can identify an additional function...{
        // Add the function to the Requirements
        Requirements += FunctionDescription
    }
    // Scrutinize functions
    For each FunctionDescription in the Requirements... {
        // Eliminate unwanted functions
        If the FunctionDescription is redundant
        Or if the FunctionDescription is undesirable,
            // Delete the function from the Requirements
            Requirements -= FunctionDescription
        // Identify preferences
        If the FunctionDescription is really a preference
            Mark the FunctionDescription as a preference
    }
}

AddAttributes(Requirements) {
    // Assign attributes to each function
    For each FunctionDescription in the Requirements... {
        For each Attribute of the FunctionDescription... {
            // Modify the function with the Attribute
            FunctionDescription += Attribute
        }
    }
}
```

Appendix A — *Cont'd*

```
AddConstraints(Requirements) {
    // Set bounds to each attribute
    For each FunctionDescription in the Requirements... {
        For each Attribute of the FunctionDescription... {
            For each Constraint of the Attribute
                Attribute += Constraint
        }
    }
}

CreateSpec(Requirements) {
    // Create an empty set of specifications
    new Spec
    // Fulfill all the requirements
    While the specifications do not meet the requirements... {
        // Identify object specifications that meet the requirements
        MeetRequirements(Spec, Requirements)
        // Make sure the specifications are consistent
        MakeConsistent(Spec)
        // Make sure the specifications are complete
        MakeComplete(Spec, Requirements)
        // Make sure the specifications only describe user views
        MakeExternal(Spec)
        // Scrutinize any added value in the specifications
        ScrutinizeAddedValue(Spec, Requirements)
    }
    return Spec
}

MeetRequirements(Spec, Requirements) {
    // Consider each requirement
    For each statement in the requirements... {
        If the spec does not address the statement
            // Alter the spec to address the statement
            Spec += StatementSolution
    }
}
```

Appendix A — *Cont'd*

```
MakeConsistent(Spec) {
    // make sure all the specification items agree with each other
    For each item in the specification... {
        For each item in the specification... {
            If the items conflict {
                Make the items consistent
            }
        }
    }
}

MakeComplete(Spec, Requirements) {
    // Identify all dimensions of the object
    new DimensionList
    For each statement in the requirements... {
        For each dimension that the statement implies... {
            If the dimension is not yet in the dimension list
                DimensionList += Dimension
        }
    }
    // Try to think of any other interesting dimensions
    While the users can identify additional dimensions... {
            If the dimension is not yet in the dimension list
                DimensionList += Dimension
    }
    // Make sure the spec addresses all the dimensions
    For each dimension in the dimension list... {
        If the dimension is not described in the specification {
            Describe the dimension in the specification
        }
    }
    // Make sure all the specification items are complete
    For each item in the specification... {
        If the item is not described completely
            ItemDescription += missing item characteristics
    }
}
```

Appendix A — *Cont'd*

```
MakeExternal(Spec) {
    // Make sure the specifications only discuss user perspectives
    For each item in the specification... {
        If the item describes the object's internals
            // Remove the item
            Spec -= item
    }
}

ScrutinizeAddedValue(Spec, Requirements) {
    // Identify unfounded specification items
    new AddedValueList
    For each item in the specification... {
        // Look through all the requirements
        For each statement in the requirements... {
            If the statement relates to the item {
                The item has foundation in the statement
            }
        }
        // If no statements related to the item
        If the item has no foundation {
            // Add the item to the added value list
                AddedValueList += item
        }
    }
    // Consider each added value item
    For each item in the added value list... {
        Determine the cost of keeping the item
        Determine the value of the item
        If nobody will pay for the item {
            Spec -= item
        }
    }
}
DesignObject(ObjectSpec) {
    // Describe the specified object in terms of its subordinates
    PseudoCode = DescribeHowObjectWorks(ObjectSpec);
    // Circle the noun phrases
    IdentifySubordinateObjects(PseudoCode);
    // Underline the verb phases
    IdentifySubordinateMethods(PseudoCode);
```

Appendix A — *Cont'd*

```
      // List the subordinate objects and methods
      CreateSubordinateRequirements(PseudoCode);
      // The PseudoCode is the design artifact
      Return PseudoCode
}

DescribeHowObjectWorks(ObjectSpec) {
      Until all review issues are resolved... {
            While the PseudoCode does not tell how the object works and
                  the PseudoCode is long (> 10 lines) and
                  the PseudoCode has too much indentation... {
                  Edit the PseudoCode
            }
            Review the PseudoCode
      }
}

IdentifySubordinateObjects(PseudoCode) {
      For each line in the PseudoCode... {
            Identify the noun phase of the line
      }
}

IdentifySubordinateMethods(PseudoCode) {
      For each line in the PseudoCode... {
            Identify the verb phrase of the line
      }
}

CreateSubordinateRequirements(PseudoCode) {
      For each line in the PseudoCode... {
            If the noun phrase has not yet been seen
                  Add the noun phase to the list of subordinate objects
            If the verb phrase has not yet been seen
                  Add the verb phase to the list of methods
                        associated with the object
      }
}
```

Appendix A — *Cont'd*

```
Code      CodeObject(ObjectDesign, Subordinates) {

          // Create a new source code file
          SourceFile = new file;
          Add magic number data members to the class definition

          TranslateDesign(SourceFile, ObjectDesign, Subordinates);

          AddClassInvariant(SourceFile);
          CheckParameter(SourceFile);
          CheckLoops(SourceFile);
          If the SourceFile contains C++,
                AddC++Features(SourceFile);

          Return SourceFile
}


TranslateDesign(Source, Design, Subordinates) {

          For each method in the design... {
                Create an empty method body
                For each design line in the method... {
                      Make a comment of the design line
                      Create source lines to implement the design line
                }
          }
}

AddClassInvariant(Source) {

          Create an invariant method
          For each data member of the class {
                Add assertions to the invariant to bound the member's values
          }
          Add the magic number assertion
```

Appendix A — *Cont'd*

```
    For each method in the source... {
        If the method is a constructor,
            Add code to turn on the magic number
            Add code to check invariant at the end of the method
        Otherwise if the method is a destructor,
            Add code to check invariant at the beginning of method
            Add code to turn off magic at the end of the method
        Otherwise
            Add code to check invariant at the beginning of method
    }
}

CheckParameter(Source) {

    For each method in the source... {
        For each parameter of the method... {
            add assertions to bound the parameter's values
        }
    }
}

CheckLoops(Source) {
    For each method in the source... {
        For each loop in the method... {
            Add assertions to loop describing the loop invariants
        }
    }
}

AddC++Features(Source) {

    For each constant parameter in the source... {
        Add the const declarative to the parameter declaration
    }
    For each non-modifying method... {
        add the const declarative to the method declaration
    }
    For each pure virtual function... {
        Add the "=0" to the function declaration
    }
}
```

Appendix A — *Cont'd*

```
CreateBlackBoxTests(TestSet) {
    For each of the objects functions... {
        For each parameter of the function... {
            Identify the groups of input
            For each group of input... {
                Select values on or near the boundaries
                // Add tests for the boundary values
                TestSet += boundary value tests
            }
            Identify invalid values for the parameter
            // Add tests for the invalid values
            TestSet += invalid value tests
        }
        TestSet += case
    }
    // Test state transitions and concurrency
    For each externally visible state of the function... {
        Call this state the source state
        For each externally visible state of the function... {
            Call this state the destination state
            // Add state transition tests
            Identify functions to move from source to destination
            TestSet += function sequence tests
            // Add concurrency tests
            Identify tests with an object in each state
            TestSet += concurrency tests
        }
    }
    // Review the verification plan
    For each statement/idea in the object's specification {
        StatementSupported = FALSE
        For each test idea in the verification plan... {
            If the test idea verifies the statement
                StatementSupported = TRUE;
        }
        If the Statement is not supported {
            // Add tests to verify the statement
            TestSet += tests to verify the statement
        }
    }
}
```

Appendix A — *Cont'd*

```
DoesPassTest(TestSet) {
    // Build the verification driver
    For each of the object's input stimulus... {
        If the driver does not support the stimulus
            Make sure the driver supports access to the stimulus
    }
    For each of the object's outputs... {
        If the driver does not represent the output
            Make sure the driver represents the output
    }
    // Build the verification cases and benchmarks
    PassTest = TRUE
    For each test in the test set... {
        Run the driver
            Create the recorded input to implement the test
            Capture the output from the driver
        If the captured output is correct
            Make the captured output the verification benchmark
        Otherwise captured output is not correct
            PassTest = FALSE
    }
    return PassTest
}

AddWhiteBoxTests(TestSet) {
    For each method in the class... {
        For condition in the method... {
            If no existing tests force a true condition,
                Create a true condition test
            If no existing tests force a false condition,
                Create a false condition test
        }
    }
}
```

ject(Requirements,
scribe the objects externals
tSpec = CreateSpec(Requiremen
the object until it passes
all veri[illegible] the [illegible] tests
Do {
// Describe how th[illegible]
ObjectDesign = DesignO[illegible]
// Find or build subordina
Subordinates = CreateSu
// Implement this objec
Code = CodeObject(O
// Create boundary v
TestSet = CreateBlac
// Create condition
[illegible]WhiteBoxTes
[illegible]ct d

Appendix B

The Example Chess Game Source Code

The following is a comprehensive listing of the source code for the example chess game. The listing includes the production source code as well as embedded design comments and conditionally compilable verification drivers.

Appendix B

```
*********************************************************************************
//
//    board.hpp - chess game board class
//

class Board;

#ifndef      BOARD_HPP
#define      BOARD_HPP

#include "global.hpp"
#include "magic.hpp"
#include "square.hpp"
#include "screen.hpp"

class Piece;

const BoardRows = 8;
const BoardCols = 8;
const BoardSquares = BoardRows*BoardCols;

class Board  {
      MAGIC                           // Magic number macro
      Square *squares[BoardRows][BoardCols];   // Squares' handles
      Screen &screen;                 // Screen handle
      // Assert the class invariants
      void   Invariant() const;
public:
      // Create a chess playing board
      Board(
             Screen&                  // Display screen handle
      );
      // Destroy the chess playing board
      ~Board();
      // Get the handle of the piece at the position
      Piece  *GetPiece(
             const Coord&             // The piece's position on the board
      ) const;
      // Place a piece on the board
      void   PlacePiece(
             Piece*,                  // Piece to place on the board
             const Coord&             // Position of placed piece
      );
      // Remove a piece from the square (return the piece's handle)
      Piece  *RemovePiece(
             const Coord&             // Location of piece to remove
      );
      // Find the location of a specified piece (return the containing square)
      Square *FindPiece(
             const Piece*             // The piece for which to search
      );
      // Try moving the piece to a new square on the board (return the piece
      //     currently at the specified location
      Piece  *TryPiece(
             const Coord&,            // Location to try
             Piece*                   // The piece to try at the location
      );
      // Restore the piece to its original square
```

Appendix B — *Cont'd*

```
      void   UntryPiece(
             const Coord&,          // The location to untry
             Piece*                 // The original piece to restore
      );
      // Select a position (return FALSE if the user quits)
      BOOLEAN SelectPosition(
             Square**               // The (returned) selected square
      ) const;
      // Determine if there are pieces between the source and destination
      BOOLEAN PiecesBetween(
             const Coord&,          // The source location
             const Coord&           // The destination location
      ) const;
      // Determine if the destination is a valid position
      BOOLEAN IsValidDestination(
             const BOOLEAN,         // True if the target piece is white
             const Coord&           // The target location
      ) const;
      // Clean up the board
      void   CleanUp();
      // Get the square associated with the row and column
      Square *GetSquare(
             const int,             // Row number
             const int              // Column number
      ) const;
      // Get the square associated with the coordinate
      Square *GetSquare(
             const Coord&           // Target coordinate
      ) const;
};

// Class for iterating through the squares on a board
class BoardIterator {
      MAGIC              // Magic number macro
      Board  &board;     // Board handle
      int    row;        // Current row
      int    col;        // Current column
      int    SquareNo;   // The number of squares iterated
      // Assert the class invariants
      void   Invariant() const;
public:
      // Create a square iterator (For each square on the board...)
      BoardIterator(
             Board&,                      // Board for iteration
             BOOLEAN UseRandom = FALSE    // Start at a random location
      );
      ~BoardIterator();
      // Get the next square
      Square*      operator++(int);
};

#endif      // BOARD_HPP
```

Appendix B — *Cont'd*

```
*********************************************************************************

//
//    board.cpp - chess game board class
//

#include <stdlib.h>
#include "board.hpp"
#include "team.hpp"
#include "command.hpp"

char  Board::MagicValue = '\0';

// Assert the class invariants
inline      void   Board::Invariant() const {
      // Check the magic number
      MagicCheck();
}

//* Create the board
Board::Board(Screen &s): screen(s) {

      MagicOn();
      //* Set the initial color to black
      BOOLEAN IsWhite = FALSE;
      //* For each row on the board...
      for (int y = 0; y < BoardRows; y++) {
             //* For each column in the row...
             for (int x = 0; x < BoardCols; x++) {
                    //* Create the square
                    squares[y][x] = new Square(IsWhite, s, Coord(y,x));
                    assert(squares[y][x] != NULL);
                    // Alternate the color
                    IsWhite = !IsWhite;
             }
             IsWhite = !IsWhite;
      }
      Invariant();
}

//* Destroy the board
Board::~Board() {

      Invariant();
      //* For each position on the board...
      BoardIterator I(*this);
      Square *S;
      while ((S = I++) != NULL) {
             //* Destroy the square
             delete S;
      }
      MagicOff();
}
```

Appendix B — *Cont'd*

```
//* Get the handle of the piece at the position
Piece *Board::GetPiece(const Coord &Location) const {

      Invariant();
      return GetSquare(Location)->GetPiece();
}

//* Place a piece on the board
void  Board::PlacePiece(Piece *piece, const Coord &Location) {

      Invariant();
      GetSquare(Location)->PlacePiece(piece);
}

//* Remove a piece from the square
Piece *Board::RemovePiece(const Coord &Location) {

      Invariant();
      Square *S = GetSquare(Location);
      return(S->GetPiece() == NULL)? NULL: S->RemovePiece();
}

//* Find the location of a specified piece
Square       *Board::FindPiece(const Piece *p) {

      Invariant();
      assert(p != NULL);
      Square *Found = NULL;

      //* For each position on the board...
      BoardIterator I(*this);
      Square *S;
      while (((S = I++) != NULL) && (Found == NULL)) {
            //* If this is the piece, return the piece's square
            if (S->GetPiece() == p) Found = S;
      }
      return Found;
}

//* Try moving the piece to a new square on the board
Piece *Board::TryPiece(const Coord &Location, Piece *p) {

      Invariant();
      return GetSquare(Location)->TryPiece(p);
}

//* Restore the piece to its original square
void  Board::UntryPiece(const Coord &Location, Piece *p) {

      Invariant();
      GetSquare(Location)->UntryPiece(p);
}

//* Select a position
BOOLEAN Board::SelectPosition(Square **S) const {

      Invariant();
      assert(S != NULL);
```

Appendix B — *Cont'd*

```
        Coord  Position((*S)->GetCoord());
        //* While not done selecting and not quitting
        BOOLEAN Quitting = FALSE;
        BOOLEAN Done = FALSE;
        UCommand c(screen);
        while ((!Done) && (!Quitting)) {
               //* Blink the current square as a prompt
               Square *Sqr = GetSquare(Position);
               Sqr->Blink();
               //* Get a command from the terminal
               c.Get();
               //* Unblink the current square
               Sqr->Unblink();

               //* Move the blinking square according to the command
               if (c.IsRightArrow()) {
                      Position.SetCol(Position.Col()+1);
                      if (Position.Col() >= BoardCols) {
                           Position.SetCol(0);
                      }
               } else if (c.IsLeftArrow()) {
                      Position.SetCol(Position.Col()-1);
                      if (Position.Col() < 0) {
                           Position.SetCol(BoardCols-1);
                      }
               } else if (c.IsUpArrow()) {
                      Position.SetRow(Position.Row()-1);
                      if (Position.Row() < 0) {
                           Position.SetRow(BoardRows-1);
                      }
               } else if (c.IsDownArrow()) {
                      Position.SetRow(Position.Row()+1);
                      if (Position.Row() >= BoardRows) {
                           Position.SetRow(0);
                      }
               } else if (c.IsQuit()) {
                      Quitting = TRUE;
               } else if (c.IsEnter()) {
                      Done = TRUE;
               } else {
                      screen.Beep();
               }
        }

        (*S) = GetSquare(Position);
        assert((*S) != NULL);
        return Quitting;
}

//* Determine if there are pieces between the source and destination
BOOLEAN Board::PiecesBetween(const Coord &Src, const Coord &Dest)
const {

        Invariant();
        int    row;
        int    col;

        BOOLEAN Between = FALSE;
```

Appendix B — *Cont'd*

```
	//* Calculate the horizontal movement
	int Horz = (Src.Col() == Dest.Col())? 0: (Src.Col() < Dest.Col())?1:-1;
	//* Calculate the vertical movement
	int Vert = (Src.Row() == Dest.Row())? 0: (Src.Row() < Dest.Row())?1:-1;
	//* For each position between the start and end...
	for (col = Src.Col() + Horz, row = Src.Row() + Vert;
		(!Between) && !((row == Dest.Row()) && (col == Dest.Col()));
		col += Horz, row += Vert) {
		//* If there is a piece at the location,
		Coord  Position(row, col);
		if (GetPiece(Position) != NULL) {
			//* There are pieces between the source and destination
			Between = TRUE;
		}
	}
	return Between;
}

//* Determine if the destination is a valid position
BOOLEAN Board::IsValidDestination(const BOOLEAN white,
					const Coord &Location)
const {

	Invariant();
	Piece *p = GetSquare(Location)->GetPiece();
	return((p == NULL) || !p->IsSameColor(white));
}

//* Clean up the board
void  Board::CleanUp() {

	Invariant();
	//* For each square on the board...
	BoardIterator I(*this);
	Square *S;
	while ((S = I++) != NULL) {
		//* Remove any piece from the square
		RemovePiece(S->GetCoord());
	}
}

//* Get the square associated with the row and column
Square		*Board::GetSquare(const int row, const int col) const {

	Invariant();
	assert((row >= 0) && (row < BoardRows));
	assert((col >= 0) && (col < BoardCols));
	Square *S = squares[row][col];
	assert(S != NULL);
	return S;
}

//* Get the square associated with the coordinate
Square		*Board::GetSquare(const Coord &Location) const {

	Invariant();
	return GetSquare(Location.Row(), Location.Col());
}
```

Appendix B — *Cont'd*

```
char  BoardIterator::MagicValue = '\0';

// Assert the class invariants
inline       void   BoardIterator::Invariant() const {
      // Check the magic number
      MagicCheck();
      assert(SquareNo >= 0);
      assert(SquareNo <= BoardSquares+1);
      assert(row >= 0);
      assert(row < BoardRows);
      assert(col >= 0);
      assert(col < BoardCols);
}

//* Create a square iterator (For each square on the board...)
BoardIterator::BoardIterator(Board &b, BOOLEAN UseRandom):
      board(b),
      row(UseRandom? rand() % BoardRows: 0),
      col(UseRandom? rand() % BoardCols: 0),
      SquareNo(0)
{
      MagicOn();
      Invariant();
}

//* Destroy the square iterator
BoardIterator::~BoardIterator() {
      Invariant();
      MagicOff();
}

//* Get the next square
Square*      BoardIterator::operator ++ (int) {

      Invariant();
      Square *S = (SquareNo++ < BoardSquares)?
             board.GetSquare(row++, col): NULL;
      if (row >= BoardRows) {
             row = 0;
             col++;
             if (col >= BoardCols) col = 0;
      }
      return S;
}


#ifdef       DRIVER

#include <stdio.h>
#include <stdlib.h>
#include "drivtool.hpp"

Screen       Scr;
Status       Sta(Scr);
Board        board(Scr);
Team         black(FALSE, board, Sta);
Team         white(TRUE, board, Sta);
```

Appendix B — *Cont'd*

```
Piece *NewPiece(FILE *Record) {

      Piece  *P;
      BOOLEAN White = GetChar("White or Black (W/B) => ", Record) == 'W';
      char c = GetChar("Piece Type: King Queen Bishop kNight Castle Pawn => ",
                        Record);

      switch (c) {
      case 'K':
            P = new King(White?&white:&black, White, board);
            break;
      case 'Q':
            P = new Queen(White?&white:&black, White, board);
            break;
      case 'B':
            P = new Bishop(White?&white:&black, White, board);
            break;
      case 'N':
            P = new Knight(White?&white:&black, White, board);
            break;
      case 'C':
            P = new Castle(White?&white:&black, White, board);
            break;
      default:
            P = new Pawn(White?&white:&black, White, board);
            break;
      }
      return P;
}

void GetCoord(char *name, Coord &c, FILE *Record) {
      char buffer[80];
      sprintf(buffer, "Enter %s row => ", name);
      c.SetRow(GetInt(buffer, Record));
      sprintf(buffer, "Enter %s column => ", name);
      c.SetCol(GetInt(buffer, Record));
}

const NHandles = 10;

// Test driver
void main(int argc, char *argv[]) {

      Board  *Hans[NHandles];
      for (int i = 0; i < NHandles; i++) Hans[i] = NULL;
      FILE   *Record;

      // If there is an input recording file,
      if (argc == 2) {
            // Open the file
            Record = fopen(argv[1],"w");
      } else {
            // Otherwise mark the file as not open
            Record = NULL;
      }
```

Appendix B — *Cont'd*

```
Coord          Src;
Coord          Dst;
Piece          *p;
Square         *Sqr;
BOOLEAN Quit;
Piece          *P;
int     Handle = 0;
// Drive until the user is done
for (int Done = 0; !Done; ) {
       switch (GetChar("Board => ", Record)) {
       case 'B':   // Board()
              Hans[Handle] = new Board(Scr);
              break;
       case 'C':   // CleanUp()
              Hans[Handle]->CleanUp();
              break;
       case 'E':   // PiecesBetween()
              GetCoord("Source", Src, Record);
              GetCoord("Destination", Dst, Record);
              printf("There are %spieces between\n",
                   Hans[Handle]->PiecesBetween(Src, Dst)?
                   "": "no ");
              break;
       case 'F':   // FindPiece()
              printf("using the last referenced piece...\n");
              Sqr = Hans[Handle]->FindPiece(P);
              if (Sqr == NULL) {
                   printf("Piece not found\n");
              } else {
                   Dst = Sqr->GetCoord();
                   printf("Found at row %d, column %d\n",
                        Dst.Row(), Dst.Col());
              }
              break;
       case 'G':   // GetPiece()
              GetCoord("Piece's", Src, Record);
              P = Hans[Handle]->GetPiece(Src);
              if (P == NULL) {
                   printf("No piece found\n");
              } else {
                   printf("Found a %s %s\n",
                        P->IsWhite()? "White": "Black",
                        P->Name());
              }
              break;
       case 'H':   // Handle
              printf("The current handle is %d\n", Handle);
              Handle = GetInt("Enter the new handle => ", Record);
              printf("Now the handle is %d\n", Handle);
              break;
       case 'I':   // IsValidDestination()
              BOOLEAN White = GetChar("Target (W/B) => ",
                        Record) == 'W';
              GetCoord("Target's", Src, Record);
              printf("The target is %svalid\n",
                   Hans[Handle]->IsValidDestination(White, Src)?
                        "": "not ");
              break;
```

Appendix B — *Cont'd*

```
case 'P':   // PlacePiece()
        P = NewPiece(Record);
        GetCoord("Destination", Dst, Record);
        Hans[Handle]->PlacePiece(P, Dst);
        break;
case 'Q':   // Quit
        Done = 1;
        break;
case 'R':   // RemovePiece()
        GetCoord("Source", Src, Record);
        P = Hans[Handle]->RemovePiece(Src);
        if (P != NULL) {
            printf("Piece is a %s %s\n",
            P->IsWhite()?"white":"black", P->Name());
        }
        if (GetChar("Delete Piece? => ", Record) == 'Y') {
            delete P;
        }
        break;
case 'S':   // SelectPosition()
        Quit = Hans[Handle]->SelectPosition(&Sqr);
        if (Quit) {
            printf("The user quit\n");
        } else {
            Dst = Sqr->GetCoord();
            printf("The square is row %d, column %d\n",
                Dst.Row(), Dst.Col());
        }
        break;
case 'T':   // TryPiece()
        GetCoord("Source", Src, Record);
        P = NewPiece(Record);
        P = Hans[Handle]->TryPiece(Src, P);
        if (P != NULL) {
            printf("Piece is a %s %s\n",
            P->IsWhite()?"white":"black", P->Name());
        }
        break;
case 'U':   // UntryPiece()
        printf("Restoring the last used piece\n");
        GetCoord("Source", Src, Record);
        Hans[Handle]->TryPiece(Src, P);
        if (P != NULL) {
            printf("Piece is a %s %s\n",
            P->IsWhite()?"white":"black", P->Name());
        }
        break;
case '~':   // ~Board()
        delete Hans[Handle];
        break;
case '1':   // GetSquare(r, c)
        int R = GetInt("Enter the row => ", Record);
        int C = GetInt("Enter the column => ", Record);
        Sqr = Hans[Handle]->GetSquare(R, C);
        Dst = Sqr->GetCoord();
        printf("The square is row %d, column %d\n",
            Dst.Row(), Dst.Col());
        break;
```

Appendix B — *Cont'd*

```
            case '2':   // GetSquare(coord)
                  GetCoord("Source", Src, Record);
                  Sqr = Hans[Handle]->GetSquare(Src);
                  Dst = Sqr->GetCoord();
                  printf("The square is row %d, column %d\n",
                      Dst.Row(), Dst.Col());
                  break;
            default:    // Help
                  printf("Valid commands are...\n");
                  printf("\tB - Board (create a board)\n");
                  printf("\tC - CleanUp (clean up board)\n");
                  printf("\tE - PiecesBetween (pieces between?)\n");
                  printf("\tF - FindPiece (find the piece)\n");
                  printf("\tG - GetPiece (get the piece)\n");
                  printf("\tH - Handle (change the handle)\n");
                  printf("\tI - IsValidDestination (move ok?)\n");
                  printf("\tP - PlacePiece (place the piece)\n");
                  printf("\tQ - Quit (quit the driver)\n");
                  printf("\tR - RemovePiece (remove the piece)\n");
                  printf("\tS - SelectPosition (select a position)\n");
                  printf("\tT - TryPiece (try a piece)\n");
                  printf("\tU - UntryPiece (untry a piece)\n");
                  printf("\t~ - Destroy (destroy the board)\n");
                  printf("\t1 - GetSquare(r,c) (get square handle)\n");
                  printf("\t2 - GetSquare(coord) (get square handle)\n");
                  break;
            }
      }

      // If the user is recording input,
      if (Record != NULL) {
            // Close the recording file
            fclose(Record);
      }
}

#endif        //DRIVER

********************************************************************************

//
//    bishop.hpp - the bishop chess piece class
//

class         Bishop;

#ifndef       BISHOP_HPP
#define       BISHOP_HPP

#include "global.hpp"
#include "magic.hpp"
#include "piece.hpp"
#include "team.hpp"
#include "board.hpp"
```

Appendix B — *Cont'd*

```
class       Bishop:public Piece    {
      MAGIC             // Magic number macro
      Board  &board;    // Board handle
      // Assert the class invariants
      void   Invariant() const;
public:
      // Create a bishop
      Bishop(
             Team*,      // Bishop's team handle
             BOOLEAN,    // Color indicator (true if white)
             Board&      // Playing board handle
      );
      // Destroy the bishop
      virtual ~Bishop();
      // Return the bishop's name
      char   *Name() const;
      // Return the bishop's value
      int    Value() const;
      // Return that this is a bishop
      PieceType    GetType() const;
      // Determine if the proposed move is legal
      BOOLEAN IsLegalMove(
             const Coord&,    // Source location
             const Coord&     // Destination location
      ) const;
};

#endif      // BISHOP_HPP

******************************************************************************

//
//    bishop.cpp - the chess game bishop piece
//

#include "bishop.hpp"

char        Bishop::MagicValue = '\0';

// Assert the class invariants
inline      void   Bishop::Invariant() const {
      // Check the magic number
      MagicCheck();
}

//* Create a bishop
Bishop::Bishop(Team *t, BOOLEAN white, Board &b):board(b), Piece(t, white) {
      MagicOn();
      Invariant();
}

//* Destroy the bishop
Bishop::~Bishop() {
      Invariant();
      MagicOff();
}
```

Appendix B — *Cont'd*

```
//* Return the name of the piece
char  *Bishop::Name() const {

      Invariant();
      return("Bishop");
}

//* Return the value of this type of piece
int   Bishop::Value() const {

      Invariant();
      return(5);
}

//* Return the type of the piece
PieceType    Bishop::GetType() const {

      Invariant();
      return(BISHOP);
}

//* Determine if this is a legal move
BOOLEAN Bishop::IsLegalMove(const Coord &src, const Coord &dest) const
{

      Invariant();
      //* The move is legal if -
      return(
             //* The source is not the destination and
             (src != dest) &&
             //* The move is diagonal and
             (
                    ((src.Col()-dest.Col()) == (src.Row()-dest.Row())) ||
                    ((src.Col()-dest.Col()) == -(src.Row()-dest.Row()))
             ) &&
             //* There is no piece between the source and destination and
             (!board.PiecesBetween(src, dest)) &&
             //* The destination does not contain the same team and
             (board.IsValidDestination(IsWhite(), dest)) &&
             //* The move does not cause (self-inflicted) checkmate
             (!CausesCheckmate(src, dest))
      );
}

*******************************************************************************
//
//    castle.hpp - the castle chess piece class
//
class       Castle;

#ifndef     CASTLE_HPP
#define     CASTLE_HPP

#include "global.hpp"
#include "magic.hpp"
#include "piece.hpp"
#include "team.hpp"
#include "board.hpp"
```

Appendix B — *Cont'd*

```
class Castle:public Piece     {
      MAGIC              // Magic number macro
      Board  &board;     // Board handle
      // Assert the class invariants
      void   Invariant() const;
public:
      // Create a castle
      Castle(
             Team*,      // Castle's team handle
             BOOLEAN,    // Color indicator (true if white)
             Board&      // Playing board handle
      );
      // Destroy the castle
      virtual        ~Castle();
      // Return the castle's name
      char           *Name() const;
      // Return the castle's value
      int            Value() const;
      // Return that this is a castle
      PieceType      GetType() const;
      // Determine if the proposed move is legal
      BOOLEAN IsLegalMove(
             const  Coord&,  // Source location
             const  Coord&   // Destination location
      ) const;
};

#endif       // CASTLE_HPP

******************************************************************************

//
//    castle.cpp - the chess game castle piece
//

#include "castle.hpp"

char  Castle::MagicValue = '\0';

// Assert the class invariants
inline       void   Castle::Invariant() const {
      // Check the magic number
      MagicCheck();
}

//* Create a castle
Castle::Castle(Team *t, BOOLEAN white, Board &b): board(b), Piece(t, white) {

      MagicOn();
      Invariant();
}

//* Destroy the castle
Castle::~Castle() {
      Invariant();
      MagicOff();
}
```

Appendix B — *Cont'd*

```
//* Return the name of the piece
char  *Castle::Name() const {

      Invariant();
      return("Castle");
}

//* Return the value of this type of piece
int   Castle::Value() const {

      Invariant();
      return(2);
}

//* Return the type of the piece
PieceType   Castle::GetType() const {

      Invariant();
      return(CASTLE);
}

//* Determine if this is a legal move
BOOLEAN Castle::IsLegalMove(const Coord &src, const Coord &dest) const
{

      Invariant();
      //* The move is legal if -
      return(
             //* The source is not the destination and
             (src != dest) &&
             //* The move is
             (
                    //* Horizontal or
                    (src.Row() == dest.Row()) ||
                    //* Vertical
                    (src.Col() == dest.Col())
             //* And
             ) &&
             //* There is no piece between the source and destination and
             (!board.PiecesBetween(src, dest)) &&
             //* The destination does not contain the same team and
             (board.IsValidDestination(IsWhite(), dest)) &&
             //* The move does not cause (self-inflicted) checkmate
             (!CausesCheckmate(src, dest))
      );
}

*******************************************************************************

//
//    chess.cpp - main for the chess game example
//

#include "global.hpp"
#include "screen.hpp"
#include "status.hpp"
#include "game.hpp"
```

Appendix B — *Cont'd*

```
//* Chess game main entry point
void  main() {

      //* Initialize the screen
      Screen screen;
      //* Create the user interaction line
      Status status(screen);
      //* Create the game
      Game   game(screen, status);
      BOOLEAN Quitting;
      BOOLEAN PlayAgain;
      Winner Result;

      //* Until the user does not want to play again or quitting...
      do {
             //* Initialize the game
             game.Initialize();
             //* Play the game
             Quitting = game.Play(Result);
             //* If the user does not want to quit,
             if (!Quitting) {
                    //* Determine if the user wants to play again
                    PlayAgain = status.PlayAgain(Result);
             }
             //* Clean up the game
             game.CleanUp();
      } while (PlayAgain && !Quitting);
}

********************************************************************************

//
//    command.hpp - user interaction command
//

#ifndef      COMMAND_HPP
#define      COMMAND_HPP

#include "global.hpp"
#include "magic.hpp"
#include "screen.hpp"

// Interactive user command class
class        UCommand    {
      MAGIC                // Magic number macro
      Screen  &screen;
      int     c1;
      int     c2;
      // Assert the class invariants
      void    Invariant() const;
public:
      // Create a command
      UCommand(Screen&);
      // Destroy the command
      ~UCommand();
      // Get the command from the user
      void    Get();
      // Determine if the command is an up arrow
```

Appendix B — *Cont'd*

```
      BOOLEAN IsUpArrow() const;
      // Determine if the command is a down arrow
      BOOLEAN IsDownArrow() const;
      // Determine if the command is a left arrow
      BOOLEAN IsLeftArrow() const;
      // Determine if the command is a right arrow
      BOOLEAN IsRightArrow() const;
      // Determine if the command is an arrow
      BOOLEAN IsArrow() const;
      // Determine if the command is a quit command
      BOOLEAN IsQuit() const;
      // Determine if the command is a white selection command
      BOOLEAN       IsWhite() const;
      // Determine if the command is a black selection command
      BOOLEAN       IsBlack() const;
      // Determine if the command is a yes command
      BOOLEAN IsYes() const;
      // Determine if the command is a no command
      BOOLEAN IsNo() const;
      // Determine if the command is an enter command
      BOOLEAN IsEnter() const;
};
#endif       // COMMAND_HPP
*******************************************************************************
//
//    command.cpp - user interaction command class
//

#include "command.hpp"

char         UCommand::MagicValue = '\0';

// Assert the class invariants
inline       void   UCommand::Invariant() const {
      // Check the magic number
      MagicCheck();
}

//* Create a command
UCommand::UCommand(
      Screen &scr
): screen(scr), c1(0), c2(0) {
      MagicOn();
      Invariant();
}

//* Destroy the command
UCommand::~UCommand() {
      Invariant();
      MagicOff();
}

//* Create a command
void         UCommand::Get() {
      Invariant();
      c1 = screen.GetCh();
      c2 = (c1 == 0)? screen.GetCh(): 0;
}
```

Appendix B — *Cont'd*

```
//* Determine if the command is an up arrow
BOOLEAN UCommand::IsUpArrow() const {
      Invariant();
      return (c1 == 0) && (c2 == 0x48);
}

//* Determine if the command is a down arrow
BOOLEAN UCommand::IsDownArrow() const {
      Invariant();
      return (c1 == 0) && (c2 == 0x50);
}

//* Determine if the command is a left arrow
BOOLEAN UCommand::IsLeftArrow() const {
      Invariant();
      return (c1 == 0) && (c2 == 0x4B);
}

//* Determine if the command is a right arrow
BOOLEAN UCommand::IsRightArrow() const {
      Invariant();
      return (c1 == 0) && (c2 == 0x4D);
}

//* Determine if the command is an arrow
BOOLEAN UCommand::IsArrow() const {
      Invariant();
      return IsUpArrow() || IsDownArrow() || IsLeftArrow() || IsRightArrow();
}

//* Determine if the command is a quit command
BOOLEAN UCommand::IsQuit() const {
      Invariant();
      return (c1 == 'q') || (c1 == 'Q');
}

//* Determine if the command is a white selection command
BOOLEAN UCommand::IsWhite() const {
      Invariant();
      return (c1 == 'w') || (c1 == 'W');
}

//* Determine if the command is a black selection command
BOOLEAN      UCommand::IsBlack() const {
      Invariant();
      return (c1 == 'b') || (c1 == 'B');
}

//* Determine if the command is a yes command
BOOLEAN UCommand::IsYes() const {
      Invariant();
      return (c1 == 'y') || (c1 == 'Y');
}

//* Determine if the command is a no command
BOOLEAN UCommand::IsNo() const {
      Invariant();
      return (c1 == 'n') || (c1 == 'N');
}
```

Appendix B — *Cont'd*

```
//* Determine if the command is an enter command
BOOLEAN UCommand::IsEnter() const {
      Invariant();
      return (c1 == '\n') || (c1 == '\r');
}

#ifdef      DRIVER

#include <stdio.h>
#include <stdlib.h>
#include "drivtool.hpp"

const NHandles = 10;

// Test driver
void main(int argc, char *argv[]) {

      UCommand      *Hans[NHandles];
      for (int i = 0; i < NHandles; i++) Hans[i] = NULL;
      FILE   *Record;

      // If there is an input recording file,
      if (argc == 2) {
            // Open the file
            Record = fopen(argv[1],"w");
      } else {
            // Otherwise mark the file as not open
            Record = NULL;
      }

      Screen Scr;
      int    Handle = 0;
      // Drive until the user is done
      for (int Done = 0; !Done; ) {
            switch (GetChar("Command => ", Record)) {
            case 'A':   // IsArrow()
                  printf("The command is %san arrow\n",
                       Hans[Handle]->IsArrow()? "": "not ");
                  break;
            case 'B':   // IsBlack()
                  printf("The command is %sa black\n",
                       Hans[Handle]->IsBlack()? "": "not ");
                  break;
            case 'C':   // UCommand()
                  Hans[Handle] = new UCommand(Scr);
                  break;
            case 'D':   // IsDownArrow()
                  printf("The command is %sa down arrow\n",
                       Hans[Handle]->IsDownArrow()? "": "not ");
                  break;
            case 'E':   // IsEnter()
                  printf("The command is %sa enter\n",
                       Hans[Handle]->IsEnter()? "": "not ");
                  break;
            case 'G':   // Get()
                  printf("Enter a command\n");
                  Hans[Handle]->Get();
                  break;
```

Appendix B — *Cont'd*

```
        case 'H':   // Handle
              printf("The current handle is %d\n", Handle);
              Handle = GetInt("Enter the new handle => ", Record);
              printf("Now the handle is %d\n", Handle);
              break;
        case 'I':   // IsQuit()
              printf("The command is %s quit\n",
                  Hans[Handle]->IsQuit()? "": "not ");
              break;
        case 'L':   // IsLeftArrow()
              printf("The command is %sa left arrow\n",
                  Hans[Handle]->IsLeftArrow()? "": "not ");
              break;
        case 'N':   // IsNo()
              printf("The command is %sa no\n",
                  Hans[Handle]->IsNo()? "": "not ");
              break;
        case 'Q':   // Quit
              Done = 1;
              break;
        case 'R':   // IsRightArrow()
              printf("The command is %sa right arrow\n",
                  Hans[Handle]->IsRightArrow()? "": "not ");
              break;
        case 'U':   // IsUpArrow()
              printf("The command is %san up arrow\n",
                  Hans[Handle]->IsUpArrow()? "": "not ");
              break;
        case 'W':   // IsWhite()
              printf("The command is %sa white\n",
                  Hans[Handle]->IsWhite()? "": "not ");
              break;
        case 'Y':   // IsYes()
              printf("The command is %sa yes\n",
                  Hans[Handle]->IsYes()? "": "not ");
              break;
        case '~':   // ~UCommand()
              delete Hans[Handle];
              break;
        default:    // Help
              printf("Valid commands are...\n");
              printf("\tA - IsArrow (is command an arrow)\n");
              printf("\tB - IsBlack (is command a black)\n");
              printf("\tC - Command (create a command)\n");
              printf("\tD - IsDownArrow (is command a down arrow)\n");
              printf("\tE - IsEnter (is command an enter)\n");
              printf("\tG - Get (get command input)\n");
              printf("\tH - Handle (change the current handle)\n");
              printf("\tI - IsQuit (is command quit)\n");
              printf("\tL - IsLeftArrow (is command a left arrow)\n");
              printf("\tN - IsNo (is command a no)\n");
              printf("\tQ - Quit (quit the driver)\n");
              printf("\tR - IsRightArrow (is command right arrow)\n");
              printf("\tU - IsUpArrow (is command an up arrow)\n");
              printf("\tW - IsWhite (is command a white)\n");
              printf("\tY - IsYes (is command a yes)\n");
              printf("\t~ - Destroy (destroy the command)\n");
              break;
        }
}
```

Appendix B — *Cont'd*

```
        // If the user is recording input,
        if (Record != NULL) {
                // Close the recording file
                fclose(Record);
        }
}

#endif          // DRIVER

*********************************************************************************
//
//      coord.hpp - coordinate (row/column) class
//

class Coord;

#ifndef         COORD_HPP
#define         COORD_HPP

#include "global.hpp"

class Coord {
        int     R;                      // Row index
        int     C;                      // Column index
public:
        // Create a coordinate from a row and column
        Coord(
                const int r = 0,        // Row value
                const int c = 0         // Column value
        ): R(r), C(c) {}
        // Create a coordinate as a duplicate
        Coord(
                const Coord &c          // Coordinate to duplicate
        ): R(c.Row()), C(c.Col()) {}
        // Get the coordinate's row
        int     Row() const {return R;}
        // Get the coordinate's column
        int     Col() const {return C;}
        // Set the coordinate's row to the specific value
        void    SetRow(
                const int row           // Row value
        ) { R = row; }
        // Set the coordinate's column to the specific value
        void    SetCol(
                const int col           // Column value
        ) { C = col; }
        // Determine if two coordinates have the same value
        BOOLEAN operator == (
                const Coord &c          // Comparison Coordinate
        ) const {
                return ((R==c.R)&&(C==c.C));
        }
        // Determine if two coordinates do not have the same value
        BOOLEAN operator != (
                const Coord &c          // Comparison Coordinate
        ) const {
                return ((R!=c.R)||(C!=c.C));
        }
```

Appendix B — *Cont'd*

```
	// Copy the contents of one coordinate to another
	Coord& operator = (
		const Coord &c		// Coordinate to copy
	) {
		R = c.R;
		C = c.C;
		return *this;
	}
};

#endif		// COORD_HPP
********************************************************************************

//
//	drivtool.cpp - Common test driver functions
//

#include <stdio.h>
#include <stdlib.h>
#include <string.h>
#include <ctype.h>
#include "drivtool.hpp"


void GetLine(char *Prompt, char *Buffer, FILE *Record) {
	char	Resp[2];

	// Until the input is not a comment...
	do {
		// Prompt for the input
		printf(Prompt);
		// Get the entire input line
		gets(Buffer);
		// If input is being recorded,
		if (Record != NULL) {
			// Save the entire input line
			fprintf(Record, "%s\n", Buffer);
		}
		// Strip off the first meaningful character
		if (strlen(Buffer) > 0) {
			sscanf(Buffer, "%1s", Resp);
		} else {
			Resp[0] = '\0';
		}
	} while (*Resp == '#');
}

char GetChar(char *Prompt, FILE *Record) {
	char	Buffer[MaxLine];
	char	C;

	// Get a non-comment line
	GetLine(Prompt, Buffer, Record);
	if (strlen(Buffer) > 0) {
		// Get the first character
		char	Resp[2];
		sscanf(Buffer, "%1s", Resp);
		// Normalize the character
```

Appendix B — *Cont'd*

```
            C = islower(*Resp)? toupper(*Resp): *Resp;
      } else {
            C = '\0';
      }
      // Return the character
      return C;
}

int   GetInt(char *Prompt, FILE *Record) {
      char   Buffer[MaxLine];
      int    N;

      // Get a non-comment line
      GetLine(Prompt, Buffer, Record);
      if (strlen(Buffer) > 0) {
            // Get the int out of the line
            sscanf(Buffer, "%d", &N);
      } else {
            N = 0;
      }
      // return the int
      return N;
}

********************************************************************************

//
//    drivtool.hpp - Common test driver functions
//

#ifndef      DRIVTOOL_HPP
#define      DRIVTOOL_HPP

const MaxLine = 132;

// Get a line of input and process comments
void  GetLine(
      char *,        // Prompt string
      char *,        // Output buffer
      FILE *         // Recording file handle (NULL means no file)
);

// Get an input character and process comments
char  GetChar(
      char *,        // Prompt string
      FILE *         // Recording file handle (NULL means no file)
);

// Get an input integer and process comments
int   GetInt(
      char *,        // Prompt string
      FILE *         // Recording file handle (NULL means no file)
);

#endif       //DRIVTOOL_HPP
```

Appendix B — *Cont'd*

```
********************************************************************************
//
//    game.hpp - Chess game class
//

class Game;

#ifndef      GAME_HPP
#define      GAME_HPP

#include "global.hpp"
#include "magic.hpp"
#include "board.hpp"
#include "screen.hpp"
#include "status.hpp"
#include "team.hpp"

class Game  {
      MAGIC                         // Magic number macro
      Board        board;           // game board
      Screen       &screen;         // Screen handle
      Status       &status;         // User interaction line handle
      Team         *White;          // White team handle
      Team         *Black;          // Black team handle
      // Assert the class invariants
      void   Invariant() const;
public:
      // Create the game
      Game(
             Screen&,    // Screen handle
             Status&     // Status line handle
      );
      // Destroy the game
      ~Game();
      // Initialize the game
      void   Initialize();
      // Play the game (return FALSE if the user quits)
      BOOLEAN Play(
             Winner&     // Win-lose-draw indicator
      );
      // Clean up the game
      void   CleanUp();
};

#endif      // GAME_HPP
********************************************************************************
//
//    game.cpp - Chess game class
//

#include "game.hpp"

char  Game::MagicValue = '\0';

// Assert the class invariants
inline       void   Game::Invariant() const {
      // Check the magic number
      MagicCheck();
}
```

Appendix B — *Cont'd*

```
//* Create the game
Game::Game(Screen &s, Status &st):
      screen(s),
      board(s),
      status(st)
{
      MagicOn();
      Invariant();
}

// Destroy the game
Game::~Game() {
      Invariant();
      MagicOff();
}

//* Initialize the game
void Game::Initialize() {

      Invariant();
      //* Create a white team
      White = new Team(TRUE, board, status);
      assert(White != NULL);
      //* Create a black team
      Black = new Team(FALSE, board, status);
      assert(Black != NULL);
      //* If the user wants to be white,
      if (status.GetIsWhite()) {
              //* Tell white team to play manually
              White->PlayManually();
              //* Tell black team to play automatically
              Black->PlayAutomatically();
      //* Otherwise the user wants black,
      } else {
              //* Tell white team to play automatically
              White->PlayAutomatically();
              //* Tell black team to play manually
              Black->PlayManually();
      }
}

//* Play the game
BOOLEAN Game::Play(Winner &WinResult) {

      Invariant();
      BOOLEAN Quitting = FALSE;
      BOOLEAN Checkmate;
      BOOLEAN Stalemate;

      // set the default result in case of a quit
      WinResult = WinDraw;
      //* Initialize the current team to white
      Team *Current = White;
      //* While the current team is not in checkmate and
      while ((!(Checkmate = Current->IsCheckmate())) &&
          //* The current team is not in stalemate and
          (!(Stalemate = Current->IsStalemate())) &&
          //* Not quitting...
```

Appendix B — *Cont'd*

```
            (!Quitting)) {
                //* Have the current team make a move
                Quitting = Current->Move();
                //* Change the current team to the other team
                Current = (Current == White)? Black: White;
        }
        //* If the user did not quit,
        if (!Quitting) {
                //* Figure out who won
                if (Stalemate) {
                        WinResult = WinDraw;
                } else {
                        assert(Checkmate);
                        if (Current->IsManual()) {
                            WinResult = WinComputer;
                        } else {
                            WinResult = WinUser;
                        }
                }
        }
        return(Quitting);
}

//* Clean up the game
void  Game::CleanUp() {

        Invariant();
        //* Clean up the board
        board.CleanUp();
        //* Destroy black team
        delete White;
        //* Destroy white team
        delete Black;
}

#ifdef        DRIVER

#include <stdio.h>
#include <stdlib.h>
#include "drivtool.hpp"

const         NHandles = 10;

// Test driver
void          main(int argc, char *argv[]) {

        Game   *Hans[NHandles];
        for (int i = 0; i < NHandles; i++) Hans[i] = NULL;
        FILE   *Record;

        // If there is an input recording file,
        if (argc == 2) {
                // Open the file
                Record = fopen(argv[1],"w");
        } else {
                // Otherwise mark the file as not open
                Record = NULL;
        }
```

Appendix B — *Cont'd*

```
    Screen        Scr;
    Status        Sta(Scr);
    int           Handle = 0;
    // Drive until the user is done
    for (int Done = 0; !Done; ) {
            switch (GetChar("Game => ", Record)) {
            case 'C':   // CleanUp()
                    Hans[Handle]->CleanUp();
                    break;
            case 'G':   // Game()
                    Hans[Handle] = new Game(Scr, Sta);
                    break;
            case 'H':   // Handle
                    printf("The current handle is %d\n", Handle);
                    Handle = GetInt("Enter the new handle => ", Record);
                    printf("Now the handle is %d\n", Handle);
                    break;
            case 'I':   // Initialize()
                    Hans[Handle]->Initialize();
                    break;
            case 'P':   // Play()
                    Winner    W;
                    BOOLEAN Quit = Hans[Handle]->Play(W);
                    printf("The user did %squit\n",Quit? "": "not ");
                    if (!Quit) {
                         if (W == WinUser) printf("User\n");
                         else if (W == WinComputer) printf("Computer\n");
                         else if (W == WinDraw) printf("Draw\n");
                    }
                    break;
            case 'Q':   // Quit
                    Done = 1;
                    break;
            case '~':   // ~Game()
                    delete Hans[Handle];
                    break;
            default:    // Help
                    printf("Valid commands are...\n");
                    printf("\tC - CleanUp (cleanup the game)\n");
                    printf("\tG - Game (create a game)\n");
                    printf("\tH - Handle (change the handle)\n");
                    printf("\tI - Initialize (Initialize the game)\n");
                    printf("\tQ - Quit (quit the driver)\n");
                    printf("\t~ - Destroy (destroy the game)\n");
                    break;
            }
    }

    // If the user is recording input,
    if (Record != NULL) {
            // Close the recording file
            fclose(Record);
    }
}

#endif        //DRIVER
```

Appendix B — *Cont'd*

```
******************************************************************************

//
//   global.hpp - global definitions
//

#ifndef      GLOBAL_HPP
#define      GLOBAL_HPP

const        FALSE = 0;
const        TRUE = (!FALSE);
typedef      int    BOOLEAN;

#include <stdlib.h>
#include <iostreams.h>
#include <conio.h>


// Turn off assertions for optimization
#ifdef       OPTIMIZE
#define      assert(b)
#else        // OPTIMIZE
#define      assert(b)   MyAssert((b),__FILE__,__LINE__)
#endif       // OPTIMIZE

// Assertion function outputs a message and waits for interaction
inline       void   MyAssert(
      BOOLEAN b,         // Assertion condition (should be true)
      char    *File,     // File name
      int     Line       // Line number
      ) {
      if (!b) {
             cout << "assertion failed - ";
             cout << File << ":" << Line << endl;
             getch();
             exit(-1);
      }
}

#endif       // GLOBAL_HPP
******************************************************************************

//
//   king.hpp - the king chess piece class
//

class        King;

#ifndef      KING_HPP
#define      KING_HPP

#include "global.hpp"
#include "magic.hpp"
#include "piece.hpp"
#include "team.hpp"
#include "board.hpp"
```

Appendix B — *Cont'd*

```
class       King:public Piece       {
      MAGIC              // Magic number macro
      Board  &board;     // Board handle
      // Assert the class invariants
      void   Invariant() const;
public:
      // Create a king
      King(
             Team*,      // King's team handle
             BOOLEAN,    // Color indicator (true if white)
             Board&      // Playing board handle
      );
      // Destroy the king
      virtual ~King();
      // Return the king's name
      char   *Name() const;
      // Return the king's value
      int    Value() const;
      // Return that this is a king
      PieceType      GetType() const;
      // Determine if the proposed move is legal
      BOOLEAN  IsLegalMove(
             const Coord&,    // Source location
             const Coord&     // Destination location
      ) const;
};

#endif      // KING_HPP
*********************************************************************************

//
//    king.cpp - the chess game king piece
//

#include "king.hpp"

char  King::MagicValue = '\0';

// Assert the class invariants
inline      void   King::Invariant() const {
      // Check the magic number
      MagicCheck();
}

//* Create a king
King::King(Team *t, BOOLEAN white, Board &b): board(b), Piece(t, white)
{
      MagicOn();
      Invariant();
}

//* Destroy the king
King::~King() {
      Invariant();
      MagicOff();
}
```

Appendix B — *Cont'd*

```
//* Return the name of the piece
char  *King::Name() const {

      Invariant();
      return("King");
}

//* Return the value of this type of piece
int   King::Value() const {

      Invariant();
      return(7);
}

//* Return the type of the piece
PieceType    King::GetType() const {

      Invariant();
      return(KING);
}
//* Determine if this is a legal move
BOOLEAN King::IsLegalMove(const Coord &src, const Coord &dest) const
{

      Invariant();
      //* The move is legal if -
      return(
             //* The new square is not the old one and
             (src != dest) &&
             (
                    //* The destination is less than one row/column away or
                    (
                         (dest.Row() <= (src.Row()+1)) &&
                         (dest.Row() >= (src.Row()-1)) &&
                         (dest.Col() <= (src.Col()+1)) &&
                         (dest.Col() >= (src.Col()-1))
                    ) ||
                    //* The new position is a legal castle move
                    (FALSE)
             ) &&
             //* And
             //* The destination does not contain the same team and
             (board.IsValidDestination(IsWhite(), dest)) &&
             //* The move does not cause (self-inflicted) checkmate
             (!CausesCheckmate(src, dest))
      );
}
*******************************************************************************

//
//    knight.hpp - the knight chess piece class
//

class Knight;

#ifndef      KNIGHT_HPP
#define      KNIGHT_HPP
```

Appendix B — *Cont'd*

```
#include "global.hpp"
#include "magic.hpp"
#include "piece.hpp"
#include "team.hpp"
#include "board.hpp"

class Knight:public Piece     {
      MAGIC              // Magic number macro
      Board  &board;     // Board handle
      // Assert the class invariants
      void   Invariant() const;
public:
      // Create a knight
      Knight(
             Team*,      // Knight's team handle
             BOOLEAN,    // Color indicator (true if white)
             Board&      // Playing board handle
      );
      // Destroy the knight
      virtual ~Knight();
      // Return the knight's name
      char   *Name() const;
      // Return the knight's value
      int    Value() const;
      // Return that this is a knight
      PieceType     GetType() const;
      // Determine if the proposed move is legal
      BOOLEAN IsLegalMove(
             const Coord&,    // Source location
             const Coord&     // Destination location
      ) const;
};

#endif       // KNIGHT_HPP
*******************************************************************************

//
//    knight.cpp - the chess game knight piece
//

#include "knight.hpp"

char         Knight::MagicValue = '\0';

// Assert the class invariants
inline       void   Knight::Invariant() const {
      // Check the magic number
      MagicCheck();
}

//* Create a knight
Knight::Knight(Team *t, BOOLEAN white, Board &b): board(b), Piece(t, white) {

      MagicOn();
      Invariant();
}
```

Appendix B — *Cont'd*

```
//* Destroy the knight
Knight::~Knight() {
      Invariant();
      MagicOff();
}

//* Return the name of the piece
char  *Knight::Name() const {

      Invariant();
      return("Knight");
}

//* Return the value of this type of piece
int   Knight::Value() const {

      Invariant();
      return(4);
}

//* Return the type of the piece
PieceType    Knight::GetType() const {

      Invariant();
      return(KNIGHT);
}

//* Determine if this is a legal move
BOOLEAN Knight::IsLegalMove(const Coord &src, const Coord &dest) const
{

      Invariant();
      //* The move is legal if -
      return(
             //* The source is not the destination and
             (src != dest) &&
             //* The move is
             (
                    //* A move up or
                    (
                         (dest.Row() == (src.Row()+2)) &&
                         (
                              (dest.Col() == (src.Col()+1)) ||
                              (dest.Col() == (src.Col()-1))
                         )
                    ) ||
                    //* A move down or
                    (
                         (dest.Row() == (src.Row()-2)) &&
                         (
                              (dest.Col() == (src.Col()+1)) ||
                              (dest.Col() == (src.Col()-1))
                         )
                    ) ||
                    //* A move left or
                    (
                         (dest.Col() == (src.Col()-2)) &&
                         (
```

Appendix B — *Cont'd*

```
                            (dest.Row() == (src.Row()+1)) ||
                            (dest.Row() == (src.Row()-1))
                        )
                    ) ||
                    //* A move right
                    (
                        (dest.Col() == (src.Col()+2)) &&
                        (
                            (dest.Row() == (src.Row()+1)) ||
                            (dest.Row() == (src.Row()-1))
                        )
                    )
            //* And
            ) &&
            //* The destination does not contain the same team and
            (board.IsValidDestination(IsWhite(), dest)) &&
            //* The move does not cause (self-inflicted) checkmate
            (!CausesCheckmate(src, dest))
      );
}

*******************************************************************************

//
//    magic.hpp - Included in a class structure for magic number checking
//

#ifndef      MAGIC_HPP
#define      MAGIC_HPP

#define      MAGIC                                         \
      static char   MagicValue;                            \
      char   *Magic;                                       \
      void   MagicOn() { Magic = &MagicValue; }            \
      void   MagicOff() { Magic = NULL; }                  \
      void   MagicCheck() const {                          \
             assert(this != NULL);                         \
             assert(Magic == &MagicValue); }

#endif       // MAGIC_HPP
*******************************************************************************

//
//    pawn.hpp - the pawn chess piece class
//

class Pawn;

#ifndef      PAWN_HPP
#define      PAWN_HPP

#include "global.hpp"
#include "magic.hpp"
#include "piece.hpp"
#include "team.hpp"
#include "board.hpp"
```

Appendix B — *Cont'd*

```
class Pawn:public Piece  {
      MAGIC               // Magic number macro
      Board  &board;      // Board handle
      // Assert the class invariants
      void   Invariant() const;
public:
      // Create a pawn
      Pawn(
             Team*,       // Pawn's team handle
             BOOLEAN,     // Color indicator (true if white)
             Board&       // Playing board's handle
      );
      // Destroy the pawn
      virtual ~Pawn();
      // Return the pawn's name
      char   *Name() const;
      // Return the pawn's value
      int    Value() const;
      // Return that this is a pawn
      PieceType     GetType() const;
      // Determine if the proposed move is legal
      BOOLEAN IsLegalMove(
             const Coord&,    // Source location
             const Coord&     // Destination location
      ) const;
      // Determine if this is a legal initial move
      BOOLEAN IsInitial(
             const Coord&,    // Source location
             const Coord&     // Destination location
      ) const;
      // Determine if this is a legal striking move
      BOOLEAN IsStriking(
             const Coord&,    // Source location
             const Coord&     // Destination location
      ) const;
      // Determine if this is a legal normal move
      BOOLEAN       IsNormal(
             const Coord&,    // Source location
             const Coord&     // Destination location
      ) const;
};

#endif      // PAWN_HPP
*******************************************************************************


//
//    pawn.cpp - the chess game pawn piece
//

#include <stdlib.h>
#include <math.h>
#include "pawn.hpp"

char  Pawn::MagicValue = '\0';

// Assert the class invariants
inline      void   Pawn::Invariant() const {
```

Appendix B — *Cont'd*

```
	// Check the magic number
	MagicCheck();
}

//* Create a pawn
Pawn::Pawn(Team *t, BOOLEAN white, Board &b): board(b), Piece(t, white)
{
	MagicOn();
	Invariant();
}

//* Destroy the pawn
Pawn::~Pawn() {
	Invariant();
	MagicOff();
}

//* Return the name of the piece
char  *Pawn::Name() const {

	Invariant();
	return("Pawn");
}

//* Return the value of this type of piece
int   Pawn::Value() const {

	Invariant();
	return(2);
}

//* Return the type of the piece
PieceType    Pawn::GetType() const {

	Invariant();
	return(PAWN);
}

//* Determine if this is a legal move
BOOLEAN Pawn::IsLegalMove(const Coord &src, const Coord &dest) const
{
	Invariant();
	//* The move is legal if -
	return(
		//* The source is not the destination and
		(src != dest) &&
		//* The move is
		(
			//* An initial move or
			IsInitial(src, dest) ||
			//* A striking move or
			IsStriking(src, dest) ||
			//* A normal move
			IsNormal(src, dest)
		//* And
		) &&
		//* The move does not cause (self-inflicted) checkmate
		(!CausesCheckmate(src, dest))
	);
}
```

Appendix B — *Cont'd*

```
//* Determine if this is an initial move
BOOLEAN Pawn::IsInitial(const Coord &src, const Coord &dest) const
{

      Invariant();
      int    Delta = dest.Col() - src.Col();
      //* The move is a legal initial move if -
      return(
             //* The pawn is in the initial position and
             !HasMoved() &&
             //* The move has no vertical component and
             (src.Row() == dest.Row()) &&
             //* The move has a horizontal component of two or less and
             ((abs(Delta) > 0) && (abs(Delta) <= 2)) &&
             //* The horizontal component is in the right direction and
             ((IsWhite() && (Delta > 0)) || ((!IsWhite()) && (Delta < 0))) &&
             //* The destination is not occupied and
             (board.GetPiece(dest) == NULL) &&
             //* There is no piece between the source and destination
             (!board.PiecesBetween(src, dest))
      );
}

//* Determine if this is a striking move
BOOLEAN Pawn::IsStriking(const Coord &src, const Coord &dest) const
{
      Invariant();
      int    Delta = dest.Col() - src.Col();
      //* The move is a legal striking move if -
      return(
             //* The move has a horizontal component of one and
             (abs(Delta) == 1) &&
             //* The horizontal component is in the right direction and
             ((IsWhite() && (Delta > 0)) || ((!IsWhite()) && (Delta < 0))) &&
             //* The move has a vertical component of one and
             (abs(src.Row() - dest.Row()) == 1) &&
             //* The destination is occupied and
             (board.GetPiece(dest) != NULL) &&
             //* The destination does not contain the same team
             (board.IsValidDestination(IsWhite(), dest))
      );
}

//* Determine if this is a normal pawn move
BOOLEAN Pawn::IsNormal(const Coord &src, const Coord &dest) const
{
      Invariant();
      int    Delta = src.Col() - dest.Col();
      //* The move is a normal move if -
      return(
             //* The move has no vertical component and
             (src.Row() == dest.Row()) &&
             //* The move has a horizontal component of one and
             (abs(Delta) == 1) &&
             //* The horizontal component is in the right direction and
             ((IsWhite() && (Delta < 0)) || ((!IsWhite()) && (Delta > 0))) &&
             //* The destination is not occupied
             (board.GetPiece(dest) == NULL)
      );
}
```

Appendix B — *Cont'd*

```
********************************************************************************

//
//    piece.hpp - generic chess piece base class
//

class Piece;

#ifndef      PIECE_HPP
#define      PIECE_HPP

#include "global.hpp"
#include "magic.hpp"
#include "square.hpp"

// List of piece types
enum  PieceType     {
      KING,
      QUEEN,
      BISHOP,
      KNIGHT,
      CASTLE,
      PAWN,
      UNDEFINED
};

class Team;

class Piece  {
      MAGIC         // Magic number macro
      BOOLEAN White;// Is this piece white?
      BOOLEAN Moved;// Has this piece moved?
      Team   *team; // Piece's team handle
      // Assert the class invariants
      void   Invariant() const;
public:
      // Create a piece
      Piece(
             Team*,      // Piece's team handle
             BOOLEAN // True if the piece is white
      );
      // Destroy a piece
      virtual~Piece() = 0;
      // Determine if the piece is a member of the team
      BOOLEAN IsMember(
             const Team* // Team in question
      ) const;
      // Mark the piece as having moved
      void   Move();
      // Determine if the piece has moved
      BOOLEAN HasMoved() const;
      // Determine the piece type
      virtualPieceType   GetType() const = 0;
      // Get the name of the piece
      virtualchar   *Name() const = 0;
      // Return the value of this piece
      virtualint    Value() const = 0;
      // Determine if the piece is the same color as that specified
```

Appendix B — *Cont'd*

```
      BOOLEAN       IsSameColor(
            const BOOLEAN // Color indicator (true if white)
      ) const;
      // Determine if the piece is white
      BOOLEAN       IsWhite() const;
      // Determine if this is a legal move for this piece
      virtualBOOLEAN IsLegalMove(
            const Coord&,    // Source location
            const Coord&     // Destination location
      ) const = 0;
      // Determine if this move causes checkmate
      BOOLEAN CausesCheckmate(
            const Coord&,    // Source location
            const Coord&     // Destination location
      ) const;
};

#endif      // PIECE_HPP
********************************************************************************
//
//    piece.cpp - generic chess piece base class
//

#include "piece.hpp"
#include "team.hpp"

char  Piece::MagicValue = '\0';

// Assert the class invariants
inline      void   Piece::Invariant() const {
      // Check the magic number
      MagicCheck();
}

//* Create a piece
Piece::Piece(Team *t, BOOLEAN white):team(t), White(white), Moved(FALSE)
{
      MagicOn();
      Invariant();
}

//* Destroy the piece
Piece::~Piece() {
      Invariant();
      MagicOff();
}

//* Determine if the piece is a member of the team
BOOLEAN Piece::IsMember(const Team *t) const {

      Invariant();
      return(t == team);
}

//* Mark the piece as having moved
void  Piece::Move() {

      Invariant();
      Moved = TRUE;
}
```

Appendix B — *Cont'd*

```
//* Determine if the piece has moved
BOOLEAN Piece::HasMoved() const {

      Invariant();
      return Moved;
}

//* Determine if the piece is the same color as that specified
BOOLEAN Piece::IsSameColor(const BOOLEAN white) const {

      Invariant();
      return((white && White) || ((!white) && (!White)));
}

//* Determine if the piece is white
BOOLEAN Piece::IsWhite() const {

      Invariant();
      return(White);
}

//* Determine if this move causes checkmate
BOOLEAN Piece::CausesCheckmate(const Coord &src, const Coord &dest)
const {

      Invariant();
      return team->CausesCheckmate(src, dest);
}


#ifdef       DRIVER

#include <stdio.h>
#include <stdlib.h>
#include "drivtool.hpp"

Screen       Scr;
Status       Sta(Scr);
Board        board(Scr);
Team         black(FALSE, board, Sta);
Team         white(TRUE, board, Sta);

Piece        *CreatePiece(FILE *Record) {

      Piece  *P;
      char c = GetChar("Enter Piece Type (K/Q/B/N/C/P) => ", Record);
      BOOLEAN White = (GetChar("Enter color (B/W) => ", Record) == 'W');

      switch (c) {
      case 'K':     // King
             P = new King(White?&white:&black, White, board);
             break;
      case 'Q':     // Queen
             P = new Queen(White?&white:&black, White, board);
             break;
      case 'B':     // Bishop
             P = new Bishop(White?&white:&black, White, board);
```

Appendix B — *Cont'd*

```
            break;
        case 'N':      // Knight
            P = new Knight(White?&white:&black, White, board);
            break;
        case 'C':      // Castle
            P = new Castle(White?&white:&black, White, board);
            break;
        case 'P':      // Pawn
            P = new Pawn(White?&white:&black, White, board);
            break;
        }
        return P;
}

void GetCoord(char *name, Coord &c, FILE *Record) {
        char buffer[80];
        sprintf(buffer, "Enter %s row => ", name);
        c.SetRow(GetInt(buffer, Record));
        sprintf(buffer, "Enter %s column => ", name);
        c.SetCol(GetInt(buffer, Record));
}

const NHandles = 10;

// Test driver
void main(int argc, char *argv[]) {

        Piece   *Hans[NHandles];
        for (int i = 0; i < NHandles; i++) Hans[i] = NULL;
        FILE    *Record;

        // If there is an input recording file,
        if (argc == 2) {
                // Open the file
                Record = fopen(argv[1],"w");
        } else {
                // Otherwise mark the file as not open
                Record = NULL;
        }

        int     Handle = 0;
        // Drive until the user is done
        for (int Done = 0; !Done; ) {
                char c = GetChar("Piece => ", Record);
                switch (c) {
                case 'A':   // HasMoved()
                        printf("piece is marked as %shaving moved\n",
                            Hans[Handle]->HasMoved()? "": "not ");
                        break;
                case 'G':   // GetType()
                        PieceType pt = Hans[Handle]->GetType();
                        printf("Piece type has a %d value\n", (int) pt);
                        break;
                case 'H':   // Handle
                        printf("The current handle is %d\n", Handle);
                        Handle = GetInt("Enter the new handle => ", Record);
                        printf("Now the handle is %d\n", Handle);
                        break;
```

Appendix B — *Cont'd*

```
        case 'I':   // IsMember()
              char t = GetChar("Enter team color (W/B) => ", Record);
              printf("Piece is %sa team member\n",
                  Hans[Handle]->IsMember(
                      (t == 'W')? &white: &black
                  )? "": "not "
              );
              break;
        case 'M':   // Move()
              Hans[Handle]->Move();
              break;
        case 'N':   // Name()
              printf("The piece's name is %s\n",Hans[Handle]->Name());
              break;
        case 'P':   // Piece()
              Hans[Handle] = CreatePiece(Record);
              break;
        case 'Q':   // Quit
              Done = 1;
              break;
        case 'S':   // IsSameColor()
              char c = GetChar("Enter color (W/B) => ", Record);
              printf("The piece is %sthe same color\n",
                  Hans[Handle]->IsSameColor(c == 'W')?"":"not ");
              break;
        case 'V':   // Value()
              printf("The pieces value is %d\n",
                  Hans[Handle]->Value());
              break;
        case 'W':   // IsWhite()
              printf("The piece is %swhite\n",
                  Hans[Handle]->IsWhite()? "": "not ");
              break;
        case '~':   // ~Piece()
              delete Hans[Handle];
              break;
        default:    // Help
              printf("Valid commands are...\n");
              printf("\tA - HasMoved (has the piece moved?)\n");
              printf("\tG - GetType (get the piece type)\n");
              printf("\tH - Handle (change the handle)\n");
              printf("\tI - IsMember (is piece a team member?)\n");
              printf("\tM - Move (mark piece as moved)\n");
              printf("\tN - Name (get piece name)\n");
              printf("\tP - Piece (create a piece)\n");
              printf("\tQ - Quit (quit the driver)\n");
              printf("\tS - IsSameColor (is piece the same color)\n");
              printf("\tV - Value (get the piece value)\n");
              printf("\tW - IsWhite (is the piece white?)\n");
              printf("\t~ - Destroy (destroy the piece)\n");
              break;
        }
    }

    // If the user is recording input,
    if (Record != NULL) {
        // Close the recording file
        fclose(Record);
```

Appendix B — *Cont'd*

```
	}
}

#endif		//DRIVER

*******************************************************************************

//
//	queen.hpp - the queen chess piece class
//

class		Queen;

#ifndef		QUEEN_HPP
#define		QUEEN_HPP

#include "global.hpp"
#include "magic.hpp"
#include "piece.hpp"
#include "team.hpp"
#include "board.hpp"

class		Queen:public Piece	{
	MAGIC			// Magic number macro
	Board	&board;		// Board handle
	// Assert the class invariants
	void	Invariant() const;
public:
	// Create a queen
	Queen(
		Team*,		// King's team handle
		BOOLEAN,	// Color indicator (true if white)
		Board&		// Playing board handle
	);
	// Destroy the queen
	virtual ~Queen();
	// Return the queen's name
	char	*Name() const;
	// Return the queen's value
	int	Value() const;
	// Return that this is a queen
	PieceType	GetType() const;
	// Determine if the proposed move is legal
	BOOLEAN IsLegalMove(
		const Coord&,	// Source location
		const Coord&	// Destination location
	) const;
};

#endif		// QUEEN_HPP
*******************************************************************************

//
//	queen.cpp - the chess game queen piece
//

#include "queen.hpp"
```

Appendix B — *Cont'd*

```
char  Queen::MagicValue = '\0';

// Assert the class invariants
inline      void   Queen::Invariant() const {
      // Check the magic number
      MagicCheck();
}

//* Create a queen
Queen::Queen(Team *t, BOOLEAN white, Board &b): board(b), Piece(t,
white) {
      MagicOn();
      Invariant();
}

//* Destroy the queen
Queen::~Queen() {
      Invariant();
      MagicOff();
}

//* Return the name of the piece
char  *Queen::Name() const {

      Invariant();
      return("Queen");
}

//* Return the value of this type of piece
int   Queen::Value() const {

      Invariant();
      return(6);
}

//* Return the type of the piece
PieceType    Queen::GetType() const {

      Invariant();
      return(QUEEN);
}

//* Determine if this is a legal move
BOOLEAN Queen::IsLegalMove(const Coord &src, const Coord &dest) const
{

      Invariant();
      //* The move is legal if -
      return(
            //* The source is not the destination and
            (src != dest) &&
            //* The move is
            (
                  //* Horizontal or
                  (src.Row() == dest.Row()) ||
                  //* Vertical or
                  (src.Col() == dest.Col()) ||
                  //* Diagonal
```

Appendix B — *Cont'd*

```
                ((src.Col()-dest.Col()) == (src.Row()-dest.Row())) ||
                ((src.Col()-dest.Col()) == -(src.Row()-dest.Row()))
            ) &&
            //* And
            //* There is no piece between the source and destination and
            (!board.PiecesBetween(src, dest)) &&
            //* The destination does not contain the same team and
            (board.IsValidDestination(IsWhite(), dest)) &&
            //* The move does not cause (self-inflicted) checkmate
            (!CausesCheckmate(src, dest))
        );
}

********************************************************************************

//
//      screen.hpp - low level terminal interface
//

class           Screen;

#ifndef         SCREEN_HPP
#define         SCREEN_HPP

#include <conio.h>
#include <dos.h>
#include "global.hpp"
#include "magic.hpp"

// Screen video attributes
typedef         int     Att;
const           AttNone =   0;  // No attributes
const           AttBold =   1;  // Bold attribute
const           AttBlink =  2;  // Blink attribute
const           AttRevid =  4;  // Reverse video attribute

// Interactive terminal class
class           Screen {
        MAGIC                   // Magic number macro
        // Assert the class invariants
        void    Invariant() const;
public:
        // Initialize the screen
        Screen();
        // Close the screen
        ~Screen();
        // Clear the screen
        void    Clear() const;
        // Position the cursor
        void    GoToXY(
                const int,      // Cursor X position value
                const int       // Cursor Y position value
        ) const;
        // Output a string with the current attributes
        void    PutString(
                const char*     // String to output
        ) const;
        // Change the current attributes
```

Appendix B — *Cont'd*

```
	void	Attribute(
			const Att	// The target attribute(s)
	) const;
	// Sound a warning beep
	void	Beep() const;
	// Get a character command
	int	GetCh() const;
};


// #include "wrapper.hpp"	// verification driver

#endif		// SCREEN_HPP

*******************************************************************************

//
//	screen.cpp - low level terminal interface
//

#include "screen.hpp"

// Turn off wrapper (if it is turned on)
#ifdef		Screen
#undef		Screen
#endif		// Screen

char		Screen::MagicValue = '\0';

// Assert the class invariants
inline		void	Screen::Invariant() const {
	// Check the magic number
	MagicCheck();
}

//* Initialize the screen
Screen::Screen() {

	MagicOn();
	_setcursortype(_NOCURSOR);
	Clear();
	Invariant();
}
//* Close the screen
Screen::~Screen() {

	Invariant();
	Attribute(AttNone);
	_setcursortype(_NORMALCURSOR);
	Clear();
	MagicOff();
}
//* Clear the screen
void		Screen::Clear() const {

	Invariant();
	clrscr();
}
```

Appendix B — *Cont'd*

```
//* Position the cursor
void  Screen::GoToXY(const int x, const int y) const {

      Invariant();
      assert((x >= 0) && (x < 80));
      assert((y >= 0) && (y < 80));
      gotoxy(x+1, y+1);
}

//* Output a string with the current attributes
void  Screen::PutString(const char *str) const {

      Invariant();
      assert(str != NULL);
      cprintf(str);
}
//* Change the current attributes
void  Screen::Attribute(const Att att) const {

      Invariant();
      textbackground((att & AttRevid)? LIGHTGRAY: BLACK);
      textcolor(((att & AttBold)? WHITE:
             (att & AttRevid)? BLACK: LIGHTGRAY) |
             ((att & AttBlink)? BLINK: 0));
}
//* Sound a warning beep
void  Screen::Beep() const {

      Invariant();
      sound(440);
      delay(100);
      nosound();
}
//* Get a command
int   Screen::GetCh() const {

      Invariant();
      return getch();
}

#ifdef      DRIVER

#include <stdio.h>
#include <stdlib.h>
#include "drivtool.hpp"


// Test driver
void  main(int argc, char *argv[]) {

      Screen        *Scr;
      FILE          *Record;

      // If there is an input recording file,
      if (argc == 2) {
             // Open the file
             Record = fopen(argv[1],"w");
      } else {
```

Appendix B — *Cont'd*

```
            // Otherwise mark the file as not open
            Record = NULL;
    }
    // Drive until the user is done
    for (int Done = 0; !Done; ) {
            switch (GetChar("Screen => ", Record)) {
            case 'A':   // Attribute()
                    printf("Attributes bits are...\n");
                    printf("\t0 - None\n");
                    printf("\t1 - Bold\n");
                    printf("\t2 - Blink\n");
                    printf("\t4 - Reverse video\n");
                    Att A = GetInt("Enter attribute bits => ", Record);
                    Scr->Attribute(A);
                    break;
            case 'B':   // Beep()
                    Scr->Beep();
                    break;
            case 'C':   // Clear()
                    Scr->Clear();
                    break;
            case 'G':   // GoToXY()
                    int X = GetInt("Enter the X coordinate => ", Record);
                    int Y = GetInt("Enter the Y coordinate => ", Record);
                    Scr->GoToXY(X,Y);
                    break;
            case 'H':   // GetCh()
                    printf("Type a key => ");
                    int N = Scr->GetCh();
                    printf("Key value = %d\n", N);
                    break;
            case 'P':   // PutString()
                    char Buffer[MaxLine];
                    GetLine("Enter a string => ", Buffer, Record);
                    Scr->PutString(Buffer);
                    break;
            case 'Q':   // Quit
                    Done = 1;
                    break;
            case 'S':   // Screen()
                    Scr = new Screen();
                    break;
            case '~':   // ~Screen()
                    delete Scr;
                    break;
            default:    // Help
                    printf("Valid commands are...\n");
                    printf("\tA - Attribute (change current attribute)\n");
                    printf("\tB - Beep (sound beep)\n");
                    printf("\tC - Clear (clear the screen)\n");
                    printf("\tG - GoToXY (position the cursor)\n");
                    printf("\tH - GetCh (get a character)\n");
                    printf("\tP - PutString (output a string)\n");
                    printf("\tQ - Quit (quit the driver)\n");
                    printf("\tS - Screen (create a screen)\n");
                    printf("\t~ - ~Screen (destroy a screen)\n");
                    break;
            }
    }
```

Appendix B — *Cont'd*

```
      // If the user is recording input,
      if (Record != NULL) {
             // Close the recording file
             fclose(Record);
      }
}

#endif       // DRIVER
*********************************************************************************

//
//    Status.hpp - status line for the chess game
//

class        Status;

#ifndef      STATUS_HPP
#define      STATUS_HPP

#include "global.hpp"
#include "magic.hpp"
#include "screen.hpp"

// game conclusion states
enum         Winner {
      WinUser,               // User wins
      WinComputer,           // Computer wins
      WinDraw                // Draw
};

// User interaction (status) line
class        Status {
      MAGIC                  // Magic number macro
      Screen &screen;        // Screen handle
      // Assert the class invariants
      void   Invariant() const;
      // Prompt the user for a response
      void   Prompt(
             const char*     // Character string prompt
      ) const;
      // Show a status line
      void   Show(
             const char*     // Line to show
      ) const;
public:
      // Create the user interaction line
      Status(
             Screen &s       // Display screen
      );
      // Destroy the user interaction line
      ~Status();
      // Cause a warning beep
      void   Beep() const;
      // Clear the status line
      void   Clear() const;
      // Determine if the user wants to play again
      BOOLEAN PlayAgain(
             const Winner    // Indicator of who won
```

Appendix B — *Cont'd*

```
      ) const;
      // Get the color from the user
      BOOLEAN GetIsWhite() const;
      // Show the "Thinking" prompt
      void   Thinking() const;
      // Show the "Select piece" prompt
      void   SelectPiece() const;
      // Show the "Place piece" prompt
      void   PlacePiece() const;
      // Show the "Illegal move" prompt
      void   IllegalMove() const;
};

#endif       // STATUS_HPP
*******************************************************************************

//
//    Status.cpp - status line for the chess game
//

#include <string.h>
#include "status.hpp"
#include "command.hpp"

#define      LINE_NUMBER 24
#define      LINE_WIDTH  80

char         Status::MagicValue = '\0';

// Assert the class invariants
inline       void   Status::Invariant() const {
      // Check the magic number
      MagicCheck();
}


//* Create the user interaction line
Status::Status(Screen &s): screen(s) {

      MagicOn();
      Invariant();
}

//* Destroy the user interaction line
Status::~Status() {

      Invariant();
      MagicOff();
}

//* Cause a warning beep
void         Status::Beep() const {

      Invariant();
      screen.Beep();
}
```

Appendix B — *Cont'd*

```
//* Determine if the user wants to play again
BOOLEAN Status::PlayAgain(const Winner winner) const {

      Invariant();
      //* Ask the user to play again
      Prompt(
             (winner == WinUser)? "You win!  Play again(Y/N)?":
             (winner == WinComputer)? "I win!  Play again(Y/N)?":
             "Draw!  Play again(Y/N)?"
      );
      //* get the user's response
      UCommand c(screen);
      for (;;) {
             c.Get();
             if (c.IsYes() || c.IsNo()) break;
             screen.Beep();
      }
      Clear();
      return c.IsYes();
}

//* Get the color from the user
BOOLEAN Status::GetIsWhite() const {

      Invariant();
      //* Prompt the user for the color
      Prompt("Black or White(B/W)?");
      //* Get the user's response
      UCommand c(screen);
      for (;;) {
             c.Get();
             if (c.IsWhite() || c.IsBlack()) break;
             screen.Beep();
      }
      Clear();
      return c.IsWhite();
}

//* Prompt for input
void         Status::Prompt(const char *prompt) const {

      assert(prompt != NULL),
      // Clear the line
      Clear();
      // Output the prompt
      screen.GoToXY(0,LINE_NUMBER);
      screen.PutString(prompt);
}

//* Show a status line
void         Status::Show(const char *status) const {

      assert(status != NULL);
      // Clear the line
      Clear();
      // Output the status
      screen.GoToXY((LINE_WIDTH - strlen(status))/2,LINE_NUMBER);
      screen.PutString(status);
}
```

Appendix B — *Cont'd*

```
//* Clear the status line
void Status::Clear() const {

      Invariant();
      static char   *BlankLine = "
";

      screen.Attribute(AttNone);
      // Clear the line
      screen.GoToXY(0,LINE_NUMBER);
      screen.PutString(BlankLine);
}

//* Show the "Thinking" prompt
void Status::Thinking() const {

      Invariant();
      Show("Thinking...");
}

//* Show the "Select piece" prompt
void Status::SelectPiece() const {

      Invariant();
      Show("Select the piece to move (use arrow keys to position or enter
key to select)");
}

//* Show the "Place piece" prompt
void Status::PlacePiece() const {

      Invariant();
      Show("Select the destination (use arrow keys to position or the enter
key to select)");
}

//* Show the "Illegal move" prompt
void Status::IllegalMove() const {

      Invariant();
      Show("Illegal move (press enter to continue)");
      UCommand c(screen);
      for (;;) {
            c.Get();
            if (c.IsEnter()) break;
            screen.Beep();
      }
}

#ifdef      DRIVER

#include <stdio.h>
#include <stdlib.h>
#include "drivtool.hpp"


const       NHandles = 10;
```

Appendix B — *Cont'd*

```
// Test driver
void main(int argc, char *argv[]) {

      Status *Hans[NHandles];
      for (int i = 0; i < NHandles; i++) Hans[i] = NULL;
      FILE   *Record;

      // If there is an input recording file,
      if (argc == 2) {
             // Open the file
             Record = fopen(argv[1],"w");
      } else {
             // Otherwise mark the file as not open
             Record = NULL;
      }

      Screen Scr;
      int    Handle = 0;
      // Drive until the user is done
      for (int Done = 0; !Done; ) {
             Scr.GoToXY(0,0);
             switch (GetChar("Status => ", Record)) {
             case 'A':   // PlacePiece()
                    Hans[Handle]->PlacePiece();
                    break;
             case 'B':   // Beep()
                    Hans[Handle]->Beep();
                    break;
             case 'C':   // Clear()
                    Hans[Handle]->Clear();
                    break;
             case 'G':   // GetIsWhite()
                    BOOLEAN White = Hans[Handle]->GetIsWhite();
                    Scr.GoToXY(0,0);
                    printf("The user wants %s\n",
                         White? "white": "black");
                    break;
             case 'H':   // Handle
                    printf("The current handle is %d\n", Handle);
                    Handle = GetInt("Enter the new handle => ", Record);
                    printf("Now the handle is %d\n", Handle);
                    break;
             case 'I':   // IllegalMove()
                    Hans[Handle]->IllegalMove();
                    break;
             case 'L':   // SelectPiece()
                    Hans[Handle]->SelectPiece();
                    break;
             case 'P':   // PlayAgain()
                    Winner W;
                    char C = GetChar("Who won (User, Computer, Draw) => ",
                         Record);
                    if (C == 'U') W = WinUser;
                    else if (C == 'C') W = WinComputer;
                    else W = WinDraw;
                    BOOLEAN Play = Hans[Handle]->PlayAgain(W);
                    Scr.GoToXY(0,0);
                    printf("The user does %swant to play again\n",
```

Appendix B — *Cont'd*

```
                                Play? "": "not ");
                        break;
                case 'Q':   // Quit
                        Done = 1;
                        break;
                case 'S':   // Status()
                        Hans[Handle] = new Status(Scr);
                        break;
                case 'T':   // Thinking()
                        Hans[Handle]->Thinking();
                        break;
                case '~':   // ~Status()
                        delete Hans[Handle];
                        break;
                default:    // Help
                        printf("Valid commands are...\n");
                        printf("\tA - SelectPiece (show PlacePiece prompt)\n");
                        printf("\tB - Beep (cause a warning beep)\n");
                        printf("\tC - Clear (clear the status line)\n");
                        printf("\tG - GetIsWhite (prompt for player color)\n");
                        printf("\tH - Handle (change the handle)\n");
                        printf("\tI - IllegalMove (show IllegalMove prompt)\n");
                        printf("\tL - SelectPiece (show SelectPiece prompt)\n");
                        printf("\tP - PlayAgain (prompt for play again)\n");
                        printf("\tQ - Quit (quit the driver)\n");
                        printf("\tS - Status (create a status line)\n");
                        printf("\tT - Thinking (show thinking prompt)\n");
                        printf("\t~ - Destroy (destroy the status)\n");
                        break;
                }
        }

        // If the user is recording input,
        if (Record != NULL) {
                // Close the recording file
                fclose(Record);
        }
}

#endif          // DRIVER

********************************************************************************

//
//      square.hpp - board square class
//

class           Coord;
class           Square;

#ifndef         SQUARE_HPP
#define         SQUARE_HPP

#include "global.hpp"
#include "magic.hpp"
#include "screen.hpp"
#include "coord.hpp"

class           Piece;          // This solves the recursive header problem
```

Appendix B — *Cont'd*

```
const       SqrRows = 3;
const       SqrCols = 10;

// The chess game board's square abstraction
class       Square {
      MAGIC                                  // Magic number macro
      BOOLEAN IsWhite;                  // Is the square a white one
      Piece        *piece;              // Piece residing in square
      Screen       &screen;             // Screen handle
      Coord        coord;               // Location of this square
      Att          att;                 // Video attributes of square
      char   Name[SqrRows][SqrCols+1];  // Name shown on square
      // Assert the class invariants
      void   Invariant() const;
      // Draw the square
      void   Draw() const;
      // Place the string in the center of the name buffer
      void   CenterName(
             const int,        // Square line number [0-SqrRows]
             const char*       // String to center
      );
public:
      // Create a square
      Square(
             const BOOLEAN,         // True if this is a white square
             Screen&,               // Display screen
             const Coord&           // Location of this square
      );
      // Destroy a square
      ~Square();
      // Get the coordinate for this square
      Coord  &GetCoord();
      // Draw the square as bold
      void   Bold();
      // Draw the square as not bold
      void   Unbold();
      // Draw the square as blinking
      void   Blink();
      // Draw the square as not blinking
      void   Unblink();
      // Place a piece in the square
      void   PlacePiece(
             Piece*            // Piece to put in the square
      );
      // Get the piece the square contains
      Piece  *GetPiece() const;
      // Remove a piece from the square (return the removed piece)
      Piece  *RemovePiece();
      // Try a piece in this location (return the current piece in the
square)
      Piece  *TryPiece(
             Piece*            // Piece to try
      );
      // Stop trying the piece in this location
      void   UntryPiece(
             Piece*            // Original piece to return to square
      );
};

#endif      // SQUARE_HPP
```

Appendix B — *Cont'd*

```
********************************************************************************

//
//    square.cpp - board square class
//

#include <stdlib.h>
#include <string.h>
#include "square.hpp"
#include "team.hpp"

const        BlockChar = ((char) 219);

char         Square::MagicValue = '\0';

// Assert the class invariants
inline       void   Square::Invariant() const {
      // Check the magic number
      MagicCheck();
}

//* Create a square
Square::Square(const BOOLEAN IsW, Screen &s, const Coord &c):
      IsWhite(IsW),
      piece(NULL),
      screen(s),
      coord(c) {

      MagicOn();
      //* Set the background for the square based upon its color
      att = IsWhite? AttNone: AttRevid;
      //* Mark the square as containing no piece
      piece = NULL;
      for (int y = 0; y < SqrRows; y++) {
             for (int x = 0; x < SqrCols; x++) {
                    Name[y][x] = BlockChar;
             }
             Name[y][x] = '\0';
      }
      //* Draw the square
      Draw();
      Invariant();
}

//* Draw the square
void  Square::Draw() const {

      //* Turn on the appropriate attributes
      screen.Attribute(att);
      //* For each line in the name buffer...
      for (int i = 0; i < SqrRows; i++) {
             //* Position at the beginning of the line
             screen.GoToXY((coord.Col()*SqrCols), (coord.Row()*SqrRows + i));
             //* Output the name buffer for the line
             screen.PutString(Name[i]);
      }
}
```

Appendix B — *Cont'd*

```
//* Destroy a square
Square::~Square() {

      Invariant();
      //* Remove the piece
      if (piece != NULL) RemovePiece();
      //* Set the attribute to none
      att = AttNone;
      //* Draw the square
      Draw();
      MagicOff();
}

//* Get the coordinate for this square
Coord        &Square::GetCoord() {

      Invariant();
      return coord;
}

//* Draw the square as bold
void  Square::Bold() {

      Invariant();
      //* Turn on the bold attribute
      att |= AttBold;
      //* Redraw the square
      Draw();
}

//* Draw the square as not bold
void  Square::Unbold() {

      Invariant();
      //* Turn off the bold attribute
      att &= ~AttBold;
      //* Redraw the square
      Draw();
}

//* Draw the square as blinking
void  Square::Blink() {

      Invariant();
      //* Turn on the blink attribute
      att |= AttBlink;
      //* Redraw the square
      Draw();
}

//* Draw the square as not blinking
void  Square::Unblink() {

      Invariant();
      //* Turn off the blink attribute
      att &= ~AttBlink;
      //* Redraw the square
      Draw();
}
```

Appendix B — *Cont'd*

```
//* Place the string in the center of the name buffer
void  Square::CenterName(const int n, const char *str) {

      assert((n >= 0) && (n < SqrRows));
      assert(str != NULL);
      int    len = strlen(str);
      assert(len < SqrCols);
      int    start = (SqrCols - len) / 2;

      for (int i = 0; i < SqrCols; i++) {
             if ((i >= start) && (i < (start + len))) {
                    Name[n][i] = str[i - start];
             } else {
                    Name[n][i] = ' ';
             }
      }
      Name[n][i] = '\0';
}

//* Place a piece in the square
void  Square::PlacePiece(Piece *p) {

      Invariant();
      assert(p != NULL);
      assert(piece == NULL);
      //* Save the piece in the square
      piece = p;
      //* Paint the piece's name
      CenterName(0, piece->IsWhite()? "White": "Black");
      CenterName(1, piece->Name());
      for (int i = 0; i < SqrCols; i++) Name[2][i] = ' ';
      Name[2][i] = '\0';
      //* Redraw the square;
      if (IsWhite) {
             att |= AttRevid;
      } else {
             att &= ~AttRevid;
      }
      Draw();
}

//* Get the piece the square contains
Piece *Square::GetPiece() const {

      Invariant();
      return((Piece*) piece);
}

//* Remove a piece from the square
Piece *Square::RemovePiece() {

      Invariant();
      assert(piece != NULL);
      Piece *tmp = (Piece*) piece;
      //* Remove the piece from this square
      piece = NULL;
      //* Erase the piece's name
      for (int y = 0; y < SqrRows; y++) {
```

Appendix B — *Cont'd*

```
            for (int x = 0; x < SqrCols; x++) {
                   Name[y][x] = BlockChar;
            }
            Name[y][x] = '\0';
      }
      //* Redraw the square
      if (IsWhite) {
            att &= ~AttRevid;
      } else {
            att |= AttRevid;
      }
      Draw();
      assert(tmp != NULL);
      return(tmp);
}

//* Try a piece in this location
Piece *Square::TryPiece(Piece *TempPiece) {

      Invariant();
      //* Save the original piece
      Piece  *tmp = piece;
      //* Use the try piece without updating the screen
      piece = TempPiece;
      //* Return the piece that was in the square
      return tmp;
}

//* Stop trying the piece in this location
void  Square::UntryPiece(Piece *save) {

      Invariant();
      //* Return the original piece to its square
      piece = save;
}

#ifdef       DRIVER

#include <stdio.h>
#include <stdlib.h>
#include "drivtool.hpp"

Screen       Scr;
Status       Sta(Scr);
Board        board(Scr);
Team         black(FALSE, board, Sta);
Team         white(TRUE, board, Sta);

Piece        *NewPiece(FILE *Record) {

      Piece  *P;
      BOOLEAN White = GetChar("White or Black (W/B) => ", Record) == 'W';
      char c = GetChar("Piece Type: King Queen Bishop kNight Castle Pawn
=> ",
                                                      Record);
```

Appendix B — *Cont'd*

```
	switch (c) {
	case 'K':
		P = new King(White?&white:&black, White, board);
		break;
	case 'Q':
		P = new Queen(White?&white:&black, White, board);
		break;
	case 'B':
		P = new Bishop(White?&white:&black, White, board);
		break;
	case 'N':
		P = new Knight(White?&white:&black, White, board);
		break;
	case 'C':
		P = new Castle(White?&white:&black, White, board);
		break;
	default:
		P = new Pawn(White?&white:&black, White, board);
		break;
	}
	return P;
}

const NHandles = 10;

// Test driver
void main(int argc, char *argv[]) {

	Square *Hans[NHandles];
	for (int i = 0; i < NHandles; i++) Hans[i] = NULL;
	FILE   *Record;

	// If there is an input recording file,
	if (argc == 2) {
		// Open the file
		Record = fopen(argv[1],"w");
	} else {
		// Otherwise mark the file as not open
		Record = NULL;
	}

	Piece  *P;
	int    Handle = 0;
	// Drive until the user is done
	for (int Done = 0; !Done; ) {
		switch (GetChar("Square => ", Record)) {
		case 'B':   // Bold()
			Hans[Handle]->Bold();
			break;
		case 'E':   // GetPiece()
			P = Hans[Handle]->GetPiece();
			printf("Piece is a %s %s\n",
			     P->IsWhite()?"white":"black", P->Name());
			break;
		case 'G':   // GetCoord()
			Coord co = Hans[Handle]->GetCoord();
			printf("Row = %d, Column = %d\n", co.Row(), co.Col());
			break;
```

Appendix B — *Cont'd*

```
case 'H':   // Handle
        printf("The current handle is %d\n", Handle);
        Handle = GetInt("Enter the new handle => ", Record);
        printf("Now the handle is %d\n", Handle);
        break;
case 'L':   // Blink()
        Hans[Handle]->Blink();
        break;
case 'N':   // Unblink()
        Hans[Handle]->Unblink();
        break;
case 'P':   // PlacePiece()
        Hans[Handle]->PlacePiece(NewPiece(Record));
        break;
case 'Q':   // Quit
        Done = 1;
        break;
case 'R':   // RemovePiece()
        P = Hans[Handle]->RemovePiece();
        printf("Piece is a %s %s\n",
             P->IsWhite()?"white":"black", P->Name());
        if (GetChar("Delete Piece? => ", Record) == 'Y') {
             delete P;
        }
        break;
case 'S':   // Square()
        char c = GetChar("Square color (W/B) => ", Record);
        BOOLEAN White = (c == 'W');
        int R = GetInt("Row => ", Record);
        int C = GetInt("Column => ", Record);
        Coord Pos(R,C);
        Hans[Handle] = new Square(White, Scr, Pos);
        break;
case 'T':   // TryPiece()
        P = Hans[Handle]->TryPiece(NewPiece(Record));
        printf("Existing piece is a %s %s\n",
             P->IsWhite()?"white":"black", P->Name());
        break;
case 'U':   // Unbold()
        Hans[Handle]->Unbold();
        break;
case 'Y':   // UntryPiece
        printf("Place last used piece\n");
        printf("Piece is a %s %s\n",
             P->IsWhite()?"white":"black", P->Name());
        Hans[Handle]->UntryPiece(P);
        break;
case '~':   // ~Square()
        delete Hans[Handle];
        break;
default:    // Help
        printf("Valid commands are...\n");
        printf("\tB - Bold (bold the square)\n");
        printf("\tE - GetPiece (get the piece)\n");
        printf("\tG - GetCoord (get square's location)\n");
        printf("\tH - Handle (change the handle)\n");
        printf("\tL - Blink (blink the square)\n");
        printf("\tP - PlacePiece (place a piece)\n");
```

Appendix B — *Cont'd*

```
                printf("\tN - Unblink (unblink the square)\n");
                printf("\tQ - Quit (quit the driver)\n");
                printf("\tR - RemovePiece (remove the piece)\n");
                printf("\tS - Square (create a square)\n");
                printf("\tT - TryPiece (Try the piece)\n");
                printf("\tU - Unbold (unbold the square)\n");
                printf("\tY - UntryPiece (untry the piece)\n");
                printf("\t~ - Destroy (destroy the square)\n");
                break;
            }
    }

    // If the user is recording input,
    if (Record != NULL) {
        // Close the recording file
        fclose(Record);
    }
}

#endif      //DRIVER

********************************************************************************

//
//    team.hpp - chess team class
//

class Team;

#ifndef     TEAM_HPP
#define     TEAM_HPP

#include "global.hpp"
#include "magic.hpp"
#include "status.hpp"
#include "piece.hpp"
#include "king.hpp"
#include "queen.hpp"
#include "bishop.hpp"
#include "knight.hpp"
#include "castle.hpp"
#include "pawn.hpp"
#include "board.hpp"

const       NPawns = 8;

// Chess team class
class       Team    {
    MAGIC               // Magic number macro
    BOOLEAN Manual;         // Manual operated team
    BOOLEAN IsWhite;    // White team
    Board  &board;      // Board handle
    Status &status;     // User interaction line handle
    King   *king;       // King handle
    Queen  *queen;      // Queen Handle
    Bishop *KBishop;    // King's Bishop handle
    Bishop *QBishop;    // Queen's Bishop handle
    Knight *KKnight;    // King's knight handle
```

Appendix B — *Cont'd*

```
	Knight        *QKnight;       // Queen's knight handle
	Castle        *KCastle;       // King's castle handle
	Castle        *QCastle;       // Queen's castle handle
	Piece         *pawn[NPawns];  // Pawn handles
	// Assert the class invariants
	void          Invariant() const;
	// Determine if the team is in check
	BOOLEAN IsCheck() const;
	// Determine if a specific piece has a legal move from a given position
	BOOLEAN HasMove(
		const Piece*,         // The piece in question
		const Coord&          // The piece's location
	) const;
	// Determine if any legal moves exist
	BOOLEAN LegalMovesExist() const;
	// Select the source of the manual move (returns False if user quits)
	BOOLEAN SelectPieceToMove(
		Square**              // (Returned) selected piece's square
	) const;
	// Select the destination of the manual move (returns False-user quits)
	BOOLEAN SelectDestination(
		Square**              // (Returned) selected destination
	) const;
	//* Crown the pawn (convert it to a queen)
	void          CrownPawn(
		Piece**               // Piece to convert to a queen
	);
	// Make the move
	void          MakeMove(
		const Coord&,         // Source piece location
		const Coord&          // Destination piece location
	);
	// Determine if this is a valid destination
	BOOLEAN ValidDestination(
		Square*,              // Source piece's square
		Square*               // Destination square
	) const;
	// Make a manual move (return false if user quits)
	BOOLEAN MakeManualMove();
	// Calculate the best move from this square
	int           CalcMove(
		const Piece*,         // The piece to move
		const Coord&,         // The piece's source location
		Coord&                // The (returned) destination location
	) const;
	// Make an automatic move
	void   MakeAutomaticMove();

public:
	// Create a team
	Team(
		BOOLEAN,              // True if team is white
		Board&,               // playing board handle
		Status&               // User interaction status line
	);
	// Destroy the team
	~Team();
```

Appendix B — *Cont'd*

```
        // Tell the team to play automatically
        void          PlayAutomatically();
        // Tell the team to play manually
        void          PlayManually();
        // Determine if the team plays manually
        BOOLEAN IsManual() const;
        // Determine if the team is in checkmate
        BOOLEAN IsCheckmate() const;
        // Determine if the team is in stalemate
        BOOLEAN IsStalemate() const;
        // Have the team make a move
        BOOLEAN Move();
        // Determine if a move causes checkmate
        BOOLEAN CausesCheckmate(
               const Coord&,          // Move's source location
               const Coord&           // Move's destination location
        ) const;
};

#endif       // TEAM_HPP
********************************************************************************

//
//    team.cpp - chess team class
//

#include <stdlib.h>
#include "team.hpp"

char  Team::MagicValue = '\0';

// Assert the class invariants
inline       void   Team::Invariant() const {
        // Check the magic number
        MagicCheck();
}

//* Create a team
Team::Team(BOOLEAN white, Board &b, Status &s):
        board(b),
        IsWhite(white),
        status(s) {

        MagicOn();
        //* Create a king
        king = new King(this, IsWhite, board);
        assert(king != NULL);
        board.PlacePiece(king, Coord(4,IsWhite?0:7));
        //* Create a queen
        queen = new Queen(this, IsWhite, board);
        assert(queen != NULL);
        board.PlacePiece(queen, Coord(3,IsWhite?0:7));
        //* Create a bishop on the king's side
        KBishop = new Bishop(this, IsWhite, board);
        assert(KBishop != NULL);
        board.PlacePiece(KBishop, Coord(5,IsWhite?0:7));
        //* Create a bishop on the queen's side
        QBishop = new Bishop(this, IsWhite, board);
```

Appendix B — *Cont'd*

```
        assert(QBishop != NULL);
        board.PlacePiece(QBishop, Coord(2,IsWhite?0:7));
        //* Create a knight on the king's side
        KKnight = new Knight(this, IsWhite, board);
        assert(KKnight != NULL);
        board.PlacePiece(KKnight, Coord(6,IsWhite?0:7));
        //* Create a knight on the queen's side
        QKnight = new Knight(this, IsWhite, board);
        assert(QKnight != NULL);
        board.PlacePiece(QKnight, Coord(1,IsWhite?0:7));
        //* Create a castle on the king's side
        KCastle = new Castle(this, IsWhite, board);
        assert(KCastle != NULL);
        board.PlacePiece(KCastle, Coord(7,IsWhite?0:7));
        //* Create a castle on the queen's side
        QCastle = new Castle(this, IsWhite, board);
        assert(QCastle != NULL);
        board.PlacePiece(QCastle, Coord(0,IsWhite?0:7));
        //* For each pawn position...
        for (int i = 0; i < NPawns; i++) {
                //* Create a pawn
                pawn[i] = new Pawn(this, IsWhite, board);
                assert(pawn[i] != NULL);
                board.PlacePiece(pawn[i], Coord(i,IsWhite?1:6));
        }
        Invariant();
}

//* Destroy the team
Team::~Team() {

        Invariant();
        //* Destroy the king
        delete king;
        //* Destroy the queen
        delete queen;
        //* Destroy the bishop on the king's side
        delete KBishop;
        //* Destroy the bishop on the queen's side
        delete QBishop;
        //* Destroy the knight on the king's side
        delete KKnight;
        //* Destroy the knight on the queen's side
        delete QKnight;
        //* Destroy the castle on the king's side
        delete KCastle;
        //* Destroy the castle on the queen's side
        delete QCastle;
        //* For each pawn position...
        for (int i = 0; i < NPawns; i++) {
                //* Destroy a pawn
                delete pawn[i];
        }
        MagicOff();
}
```

Appendix B — *Cont'd*

```
//* Tell the team to play automatically
void Team::PlayAutomatically() {

      Invariant();
      //* Mark the team as an automatic player
      Manual = FALSE;
}

//* Tell the team to play manually
void Team::PlayManually() {

      Invariant();
      //* Mark the team as a manual player
      Manual = TRUE;
}

//* Determine if the team is a manual player
BOOLEAN Team::IsManual() const {

      Invariant();
      //* The team plays manually if the team is marked as a manual player
      return(Manual);
}

//* Determine if the team is in check
BOOLEAN Team::IsCheck() const {

      BOOLEAN Check = FALSE;

      //* Find the king on the board
      Square *KingSqr = board.FindPiece(king);
      assert(KingSqr != NULL);

      //* For each square on the board...
      BoardIterator I(board);
      Square *S;
      while (((S = I++) != NULL) && (!Check)) {
             //* If the square contains a piece and
             Piece *p = S->GetPiece();
             if ((p != NULL) &&
                 //* The piece is not a team member and
                 !p->IsMember(this) &&
                 //* The piece can move to the king's square,
                 (p->IsLegalMove(S->GetCoord(), KingSqr->GetCoord()))) {
                    //* This is check
                    Check = TRUE;
             }
      }
      return(Check);
}

//* Determine if a specific piece has a legal move from this square
BOOLEAN Team::HasMove(const Piece *p, const Coord &Src) const {

      assert(p != NULL);
      BOOLEAN HasMove = FALSE;
      //* For each square on the board...
      BoardIterator I(board);
```

Appendix B — *Cont'd*

```
		Square *S;
		while (((S = I++) != NULL) && (!HasMove)) {
			//* If this is a legal move for this piece,
			if (p->IsLegalMove(Src, S->GetCoord())) {
				//* This piece has a move
				HasMove = TRUE;
			}
		}
		return(HasMove);
}

//* Determine if any legal moves exist
BOOLEAN Team::LegalMovesExist() const {

		BOOLEAN MoveExists = FALSE;

		//* For each square on the board...
		BoardIterator I(board);
		Square *S;
		while (((S = I++) != NULL) && (!MoveExists)) {
			//* If the square contains a piece
			Piece *p = S->GetPiece();
			if ((p != NULL) &&
			    //* The piece is a team member and
			    p->IsMember(this) &&
			    //* The piece has a move from this square,
			    (HasMove(p, S->GetCoord()))) {
			       //* Legal moves exist
			       MoveExists = TRUE;
			}
		}
		return MoveExists;
}

//* Determine if the team is in checkmate
BOOLEAN Team::IsCheckmate() const {

		Invariant();
		//* The team is in checkmate if -
		return(
			//* The team is in check and
			IsCheck() &&
			//* No legal moves exist
			!LegalMovesExist()
		);
}

//* Determine if the team is in stalemate
BOOLEAN Team::IsStalemate() const {

		Invariant();
		//* The team is in stalemate if
		return(
			//* The team is not in checkmate and
			!IsCheckmate() &&
			//* No legal moves exist
			!LegalMovesExist()
		);
}
```

Appendix B — *Cont'd*

```
//* Select the source of the manual move
BOOLEAN Team::SelectPieceToMove(Square **Destination) const {

      assert(Destination != NULL);
      //* Find the king on the board
      Square *KingSqr = board.FindPiece(king);
      assert(KingSqr != NULL);
      (*Destination) = KingSqr;

      //* While a valid piece is not selected and not quitting...
      BOOLEAN Quitting = FALSE;
      Piece  *p = NULL;
      for (;;) {
             //* Select a square
             Quitting = board.SelectPosition(Destination);
             p = (*Destination)->GetPiece();
             if (((p != NULL) && (p->IsMember(this))) || Quitting) {
                    break;
             } else {
                    status.Beep();
             }
      }
      return Quitting;
}

//* Select the destination of the manual move
BOOLEAN Team::SelectDestination(Square **Position) const {

      assert(Position != NULL);
      //* Save the selected square
      Square *Save = (*Position);
      //* Bold the starting square
      Save->Bold();

      //* Select a square
      BOOLEAN Quitting = board.SelectPosition(Position);

      //* Unbold the starting square
      Save->Unbold();
      return Quitting;
}

//* Crown the pawn (convert it to a queen)
void Team::CrownPawn(Piece **p) {
      assert(p != NULL);
      assert((*p) != NULL);
      assert((*p)->GetType() == PAWN);
      //* For each pawn on the team...
      for (int i = 0; i < NPawns; i++) {
             //* If this is the pawn,
             if (pawn[i] == (*p)) {
                    //* Destroy the pawn
                    delete (*p);
                    //* Create a queen
                    (*p) = pawn[i] = new Queen(this, IsWhite, board);
                    assert(pawn[i] != NULL);
             }
      }
}
```

Appendix B — *Cont'd*

```
//* Make the move
void  Team::MakeMove(const Coord &Src, const Coord &Dest) {

      assert(board.GetSquare(Src)->GetPiece() != NULL);
      //* Remove any piece from the destination square
      board.RemovePiece(Dest);
      //* Remove the piece from the source square
      Piece *p = board.RemovePiece(Src);
      //* If the piece is a pawn and
      if ((p->GetType() == PAWN) &&
          //* The move is a final move,
          ((Dest.Col() == 0) || (Dest.Col() == BoardCols-1))) {
             //* Crown the pawn
             CrownPawn(&p);
      }
      //* Move the source piece to the destination
      p->Move();
      board.PlacePiece(p, Dest);
}

//* Determine if this is a valid destination
BOOLEAN Team::ValidDestination(Square *S, Square *D) const {

      Piece  *Src = S->GetPiece();
      assert(Src != NULL);
      Piece  *Dest = D->GetPiece();

      //* The destination is valid if -
      return(
             //* The move is legal and
             Src->IsLegalMove(S->GetCoord(), D->GetCoord()) &&
             (
                    //* The destination square contains no piece or
                    (Dest == NULL) ||
                    //* The destination square contains a piece and
                    //* The piece is not a member of this team
                    (!Dest->IsMember(this))
             )
      );

}

//* Make a manual move
BOOLEAN Team::MakeManualMove() {

      BOOLEAN Quitting = FALSE;
      Square *S;
      Square *D;

      //* Until a piece makes a legal move or quitting...
      for (;;) {
             //* Select the board's source for the manual move
             status.SelectPiece();
             Quitting = SelectPieceToMove(&S);
             status.Clear();
             D = S;
             //* Select the board's destination for the manual move
             if (!Quitting) {
```

Appendix B — *Cont'd*

```
                        status.PlacePiece();
                        Quitting = SelectDestination(&D);
                        status.Clear();
                }
                if (Quitting || ValidDestination(S, D)) {
                        break;
                } else {
                        status.IllegalMove();
                }
        }
        //* If not quitting,
        if (!Quitting) {
                //* Make the move
                MakeMove(S->GetCoord(), D->GetCoord());
        }
        return(Quitting);
}

//* Calculate the best move from this square
int   Team::CalcMove(const Piece *p, const Coord &Src, Coord &Dest)
const {

        int     BestMove = -1;

        assert(p != NULL);
        assert(board.GetSquare(Src)->GetPiece() == p);
        //* For each square on the board...
        BoardIterator I(board, TRUE);
        Square *S;
        while ((S = I++) != NULL) {
                //* If a move to this location is a valid move,
                if (p->IsLegalMove(Src, S->GetCoord())) {
                        //* Calculate the square's value
                        Piece *Target = S->GetPiece();
                        int Value = (Target == NULL)? 0:
                            Target->IsMember(this)? -1: Target->Value();
                        //* If the square's value represents the best move,
                        if (Value > BestMove) {
                            //* Remember this move
                            BestMove = Value;
                            Dest = S->GetCoord();
                        }
                }
        }
        return(BestMove);
}

//* Make an automatic move
void  Team::MakeAutomaticMove() {

        Coord  MoveSrc;
        Coord  MoveDest;
        int    BestMove = -1;

        status.Thinking();
        //* For each square on the board...
        BoardIterator I(board, TRUE);
        Square *S;
```

Appendix B — *Cont'd*

```
	while ((S = I++) != NULL) {
		//* If the square contains a piece and
		Piece *p = S->GetPiece();
		if ((p != NULL) &&
		    //* The piece is a member of this team,
		    p->IsMember(this)) {
			//* Calculate the best move for this square
			Coord Dest;
			int Move = CalcMove(p, S->GetCoord(), Dest);
			//* If this move is better than the best so far,
			if (Move > BestMove) {
				//* Remember this move as the best
				BestMove = Move;
				MoveSrc = S->GetCoord();
				MoveDest = Dest;
			}
		}
	}
	assert(BestMove >= 0);
	//* Make the move
	MakeMove(MoveSrc, MoveDest);
	status.Clear();
}

//* Have the team make a move
BOOLEAN Team::Move() {

	Invariant();
	BOOLEAN Quitting = FALSE;

	//* If this team is a manual player,
	if (Manual) {
		//* Make manual move
		Quitting = MakeManualMove();
	//* Otherwise the team is an automatic player
	} else {
		//* Make automatic move
		MakeAutomaticMove();
	}
	return Quitting;
}

//* Determine if a move causes checkmate
BOOLEAN Team::CausesCheckmate(const Coord &Src, const Coord &Dest)
const {

	Invariant();
	BOOLEAN Checkmate;

	//* Try moving the piece to the new square
	Piece *p = board.TryPiece(Src, NULL);
	assert(p != NULL);
	Piece *SaveDest = board.TryPiece(Dest, p);

	//* See if this puts the king in check
	// If the piece we are taking is a king, no checkmate
	Checkmate = ((SaveDest != NULL) && (SaveDest->GetType()) == KING)?
		// Otherwise see if this puts the king in check
```

Appendix B — *Cont'd*

```
            FALSE: IsCheck();

      //* Restore the piece to its original location
      board.UntryPiece(Dest, SaveDest);
      board.UntryPiece(Src, p);
      return Checkmate;
}

#ifdef      DRIVER

#include <stdio.h>
#include <stdlib.h>
#include "drivtool.hpp"


const       NHandles = 10;

// Test driver
void  main(int argc, char *argv[]) {

      Team   *Hans[NHandles];
      for (int i = 0; i < NHandles; i++) Hans[i] = NULL;
      FILE   *Record;

      // If there is an input recording file,
      if (argc == 2) {
             // Open the file
             Record = fopen(argv[1],"w");
      } else {
             // Otherwise mark the file as not open
             Record = NULL;
      }

      Screen Scr;
      Status Sta(Scr);
      Board  board(Scr);
      int    Handle = 0;
      // Drive until the user is done
      for (int Done = 0; !Done; ) {
             switch (GetChar("Team => ", Record)) {
             case 'A':  // PlayAutomatically()
                    Hans[Handle]->PlayAutomatically();
                    break;
             case 'C':  // IsCheckmate()
                    printf("The team is %sin checkmate\n",
                        Hans[Handle]->IsCheckmate()? "": "not ");
                    break;
             case 'E':  // CausesCheckmate()
                    int R = GetInt("Initial Row => ", Record);
                    int C = GetInt("Initial Column => ", Record);
                    Coord Src(R,C);
                    R = GetInt("Destination Row => ", Record);
                    C = GetInt("Destination Column => ", Record);
                    Coord Dst(R,C);
                    printf("The move does %scause checkmate\n",
                        Hans[Handle]->CausesCheckmate(Src, Dst)?
                        "": "not ");
                    break;
```

Appendix B — *Cont'd*

```
            case 'H':   // Handle
                    printf("The current handle is %d\n", Handle);
                    Handle = GetInt("Enter the new handle => ", Record);
                    printf("Now the handle is %d\n", Handle);
                    break;
            case 'I':   // IsManual()
                    printf("The team plays %s\n",
                         Hans[Handle]->IsManual()?
                         "manually": "automatically");
                    break;
            case 'M':   // PlayManually()
                    Hans[Handle]->PlayManually();
                    break;
            case 'O':   // Move()
                    Hans[Handle]->Move();
                    break;
            case 'Q':   // Quit
                    Done = 1;
                    break;
            case 'S':   // IsStalemate()
                    printf("The team is %sin stalemate\n",
                         Hans[Handle]->IsStalemate()? "": "not ");
                    break;
            case 'T':   // Team()
                    BOOLEAN White = GetChar("W/B => ", Record) == 'W';
                    Hans[Handle] = new Team(White, board, Sta);
                    break;
            case '~':   // ~Team()
                    delete Hans[Handle];
                    break;
            default:    // Help
                    printf("Valid commands are...\n");
                    printf("\tA - PlayAutomatically (computer play)\n");
                    printf("\tC - IsCheckmate (in checkmate?)\n");
                    printf("\tE - CausesCheckmate (move causes mate?)\n");
                    printf("\tH - Handle (change the handle)\n");
                    printf("\tI - IsManual (user play?)\n");
                    printf("\tM - PlayManually (user play)\n");
                    printf("\tO - Move (make a move)\n");
                    printf("\tQ - Quit (quit the driver)\n");
                    printf("\tS - IsStalemate (in stalemate?)\n");
                    printf("\tT - Team (create a team)\n");
                    printf("\t~ - Destroy (destroy the team)\n");
                    break;
            }
        }

        // If the user is recording input,
        if (Record != NULL) {
            // Close the recording file
            fclose(Record);
        }
}

#endif      //DRIVER
```

Appendix B — *Cont'd*

```
*********************************************************************************

//
//   wrapper.hpp - chess game wrapper/stub class for the verification
driver
//

#ifndef      WRAPPER_HPP
#define      WRAPPER_HPP

//#define    VERIFICATION
#ifdef       VERIFICATION     // define VERIFICATION to turn on the driver

#include <fstream.h>
#include "magic.hpp"

// NewScreen class intercepts calls to screen for verification purposes
class NewScreen {
      MAGIC              // Magic number macro
      Screen screen;
      // Assert the class invariants
      void   Invariant() const {
             // Check the magic number
             MagicCheck();
      }
public:
      // Create the screen interceptor
      NewScreen() {
             MagicOn();
             Invariant();
      }
      // Destroy the interceptor
      ~NewScreen() {
             Invariant();
             MagicOff();
      }
      // Clear the screen (with echo)
      void   Clear() const {
             Invariant();
             cout << "clear()" << endl;
             screen.Clear();
      }
      // Position the cursor (with echo)
      void   GoToXY(
             const int x,
             const int y
      ) const {
             Invariant();
             cout << "GoToXY(" << x << "," << y << ")" << endl;
             screen.GoToXY(x, y);
      }
      // Output a string with the current attributes (with echo)
      void   PutString(
             const char *str
      ) const {
             Invariant();
             cout << "PutString(" << str << ")" << endl;
             screen.PutString(str);
```

Appendix B — *Cont'd*

```
        }
        // Change the current attributes (with echo)
        void    Attribute(
                const Att att
        ) const {
                Invariant();
                cout << "Attribute(";
                if (att == AttNone)  cout << "AttNone";
                if (att & AttBold) cout << "AttBold";
                if (att & AttBlink) cout << "AttBlink";
                if (att & AttRevid) cout << "AttRevid";
                cout << ")" << endl;
                screen.Attribute(att);
        }
        // Sound a warning beep
        void    Beep() const {
                Invariant();
                cout << "Beep()" << endl;
                screen.Beep();
        }
        // Get a character
        int     GetCh() const {
                Invariant();
                int c = screen.GetCh();
                return c;
        }
};

// Redirect the old function calls to the new ones
#define         Screen NewScreen
#define         main   OldMain
#define         getch  GetChIntercept
int             GetChIntercept();

#endif          // VERIFICATION
#endif          // WRAPPER_HPP

*******************************************************************************

//
//     wrapper.cpp - Verification wrapper/stub code for the chess game
//

#include <stdio.h>
#include <string.h>
#include <ctype.h>
#include "screen.hpp"

#ifdef          VERIFICATION

// Undo the redefinitions
#ifdef          main
#undef          main
#undef          Screen
#undef          getch
#endif          // main

char  NewScreen::MagicValue = '\0';
```

Appendix B — *Cont'd*

```
extern      void   OldMain();      // the chess main

static      FILE   *Recording;     // recording stream handle

const       char   *ProcOn = "Processing_On";
cons t      MAXLINE = 128;

// Get a line of input
void        GetLine(char buffer[]) {

      int i = 0;
      int c;
      while (((c = getch()) != '\r') && (c != '\n')) {
             // Truncate lines that are too long
             if (i < (MAXLINE-1)) {
                    buffer[i++] = c;
             }
      }
      // Strip the newline
      if (c == '\r') c = getch();
      buffer[i] = '\0';
}

// intercepting character getting routine to record input and process
comments
int         GetChIntercept() {

      int    c;
      char   buffer[MAXLINE];
      static BOOLEAN Processing = FALSE;

      // get a character and eat all the comment lines
      while ((c = getch()) == '#') {
             // Put the comment into a buffer
             GetLine(buffer);
             // Turn on processing if necessary
             if (strcmp(buffer, ProcOn) == 0) Processing = TRUE;
             // Echo the comment
             if (Recording != NULL) {
                    fprintf(Recording, "#%s\n", buffer);
             }
      }
      // If processing has been turned on
      if (Processing) {
             // Get the whole line
             buffer[0] = c;
             GetLine(&buffer[1]);
             // Convert the processed input to non-processed form
             sscanf(buffer, "%d", &c);
             // Echo the line if necessary
             if (Recording != NULL) fprintf(Recording, "%s\n", buffer);
      } else {
             // Record the input if necessary
             if (Recording != NULL) {
                    // Mark recorded input as processed
                    static   BOOLEAN FirstTime = TRUE;
                    if (FirstTime) {
                         FirstTime = FALSE;
```

Appendix B — *Cont'd*

```
                    fprintf(Recording, "#%s\n", ProcOn);
                }
                fprintf(Recording, "%d %c\n",c,isalnum(c)?(char)c:'!');
            }
    }

    return c;
}

// This is the driver main (wrapper)
void main(int argc, char *argv[]) {
    // if there is a recording file, open it
    Recording = (argc==2)? fopen(argv[1],"w"): NULL;
    // call the chess game's main
    OldMain();
}

#endif // Verification

******************************************************************************
```

```
ject(Requirements,
scribe the objects externals
tSpec = CreateSpec(Requiremen
the object until it passes
tests
all veri
Do {
    // Describe how th
    ObjectDesign = DesignO
    // Find or build subordina
    Subordinates = CreateSu
    // Implement this objec
    Code = CodeObject(O
    // Create boundary v
    TestSet = CreateBlac
    // Create condition
    WhiteBoxTest
    ct d
```

Index

D

E

M

N

O

P

W